MEN WHO MATCHED THE MOUNTAINS

MEN WHO MATCHED THE MOUNTAINS
The Forest Service in the Southwest

By Edwin A. Tucker
and
George Fitzpatrick

United States Department of Agriculture
Forest Service
Southwestern Region

Fredonia Books
Amsterdam, The Netherlands

Men Who Matched the Mountains:
The Forest Service in the Southwest

by
Edwin A. Tucker
George Fitzpatrick

ISBN: 1-4101-0860-0

Reprinted from the 1972 edition

Fredonia Books
Amsterdam, The Netherlands
http://www.fredoniabooks.com

PREFACE

It would be presumptuous to call this a history of the Forest Service in the Southwest, for no single volume can tell the whole story. Better to call it a chronicle "of and by a few of the men who quite literally blazed the trail, and of the fulfillment, frustration, and fun they found along the way," as Edwin A. Tucker phrased it.

Several years ago Fred H. Kennedy, then Regional Forester, authorized Tucker to undertake twin historical projects: a history of Region 3 and the establishment of the Forest Service Museum at the Continental Divide Training Center. Both assignments were accomplished.

For nearly a year, Tucker tape recorded interviews with early-day Rangers and other officials, some retired, some still in harness. And from newspapers and official sources he gleaned news items, letters and reports concerning early activities and people. When the material was typed, it covered more than 1500 typewritten pages—four big volumes—far too bulky a manuscript for publication as a trade book.

This book then is a distillation of that material, plus such other material and chapters that were needed to clarify and bring up to date the story of some of the people of the Forest Service in the Southwest.

Tucker has spent his adult life in the Forest Service, beginning during the period when many pioneer conditions still prevailed in the Southwest, and he knew and worked with many of the old timers and of course with the new breed of professionals who now guide the destiny of the Service.

"However spectacular the changes in the Service," Tucker wrote in a foreword to his interviews, "they were nevertheless possible only because of the kind of men involved, men who responded to the challenge of their particular environment and time. In the earliest days, for example, the men for the times were necessarily tough; they had to be to survive. At that stage, ruggedness and resourcefulness, not technology, were the requisites. Despite public apathy and users' antagonism to regulations (sometimes violent), in the face of political pressures, in the absence of guidelines and for the most part with little formal education, the earliest

Rangers and Supervisors did the job that was needful at the time. They performed their work with exceptional devotion and loyalty, and with a surprising awareness of the problem of that era and their relation to the future."

Regretably, all of the interesting experiences and histories of the early-day Rangers could not be included. Insofar as possible, the material chosen for inclusion is representative of various Ranger Districts, happenings and people. Tucker compiled material that reflected not only the spirit of the times, but also the special "flavor" that was a quality of the individual involved. Every effort has been made to retain that special flavor in the historical chapters. The current operations of the Forest Service are explained briefly so that the general reader may have an overall picture of the Forest Service, not only of its beginnings and growth but its complex management operations today.

Much of the material deals with Rangers as the focal point of the narrative—but in a sense all of the employees of the Forest Service are "Rangers." A remarkable circumstance of research for this volume was the discovery of the high degree of dedication of Forest Service people—whether the title is Ranger, fire guard, clerk, Supervisor, or Chief of a Division. They are wedded to their jobs and dedicated to the philosophies of the Forest Service even when they differ personally as to the best ways to carry out the policies of the agency.

The Forest Service is a complex organization of many kinds of specialists, but the Ranger District is the principal component, and as one Supervisor put it, "the Ranger is the key to success of the Forest Service."

Today's Ranger differs from his counterpart of forty, fifty, and sixty years ago in that he is better educated in the technology of his job, and he is more of a business executive, with trained specialists to help him accomplish the job. But he is still an outdoorsman. Though he has less opportunity to do so, he can still ride a horse—and in the Ranger Districts of the Southwestern Region, horses are still plentiful. But the Ranger also calls on modern technology when needed, whether it be planes, helicopters, electronics, or computers, or all of them.

And like his predecessor who rode tall in the saddle, today's Ranger is still a man who matches the mountains.

—George Fitzpatrick

Gifford Pinchot was the first Chief of the Forest Service which was organized in 1905. Pinchot and President Theodore Roosevelt worked together in setting up the National Forest System as it exists today.

CONTENTS

Chapter I	*The Pioneers*	1
Chapter II	*Men on Horseback*	11
Chapter III	*Cattle, Sheep and People*	26
Chapter IV	*New Rangers*	41
Chapter V	*Fire!*	49
Chapter VI	*Wild Times and Wild Horses*	70
Chapter VII	*What the Well Dressed Ranger Should Wear*	83
Chapter VIII	*Six-Guns and Sons o' Guns*	88
Chapter IX	*Grazing Problems*	104
Chapter X	*Reconnaissance*	116
Chapter XI	*Timbe-r-r-r!*	121
Chapter XII	*No Lady Rangers—But Lots of Paper Work*	142
Chapter XIII	*From Horses to Horseless Carriages*	149
Chapter XIV	*CCC Days*	162
Chapter XV	*Ranger Humor*	172
Chapter XVI	*Grasslands*	182
Chapter XVII	*The National Forests of Arizona*	191
Chapter XVIII	*The National Forests in New Mexico*	200
Chapter XIV	*Lost Mines and Buried Treasure*	207
Chapter XX	*Ah Wilderness!*	212
Chapter XXI	*Recreation*	219
Chapter XXII	*Multiple Use*	230
Chapter XXIII	*Land Exchanges*	238
Chapter XXIV	*Management*	244
Chapter XXV	*Public Relations*	259
Chapter XXVI	*The Modern Ranger*	267
Chapter XXVII	*Land Grant Country*	276

"A ranger of any grade must be thoroughly sound and able-bodied, capable of enduring hardships and of performing severe labor under trying conditions. He must be able to take care of himself and his horses in regions remote from settlement and supplies."

Forest Service Use Book, 1908.

CHAPTER I
The Pioneers

The man who sat at the roll top desk bulked large above the chair back. The black coat stretched tight in accordion pleats between his shoulders as he hunched over the desk. His shaggy black hair almost covered his stand-up white collar that peeked above the coat. And when he swung his chair around and stood up at the sound of a knock on his opened door, his over-developed paunch pushed a slight spread between his vest and trousers.

"I'm headin' back for Pecos, Mr. McClure," the man at the door said.

McClure took a half-smoked cigar from his mouth that was almost hidden by a heavy mustache. "Good," he said. "Good. And remember Fletcher, keep those reports concise . . . concise. Good-bye."

McClure gave the tails of his Prince Albert a swish, sat down and swung back to his desk to resume his writing.

This was the office of the Pecos River Forest Reserve in Santa Fe in 1900 and McClure was the new Forest Supervisor, in charge of three Rangers and an area that originally covered 300,000 acres of mountain forests, and including some of the highest peaks in New Mexico.

R. C. McClure was hardly the physical type that anyone would picture—even in 1900—as a Forest Ranger. But in those early days of the Service, when it was still part of the General Land Office of the U. S. Department of the Interior, and before Civil Service covered the appointment of Rangers, McClure was one of many political appointees who launched the infant agency.

The Pecos River Forest Reserve had been set aside by proclamation of President Benjamin Harrision in January, 1892, the very first one in the Southwest and the fourth Forest Reserve in the United States. Subsequent Presidential Proclamations established Forest Reserves that later were organized into District 3—now known as Region 3 of the United States Forest Service.*

---

*Originally included National Forests in Oklahoma, Arkansas, Florida, and Puerto Rico. These were transferred in 1911 and 1913, and Region 3 now comprises only the National Forests in Arizona and New Mexico and National Grasslands in New Mexico, Oklahoma, and Texas.

Gifford Pinchot, the idealistic conservationist who became the Chief Forester of the Department of Agriculture in 1898, had the right idea in his crusade to get "forestry from the books into the woods."   But it took awhile before there were trained Foresters to tackle the tasks—and in the meantime job-seekers who were sponsored by senators or other potent political allies moved into supervisory positions in the General Land Office's Forest Reserves Division.

McClure's employment as Forest Supervisor had been made possible by Congressional appropriation in 1898, which provided for appointment of Forest Superintendents, Forest Supervisors, and Rangers for the Forest Reserves.   A resident of Kentucky, he had obtained appointment through political channels, even as had his boss, I. B. Hanna, Superintendent of Forest Reserves in the Southwest, who was from Illinois and a close friend of "Uncle Joe" Cannon, then chairman of the powerful House Appropriations Committee.

There had been two previous Superintendents for the Southwestern Region, (John D. Benedict, 1897-1899 and William B. Buntain, 1899-1900) but the new program of forest protection was slow in getting under way.

McClure's earliest reports and letters reveal that despite his lack of technical training, he was an enthusiastic and industrious supervisor, who was much concerned with seeing that the several Rangers of the Pecos Reserve put in a full day of work every day.

"We are required to make a full report of all trail work done on the Reserve, September 30, for the past quarter," he wrote Ranger Robert J. Ewing, of Glorieta, on September 23, 1900, "and as I desire to make a good showing in this line of Ranger work, I want you, in addition to your regular patrol duties, to find time this week to complete this trail (Indian Creek trail) to the top of the mountain leading to Santa Fe.   I think there is about two miles of it, not a great deal of work to be done however, and I think you can do it in two days: an ax and a pick is all that you will need."

A stickler for following the book, he was frequently critical of the reports of Rangers, and as he pointed out to Ranger S. O. Fletcher, "you will follow the instructions literally, 'describe the patrol you made, the distance traveled, and the time consumed; state length of the trail cut or blazed, the time consumed and where cut.' "

Report sheets with instructions printed on the left hand margin for guidance were supplied the Rangers.   When Rangers went beyond instructions, McClure was quick to call attention.

"I request that you make out a new report," he wrote Ranger

Fletcher, "leaving out all allusions to weather, snow, rain, etc., so that you may get pay for that day."

And to Ranger McGlone, who was stationed in Mora County, he wrote that "the phraseology of your report for the month of December is very unsatisfactory, to say nothing of your repeated reference to trespass in the grazing of goats on the Reserve, not one of which has been made the subject of special report to this office. From the reading of your report for December (1900) the Department will doubtless conclude that your District is being overrun with goats and that you are unable to keep them off, and that therefore, the order of the Hon. Secretary of the Interior excluding goats from the Pecos River Forest Reserve, New Mexico, is not being enforced by the Forest Officers in charge of this Reserve. Such is not the case, and from my personal knowledge of existing conditions, in your District, I know that they are only grazed upon that portion of territory which, by reason of the uncertainty of the exact location of the boundary line in dispute . . ." and so on at great length, being very, very touchy about any indication that all was not well on the Reserve.

And finally, "One other criticism: December 14th, you report, —'left Cleveland P. O. (Mora County) at 9:30 a.m.' Cleveland post office is a long distance from your District, and 9:30 a.m. is very late in the morning to be starting for a day's work to be commenced after you shall have ridden half the distance required in an ordinary day's patrol."

As McClure was hardly the technically-trained forester that Gifford Pinchot envisioned as Rangers, neither were the early Rangers who served under McClure. But they were rugged outdoorsmen, ex-cowboys, ex-miners, men who loved the outdoors. They were men rugged enough to match the mountains they patrolled, and the technically-trained foresters who came later learned from them and had to match their ruggedness and stamina or they fell by the wayside.

Writing of the early years of the Forest Service in Arizona, Fred Winn* once pointed out that "the Forest Officers in the early days of the Land Office regime were a motley collection of humanity. It stood to reason that the Forest Reserves could not be administered in the field without the presence of at least some men who had an intimate knowledge of the country and were able to

---

*The late Fred Winn, after his retirement from the office of Supervisor of the Coronado National Forest, started to prepare a history of the early days of the Forest Service, but unfortunately died before his writings were completed. These quotations are from some of his papers now in the Museum of the Arizona Historical Society in Tucson.

Forest Supervisor's Office, Pecos River Forest Reserve, Santa Fe, New Mexico, 1900.   L to R, Supervisor McClure and third from left, I. B. Hanna, Superintendent, Southwestern Forest Reserves.

Interior of Forest Supervisor's Office, Alamo National Forest, Alamogordo, New Mexico, March 1909.

take care of themselves and their horses, could stand severe physical hardships, live under any conditions, prepare their own food, talk the language of the natives, and engage in combat when the occasion arose. In fact, these were men 'with bark on,' as Teddy Roosevelt was wont to describe them. Another class consisted of adventurous young men from other parts of the country who had come to the West in order to grow up with it and because they had an inherent liking for the wide open spaces."

In the New Mexico Forests, Rangers of the early 1900s were "a combination ranch-and-cowboy type of men, mostly with limited education," is the way Elliott Barker, a Ranger in the early days of the Forest Service, described them. "They were rugged enough to meet any situation that we had to meet. It was that type of men, believe me, that had to lay the foundation in those rugged conditions in the early days upon which the Forest Service is building now. Without that—somebody had to do it—trained foresters could never have done it."

The technically-trained men who came later turned out to be a rugged breed, too. That is, the ones who stayed. The men who didn't have "the bark on" soon left the country for less demanding careers.

"Each year we had to take on two or three of these forestry graduates and break them in and try to teach them some of the things they don't learn in school. They had to have some basic western training to build on," Barker said.

"We had some men sent to us that were graduates in forestry that made good, and others that just did not make good. They could not grasp the western outdoor way of doing things."

Handling a horse was an important part of the business of being a Ranger, and if he could not learn to handle a horse. . . . well, it would be, as Elliott Barker put it, "the same as hiring men today who didn't know how and couldn't learn to drive an automobile."

There was need for virile men in the Service, for there was much opposition to conservation regulations, and until ranchers, timber and mining companies and residents in the Forest Districts came to an acceptance of conservation practices and Forest regulations, they sought at many opportunities to discredit the Rangers— or even to drive them off.

Forest Supervisor McClure early experienced the misery of slanderous attacks on him by a rancher whom he classified as a "common informer" of all Forest Officials "and each week sends in some slanderous report against me or some of my rangers, charging inattention, neglect, drunkenness, absence from Reserve, and other alike false reports."

In a letter to the U. S. Marshall C. M. Foraker in 1901, McClure referred to the rancher as "always an enemy of Forest Reserves, is ignorant, is a blatant free-silver Democrat and divided all Government officials into two classes, openly bad and secretly bad . . . ."

The rancher in one letter to the Department even went so far as to claim that McClure and a Ranger got drunk and forced their way into the bedroom of a widow, who stood them off with a pistol.

In a long letter to the Commissioner of the General Land Office, McClure discussed the matter, denied all the allegations and called them "malicious and false and sent to your office by a man who would not, in my judgment, scruple to blister his soul with perjury in any court in the land. . . ." The Assistant U. S. Attorney followed it up with a letter to the Commissioner in which he stated that the Rangers and their Supervisor were "gentlemen and diligent officers."

The various complaints were investigated and within a month came a letter from the Commissioner exonerating the Supervisor and Ranger from the "slanderous charges."

While McClure and the Rangers were being plagued by the complaints of the rancher, the routine of Forest work went ahead as usual.

In his final report for the year 1900, McClure painted a bright picture of accomplishment for the new Forest Reserve.

"The Forest is in good condition, is for the most part covered with snow on the mountain tops, *mesas* and plateaus, while in canyons the streams are frozen over; larger streams such as the Pecos, Mora and Santa Fe are open. Cattle owned by ranchmen living in the territory near the Reserve have removed their stock to the lowlands for the balance of the winter, leaving upon the Reserve for the most part only the stock belonging to the ranchmen living inside the reservation on homesteads taken up before creation of the Reserve. Applications (for the 1901 season) relative to grazing cattle and horses will all be in by the middle of February . . .

"Rangers have been vigilant in the performance of their duties and on the alert to discover trespasses, which at this season of the year would as a rule be the cutting of timber or the taking of timber for firewood, the killing of game, etc., but not a single trespass has been discovered.

"It would seem from reading the Monthly Report of Ranger McGlone that this is a contradiction and that his District was being overrun with goats as he speaks of goats almost every other day.

Such is not the case, and from personal knowledge, had by reason of a recent visit to his District, I know that there are a few bands of goats owned by Mexican ranchmen ranging in number from 25 to 200 which are grazed upon that portion of the territory in dispute as to boundary line, the settlers claiming that it is in one place, and Ranger McGlone in another, and no one knowing exactly where it is for the reason that . . . the east line . . . was never run . . . ."

If McClure was bothered by only minor problems in the Pecos Reserve the same could not be said for the situation in Arizona, where the setting aside of Forest Reserves was met with mixed emotions. The *Arizona Weekly Journal Miner* of Prescott, discussing the new Forest Reserves in its issue of June 18, 1898, offered a friendly send-off. It reported that the Department of the Interior was formulating rules and regulations for the care of the Forests because "vast areas have been denuded by fires" and the policy of the Department "will be to preserve the Forests for the use of the people."

"The Forests will not only be preserved for use as timber but for protecting the heads of streams, holding back the snows and preventing floods," the *Journal Miner* said. The paper noted the importance of this feature of watershed protecting, relating that the small streams from the south side of the mountains are "the foundation of the Verde River, which is a strong feeder of the Salt River, and directly affects the Salt River Valley irrigation."

There was not quite the same acceptance of the Forest Reserves in the Williams area. There, a mass meeting was called, according to the *Williams News* of August 26, 1898, "to protest against the proposed setting apart of Coconino County as a reservation by the Government." The meeting proposed sending a man to Washington "who will stay there until he heads off the scheme."

The unnamed representative did not, of course, "head off the scheme," and the *Williams News* on September 6, 1898, reported "The Evil Deed Done," in a headline over a story that Mayor John M. Francis of Flagstaff had received a telegram announcing that the Forest Reserve regulations would go into effect on September 17, 1898. "To say the telegram was a surprise is putting it mildly. None dreamed that this almost fiendish piece of business was much more than in its infancy, and while people have been busy the past ten days getting their forces together to fight this matter in a legitimate way, here comes the startling news that the Department has already so ordered this section as a Forest Reserve. . . ."

The Interior Department's representative in the area, E. J. Holsinger, bore the brunt of the criticism with attacks that were highly personal in character.

The Williams *News* reported that "It's a safe 16-to-1 bet that there's one man in Arizona that—should he ever ask for bread in this section of the Territory—will be given a stone instead, and that is the United States Land Agent by the name of S. J. Holsinger . . . His actions regarding the reservation's business and his treatment of homesteaders, have, to say the least, been small, egotistical, selfish, and by no means becoming to a man in such a position. . . ."

But a couple of months later, the same paper reported that "Special Agent Holsinger visited the Prescott Forest Reserve yesterday and made the discovery that during the past winter there had been a large part of it devastated of its timber. Hundreds of mining stulls have been taken right from the Reserve, he said, despite the fact that a Forest Ranger has been employed to look after and protect it."

The same paper in June 1899, reported that "An idea of the magnitude of the forest devastation which has been going on in this section for the past few years may be had when it is known that probably no less than 25,000, and probably a greater number of these stulls have been shipped to Jerome. Each individual stull is a good sized tree."

Holsinger undertook a number of prosecutions, and on June 22, the newspapers reported that "Uncle Sam is having quite a round-up in the stull business. Special Agent Holsinger, Deputy Marshall Grindell and Forest Supervisor Thayer have been scouring the woods for the past three or four days and have placed Uncle Sam's brand on over 7,000 stulls. They estimate that they have about 5,000 more to brand."

Four civil suits involving $11,500 were filed in U. S. court and all the stulls in sight were confiscated by the U. S. Marshall. Then in July, a deposit for the full appraised value of the stulls was made, and they were released for shipment.

The man who had initiated the investigation of unauthorized timber cutting, S. J. Holsinger, was transferred to Colorado, and the Nogales *Oasis* saluted his transfer with these remarks:

"Call out the fence-cutters. The timber thieves in the southern part, have found that they could neither intimidate nor bluff from his duties, S. J. Holsinger, the inspector for the Interior Department, who has done more within the two years to bring before the eyes of the gentry a just fear of the law than all the men who preceded him in that position. . . ."

In eastern Arizona, a new Forest Reserve was set aside by Presidential proclamation in 1902, and Charles T. McGlone of the Pecos Reserve was transferred to the new Reserve early in 1903, with headquarters at Willcox. McGlone's early activities concerned permits for cutting cordwood, fence posts, recording mining claims and patrolling to guard against fires in the dry months of summer.

As in the Pecos Reserve, McGlone seemed especially concerned about goats grazing on the Reserve.

Writing to an applicant from El Paso who sought permission to graze goats on the Chiricahua Forest Reserve, McGlone replied that the Secretary of the Interior "upon the recommendation of this office has decided that sheep and goats will not be permitted to graze therein during the present year. The lesson of six years experience has taught us that sheep and goats are very injurious to the seedling growth of the Forest, especially so in these arid lands of the Southwest, where the protection of nature's forests is so essential in the course of natural irrigation. . . ."

In the early months of his tenure in Chiricahua, McGlone served alone, but in the summer of 1903, another man was assigned to the Chiricahua Reserve, and McGlone's letter of instructions to the new man Neil Erickson, reveals what was expected of a Ranger for the $60 a month he would be paid.

Besides reminding him to submit monthly reports, McGlone advised Erickson that "The regulations governing the equipping of Rangers for field service, and found on Page 90 of the Manual, require Rangers to provide themselves with a pocket compass, camp outfit, axe, shovel, and pick or mattock (a pick with a wide blade) . . .

"Your principal duty will be regular patrol service, which consists of riding through the Reserve to protect it from fire and trespass, posting fire warnings and notices of Reserve boundary line at all such points as line thereof may be approximately determined; you will also be expected to look after the needs and cases of free use of timber to be cut from Reserve lands and in view of this fact you are admonished to study carefully the rules pertaining to the free use of timber and stone.

"You will not be assigned to any particular District for the performance of such duties, as is customary in the larger Reserves but will maintain patrol throughout the entire Reserve at present, or until such time as another Ranger can be appointed and assigned to duty within a District or portion of the Reserve.

"The Department urges the thorough organization of field service during the present year to prevent forest fires that have been so destructive to the forest cover for the last few years, especially in this dry arid region of the Southwest, and to this end you are enjoined to be vigilant, use every means to prevent further destruction of the forest timber by this known enemy of the Forest."

About the time McGlone was shifted from Pecos to Arizona, Supervisor McClure was also due for transfer.   He and George C. Langenberg changed places, and McClure went to Silver City, headquarters of the Gila River Forest Reserve.   McClure, despite his several years residence in New Mexico, still dressed the part of the Kentucky colonel, with his broad-brimmed black felt hat, flowing-end black bow tie, his Prince Albert coat and gray checked trousers.   His appearance so impressed A. O. Waha, a new appointee as Forest Assistant in 1905 that he could describe his appearance in detail 35 years later.

CHAPTER II
Men on Horseback

A. O. Waha was one of the first of the technically-trained foresters to be sent to the Southwest, arriving in Silver City in July, 1905, to assume his duties as Forest Assistant at a salary of $1,000 a year.

Years later Waha recalled that Supervisor McClure received him in his office, in a small brick house that was formerly a residence, in characteristic pose, "his cigar in his mouth at an angle of 45° and his thumbs in the armholes of his vest." McClure was, of course, wearing his black Prince Albert coat, which the Rangers for some unknown reason called his "go to hell" coat.

The Reserves had been transferred from the Department of the Interior to the Department of Agriculture a few months earlier (on February 1, 1905) but McClure was still serving under his political appointment.

"While he was quite cordial in meeting me, I could not help but feel that he was not wholly pleased with my assignment," Waha recalled in recent years. "He probably was thinking that this young squirt of a technical forester was sent here 'to get my job.'"

An incident involving McClure, which had occurred some time earlier, and which Waha soon heard about "showed McClure's heart was in the right place—but which made him appear both ludicrous and ridiculous."

"I doubt if he ever lived it down," Waha said. "It was one of those things that people simply do not forget. It seems that McClure was riding horseback, and was carrying an umbrella—horsemen in those days carried a quirt and a slicker tied to the cantle of their saddle. Whether or not he actually opened up the umbrella while riding in the rain I do not know. At any rate, it was bad enough simply to be packing an umbrella while on horseback. But when he came to a pasture and saw a calf that had been born only a few hours previously and shivering in the cold rain and meanwhile bawling plaintively, McClure dismounted, wriggled through the barbed wire and on reaching the calf stood alongside with his umbrella held over it for protection against the elements.

"Evidently, so the story has it, this was too much for the mother cow grazing a few yards away. She became infuriated, and with head down chased McClure back over the fence, and the haste in which he was forced to take the fence made somewhat of a mess of his pants. Thereafter, McClure was a wiser man, but the natives could never be convinced of this."

Waha's first assignment by McClure was to take charge of all timber sale work. This was a big task since much timber that had been cut in trespass was scattered throughout the Reserve and needed to be measured for sale to the individuals who cut it and who previously had been getting their mining timbers, lumber and cordwood simply as a matter of course.

"After buying a horse, I started out on July 22 with Rangers George Whidden and Jack Case," Waha recalled. "They were two hard-boiled, hard-riding Rangers who were much older than I and who had been around considerably. Whidden had been in the Army previously and had been in skirmishes with Indians, having been stationed at Fort Custer, while Case had been an itinerant cowpuncher.

"I shall always have a sneaking suspicion that McClure had either told them to kill me off or that they themselves had planned to do so. The first day we rode 38 miles over the burning plains country. I was quite inexperienced in riding and as a result, I was so done up after this long ride, I could scarcely crawl out of the saddle, and on reaching the ground, it was extremely difficult to move, my muscles being so sore. I doubt if there was a spot on me that didn't ache.

"After the first week in the saddle, I had become hardened to riding and felt quite at ease in handling my horse."

The Rangers were required to keep a daily diary of their activities, and in addition submitted a monthly report of daily service, which they facetiously called the "bed sheet" report.

Some excerpts from Waha's diary for February, 1906, indicate the kind of conditions encountered in the timber sale work, which continued regardless of winter weather:

Saturday—February 10. Rain and snow; very disagreeable weather. As we (also Ranger Bert Goddard who later became Supervisor of the Datil and Tonto Forests) had made up our minds to start for Kingston today, rain or shine, we saddled up about 11 o'clock and started in the rain. Stopped at Fort Bayard . . . rode to Santa Rita. Decided to stay there overnight for it was already late and we were soaking wet. Watched the masked ball in the evening. Time 8 hours. Distance 18 miles.

Sunday—February 11. Still snowing and very wet and

sloppy. Were in saddles at 7 a.m., rode to Teel's place on Mimbres River, just above San Lorenzo, had dinner and fed horses. Left Teel's at 12 o'clock, starting for Kingston. All went well until we struck the higher altitudes and encountered a regular blizzard. Trail very dim and snow became deeper. In Iron Creek, it was nearly three feet deep, and we had a struggle to get through. Reached Wright's old deserted cabin near head of Iron Creek at 5 o'clock; we were wet to the skin and awfully cold, while our horses were just about all in. After much consultation and arguing we decided to stay at the cabin overnight. Spent an awful night since we had no chuck and no bedding. Brought horses into cabin with us. They had to share some of their corn with us. Place was infested with trade rats. While I was dozing during the night, Goddard shot one that was on a beam directly over me, and it fell on me causing a rude awakening. . . .

Monday—February 12. The snow was very deep, practically three feet on the level, on the west side of the range, and to make traveling still worse, the trees and bushes were covered with about a foot of snow, which one could not escape. We soon became soaking wet, and then when we reached the divide, we found the snow so deep our horses could not get through. So we led them, breaking trail through thick oak brush. This leading and breaking trail was done for at least two miles or until we reached the canyon in which Kingston is located. Took the idle people of Kingston by surprise; they could scarcely believe that we had come over the Black Range.

Apparently suffering no ill effects from their experience, Waha and Goddard spent the next four days scaling and marking trees, issuing free use permits, and inspecting some land on which an application had been made for agricultural use.

Waha recollected that his work on the Gila was not all confined to timber work. "In fact, I was assigned from time to time to grazing activities, mining claims, examinations, boundary surveys, special use cases and other miscellaneous work. I learned the language of the stockmen and miners. At times McClure would place me in charge of the office during his absences. On one of these occasions, I took the bull by the horns and wrote a letter to Washington strongly recommending increased salaries for Rangers, who were then receiving but $75 a month and had to furnish their own horse feed. McClure, of course, had recognized that we could not expect to retain good Rangers at such meager wage, but had not submitted any recommendation for increased salaries. In my work I was naturally closer to the men and knew their problems.

"There was Ranger Goddard, for example, with a wife and five children to house, clothe and feed, and also two and three horses to maintain.   Their living conditions were far from representing the abundant life.

"Whether or not my letter brought immediate results, I do not recall, but I have in mind that it was not long before the entrance salary for Rangers was raised to $1,000 a year."

Over on the Arizona section of the Forest Reserves, much the same sort of history was being written as in New Mexico.   A succession of political-appointee Supervisors and untrained Rangers were attempting to carry on the work of the Reserves in the hostile climate of pioneer cattle and sheep men, homesteaders and mining people who had previously used the Forests pretty much as they pleased.

Along with the ex-cowboys, ex-sheepherders, ex-soldiers, lumbermen, prospectors and what-not, there were, as Fred Winn recalled, a number of health seekers employed as Rangers.   These had been appointed through the efforts of some obliging politician in order to permit them to regain their health by living outdoors "and at the same time working at Uncle Sam's expense on the Forest Reserves of the West."

"Taken together, most of these men served faithfully and well, under terrific handicap, as the Rangers as a class received only $60, $75 and $90 per month, out of which they were required to house and subsist themselves and to own and maintain from two to six horses and pack animals.

"They had to deal with a generally hostile population which was constantly antagonized by the wholly unfamiliar red tape of a Government located 3,000 or more miles away on the banks of the Potomac.   Communications were slow because of the comparatively few roads and trails, lack of post offices, and an almost entire absence of telephones."

Unlike Supervisor McClure's problem of concise reports, Supervisor Mathew Rowe had trouble getting adequate reports from his Rangers in the Black Mesa Reserve, who were not long on letter writing or keeping up forms.   A letter from Supervisor Rowe to Ranger Joe Pearse on August 25, 1899, said, "You are asked by the Forest Superintendent to give an explanation of your report of July 31.   The Superintendent writes me that your report reads, 'Made report.   Shod a horse.   Time consumed, 10 hours.' "

Fred Breen, a former Manteno, Illinois, newspaperman, who became a Forest Supervisor in 1901, achieved a remarkable record with the Forest Service, first in Black Mesa Forest Reserve and later in Coconino National Forest.   Breen ran into early difficulties with the commissioners of the General Land Office and the Superintendents of Forests in Santa Fe because of the number of health seekers who were assigned to his District.   In one letter, in 1901, he complained about four of his Rangers who were "delicate in appearance" without experience in range or riding, "incapacitated for the work by lung trouble."

Nothing much was accomplished by Breen's complaints, however, until the Forest Service was organized in the Department of Agriculture in 1905 and examinations for Rangers under Civil Service became an established fact.   The early Use Books outlining qualifications for Rangers pointed out that "Invalids seeking light out-of-door employment need not apply."

But even though he had trouble getting the kind of Rangers he wanted, Breen was firm in his instructions to those he had as to what was expected of them.

Some of these instructions indicate the character of their duties:

"Rangers are employed for the purpose of protecting Government land and timber.

"A Ranger's whole time is to be devoted to the interests of the government and to no other private business.

"Rangers are expected to go to a fire at once wherever one is discovered within a reasonable distance of his district.

"Daily reports should show where he went and the purpose of his visit, the distance traveled, and the time consumed each day, or if employed in burning firebreaks, piling brush, building trails, or other similar work, state the amount of work done in a comprehensive manner, that the amount may be known.

"Settlers and others are allowed the free use of timber and wood by making proper application. . . .   Timber or wood secured by such application must be for their own private uses and not for sale or disposal at a profit, and must be cut under the supervision of a ranger. . . .

"Post fire warnings along all roads, trails and at springs or other camping places. . . .   Nail them up securely and plentifully. . . .

"Inform yourself as to what sheep and cattle men graze their stock upon your District, the number he actually owns, and whether or not he confines himself to the range described in his permit.

"Merely riding over your District does not constitute the duties of a Ranger, but he should be on the look-out for all things affecting the Reserve, find the most exposed places and remove the debris to protect the Forest from fires, and be constantly on the alert to prevent trespasses and depredations."

Jim Sizer, who served as Forest Ranger and Assistant Supervisor on the Apache National Forest from 1909 to 1943.

Typical early-day Southwestern Forest Ranger, Santa Fe National Forest, July 27, 1907.

Breen's official letters were highly informal. Writing to the Assistant U. S. Attorney John H. Campbell of Tucson in August, 1903, he said, "Am tickled to death to hear that Mr. Knave (the U. S. Attorney) is enjoying his vacation. I was under the impression from the lack of disturbance in the Territory that you also were on vacation. I had succeeded in stirring up enough disturbance to warrant my taking leave of absence. I would be very much pleased to donate you a large, juicy plug of tobacco if you could work up steam enough to inform me of the condition of all sheep trespass cases. I realize that every drop of sweat squeezed out of you is precious."

And to the Registrar of the Land Office in Prescott, Ben F. Hildreth, he wrote in October, 1903: "I return you herewith a bunch of certified-to lost souls that I have been unable to locate in this part of the country. I think all of them have left . . . and have not been heard of for the past four or five years. I hope my ironclad certificates will clinch the matter strong enough. Since I have been compelled to be a land lawyer and special agent for the Department, I am wondering what kind of a job I'll be jobbed with next. . . . If I could only have a couple Indian Reservations, a railroad, the itch, and a Waterbury watch to take care of, I really think I would be properly supplied with a few small matters to interest me now and then."

In March, 1908, Breen decided to resign and wrote a long letter of explanation to the Forester, Washington, D. C. "You see, since my salary is less now than it was about 10 years ago, after two 'promotions' in the Forest Service, I rather felt that someone was afflicted with the ingrowing salary habit, and it wouldn't be long before my creditors would notice my financial lassitude. . . .

"I thought I had a bright future before me, but that durned bright future has certainly side-stepped me along the route somewhere, and must be loafing behind.

"I was not promoted in 1905, when the transfer was made from the Land Office. I didn't think much about it at the time one way or another, but when I did get promoted in 1906, I was glad I wasn't promoted in 1905. I was getting $2371 until my promotion came along in 1906, which gave me $2200. I knew it was a promotion for my commission from the Secretary of the Interior said so right square in the middle of it.

"In 1907 I was raised to $2300; so I am still shy some of the good old salary that I started with away back in September, 1898, with only the San Francisco Mountains National Forest to handle. The fellows on the Black Mesa and Grand Canyon Forests were getting the same amount that I got; but when they fell by the wayside I fell heir to their territory and their troubles, but none of the *pesos* they were getting. . . .

"One can get a heap more money out of a little old band of sheep, or something of that kind, even if his intellect does not average over 30 percent, with a whole lot less trouble, and retain some friends; but with this job, the general public just naturally gets cross if you try to enforce the rules, and if you don't enforce the rules then you get cross; so the Supervisor gets the double cross whatever happens, and has no pension at the end of the game, to sorter ease down his old age when the pace is too fast.

"While I think a good deal of forestry, I realize that a man can't live in this country and lay up anything unless he gets a good salary; consequently believe I should go out and make money while I can. . . .

"I feel mightily relieved at the prospect of seeing some other feller being accused of prejudice, ignorance, partiality, graft, ulterior motives, laziness, salary grabbing and other such innocent pastimes. . . .

"I am glad there will be a bright young man here March 15, to separate me and my troubles and let me wander away to new fields, where the bleat of the sheep, the height of a stump, the brand of a cow nor even a special privilege can hop up and fill me with fright or woe. . . ."

Handling all those various jobs was pretty much a routine requirement in the early Forest Service days, as A. O. Waha was discovering in New Mexico.

"Our life was most hectic," Waha wrote in some reminiscences for Gifford Pinchot in 1940. "In making inspections of Forests on those days, we followed a very detailed inspection outline that had been prepared in the Washington office, which was most inclusive. It was contemplated that every timber sale, grazing allotment, special use permit, claim, etc., should be inspected, together with a review of diaries to determine if time was being spent advantageously, and also a check of office procedures, files, etc. Some of our reports were indeed voluminous—200 to 300 pages. Certain it is, however, when we completed an inspection, we surely had first-hand knowledge of conditions and personnel."

Recalling the first inspection he made of the Jemez, Pecos and Taos Forests, Waha said that the inspection required 30 days in the field and about a week in the office going through files to obtain data for the trip—which covered 800 miles on horseback.

"I practically killed two horses on this trip; the first one was too old, and after a couple of weeks I traded him for a four-year-old mare," Waha wrote.

Ranger Station in Aquachiquita Canyon, Lincoln National Forest, 1908.

Old and new cabins, Bear Canyon Ranger Station, Gila National Forest, 1908

"My longest ride in any one day on this trip covered 60 miles; it was much too far to go in a day, but in the absence of a suitable place to stop over for the night, there seemed to be nothing else to do.   High winds and rain storms slowed us up and made riding disagreeable, while swarms of flying ants made life miserable while they lasted.   I soon learned that I had made a mistake in waving my hat to keep them away from my face; they got into my hair and it was difficult to extricate them.   Fortunately when the rains came, the ants left.

"To reach Antonito, Colorado, which was my destination, the road traversed a low country that had been pretty well flooded by the heavy rains during the day.   I struck this boggy section of the road after dark when my horse was so tired that he could scarcely make headway on firm ground.   After floundering about, we managed to get through, and about 10 o'clock, I reached Antonito and most anxious to get some nourishment since I had only one sandwich since breakfast, which I had eaten about 5 a.m.

"To my dismay, the stores and restaurants were closed, and the small hotel had no dining service.   So there was nothing to do but go to bed hungry, but I was too dog tired and sleepy to let this bother me unduly."

On another trip he made in the Chiricahua National Forest with Forest Supervisor McGlone, Waha encountered a situation that demonstrated what can happen when a public official overlooks the public relations side of his job.

The headquarters of the Chiricahua Forest had been moved from Paradise, a small mining town in the mountains, to Douglas. McGlone and Waha rode the mail stage from Douglas to Paradise.

"When we approached the post office and general store there were a number of loiterers on the porch," Waha recalled. "We were greeted with a yell that went like this: 'Moldy bread and moldy ham—to hell with the Forest Service,' followed by a typical cowpuncher yell.

"This was a bit disconcerting to say the least, and after we had reached the place where we were to stay overnight, I learned upon inquiry from McGlone the significance of this most unusual greeting.   It seems that after he had moved his office to Douglas he had been interviewed by a newspaper reporter who had been interested in learning the reasons for transferring the headquarters.   After stating the principal reasons, he went on with disparaging remarks about living conditions in Paradise, particularly the poor food that one had to put up with and made reference to moldy bread and moldy ham.   Being quite naive and not having had experience with reporters, he did not realize that his remarks might appear in bold type in the newspaper.   So naturally when the residents of Paradise read the paper and saw what McGlone had said (unfortunately the article gave the impression that the compelling reasons for the transfer were due to the poor food he was able to get in Paradise mentioning specifically the moldy bread and ham), they were incensed to a fighting degree.   McGlone never lived down this indiscretion."

Waha recalled that besides inspections, he was often called out as a "trouble shooter."   One such experience occurred in the Jemez Forest.

"The Forest Service had employed an engineer to make an accurate survey of the boundaries of one of the old Spanish land grants within the Jemez National Forest," Waha related.   "As I recall the case now the engineer was drinking to excess and something was rotten in the financial management of the camp.   At any rate, I was assigned to make the necessary investigation.   The trip that I had to make on horseback after leaving Espanola, the railroad point, is quoted from my diary:

"January 2, 1908.   At Espanola; arose at 6:30 a.m., by 7:10 I was in the saddle, and it was awfully cold.   My pony which I had procured from Ranger Leese was all bowed up, but I held his head up and kept him from 'piling' me.   About three miles from town up the Rio Grande valley, I met Ramon Salazar, a butcher, and another man who were going to Cañones, which I was told was close to Coyote, my destination.   We didn't go by the regular road up the Chama River by way of Abiquiu but took a more direct route by road and trail across the mountains.   I later regretted not taking the regular road, for we got into snow and had to follow icy and rocky trails for miles.   I became awfully sore since the saddle did not fit me.   It was not long after this trip that I decided to use a McClellan saddle instead of depending on any kind of a saddle I was able to rent.   Having always used a large stock saddle, as did everybody else, I had to take some razzing when I changed to a McClellan.   One can, of course, get saddle sore from riding a McClellan, but not nearly so sore as riding a misfit stock saddle.

"Rode like the devil when we came to fairly level stretches.   Stopped at Juan Lopez's goat ranch on the Lobato Grant for dinner and also fed our horses.   For our dinner we had boiled potatoes with meat, *tortillas,* and coffee.   Since the only dishes that were set before us consisted of a cup, saucer and spoon, I ate the potatoes with a spoon and picked the meat off the bones with my fingers.   We paid $.50 for the meal.   The men I was riding with talked their lingo all day long and only occasionally spoke to me in English. After going down a steep-sided rocky canyon for about three miles, where the trail was fierce, we struck Cañones, a small plaza, about 3:45 p.m.   My *compadres* left me at about 4 o'clock at a ranch where they were going to buy cattle to drive back to Espanola, and I started for Coyote, 12 miles farther west.   It was quite gloomy at 4 o'clock because of the black snow clouds.

   "My poor little pony was about all in, but when a Mexican caught up with me about dark, my pony took a last brace and stayed up.   On the last stretch I saw a coyote about 50 yards off the road which stared at me and refused to move notwithstanding my shouts and gestures.   Reached Coyote about 6:15 after having crossed the icy Rio Puerco numerous times.   It was plumb dark.   I went to the poolroom and found a boy who took me to Garcia's where I found a pretty squalid outfit.   Only the son could speak English; he had been attending the Phoenix Indian School for three years.   Had a supper of eggs, steak and coffee, all the while the whole family standing about and talking about me.   After supper I went to my room where a blazing fire in the three-cornered fireplace was burning cheerfully.   Talked with Garcia's English-speaking son until bedtime.   Feeling better but ached all over.   My horse had been well taken care of.   I slept quite well.

   "Sunday, January 3, 1908.   Arose at 7:45 a.m.   Had a greasy breakfast of fried potatoes, *frijoles,* an egg and coffee.   Many native people in town; church bells ringing all of the time.   Can scarcely walk owing to the swelling of my legs from riding.   Dread getting in saddle again.   It is snowing, but not enough to bother. Being only *Anglo* in this *placita,* I feel as if I were in a foreign country.   Everybody stares at me.   Got my horse from the corral at 11:30, paid bills and started up the canyon for Ranger Blake's headquarters.   Stopped at the second *adobe* house where I had been told Blake made his headquarters.   On knocking, door was opened by a six year-old boy and looking in the room, I saw an old decrepit man sitting on the floor alongside the fireplace.   I asked him in Spanish if Blake lived here and he yelled out something which I did not *sabe.*   Then he got up and I saw he was terribly deformed and also blind.   He staggered to me and I allowed him to shake hands with me, but when he commenced rubbing his hands on my arm and I got a good look at his face which was most hideous, I concluded to 'hit the *adobe*' for I had a hunch he might be a leper or had some equally terrible disease. I then rode to the next house which proved to be where Blake was living.   His village friends informed me that he was about 6 miles up the canyon working on a cabin. I rode up over the slippery hilly road, met Blake and after getting warm at a camp fire, returned with Blake to his house. It snowed all afternoon. Assistant Ranger Crumb came in the evening and I was glad to see him for it saved me a considerable ride. Had a bum supper cooked by native woman. Blake turned in about 7:30 p.m. Crumb and I discussed the engineer affair and I had him write a statement regarding it. We turned in about 11 o'clock. At 1 a.m. Blake got up and rummaged about the room, rustling papers, going through trunks and boxes. At 4 o'clock he called Crumb and me to get up for breakfast. At 5 o'clock Blake was in the saddle, while I waited for daylight before starting out.

"January 4. Rode from Blake's headquarters on Coyote Creek to Abiquiu. About three miles from Coyote I got on wrong road which took me too far to the northwest, so I cut across a big open country to strike the right road. The coyotes were numerous and barked at me. My pony wanted to take me back to Coyote and it was necessary to fight him to keep him headed the way I wanted to go. It was a long wearisome ride down the Chama to Abiquiu. My legs ached so badly I could not stand riding out of a walk. Crossed river to Abiquiu intending to stay at Tomas Gonzales', but he was not home, so I crossed back and after much inquiry, found a stopping place at Jesus Martinez's *adobe* three miles below Abiquiu. Never saw so many nasty dogs as there, in and near Abiquiu. They came at us in bunches snarling and biting at my horse's heels. At Martinez's the daughter who had attended a Presbyterian mission school could speak English fairly well."

Such were the typical working conditions of the Rangers in the early days of the Service. Waha may have been a tenderfoot when he arrived in New Mexico but he was certainly learning the hard way to be a man who matched the mountains.

It was less than a couple months later that Waha was sent to the Black Mesa Forest (now Apache National Forest) in Arizona to help reorganize the office in Springerville.

After a week with Supervisor Martin he rented a horse to ride to Show Low, headquarters of the Sitgreaves National Forest.

"I thought I would have no difficulty in reaching Show Low by dark," Waha related. "But the day turned out to be pretty bad, high winds and snow storms, and muddy roads. I was in the saddle $13\frac{1}{2}$ hours; no, it was probably 12 hours, for I had to walk and lead my horse as he had gone lame in one foot and was about to give out. At 10 p.m. I decided it was impracticable to attempt going further, so I made camp on a gently rolling ridge on which there was a scattering of pine trees. First, I gathered needles and twigs and built a small fire and then rustled around in the darkness for some good-size chunks for making a big fire, since the night was cold and windy. All I could find was a rather large log and not having an axe, I had to exert all of the strength still left in me to drag it in.

"After unsaddling and feeding my horse—luckily I had brought a feed of oats on my saddle—I tied him up and then started out afoot to reconnoiter. I felt quite positive that I was on the right trail and also that I must have covered about 50 miles and should therefore be somewhere in the vicinity of Show Low. However, after scouting about for an hour or so, I returned to my camp, hobbled my horse, laid my saddle blanket on some pine needles which I had scraped together to soften the *malpais* rocks a bit, sat down before the fire to think it over. It was surely a lonesome night and while I managed to doze a little, I couldn't sleep. A bunch of coyotes prowling around would howl heathenishly and make one feel a bit shivery. I had a sandwich in my saddle bags which I had saved out from my lunch but refrained from eating, believing that I would be more hungry in the morning. And besides, if my horse got away from me during the night, I figured it wouldn't be so good to be afoot and perhaps lost and with no food whatever.

"Along about 2:30 a.m. I was dreamily thinking of the good bed I was missing and many other things when I realized that I could not hear my horse. Immediately I aroused myself and started out to find him, and much to my surprise, for I had thought he was about worn out, I found him about ¾ of a mile from camp and making hurried tracks to Springerville. I brought him back to camp, tied him up and let him feed on 'post' hay for the remainder of the night. He was really good company for me and I was amused in watching him for he seemed to have me sized up for somewhat of an idiot, and by his looks I imagined he was rather sneering at me. I certainly couldn't blame him a bit. . . .

"Daylight came none too soon to suit me. I prepared a hurried breakfast, which consisted of a toasted tongue sandwich, then I saddled up and started. After riding two miles, I found myself in Show Low. I had been on the hill above Show Low when I was out reconnoitering and could have seen the town if there had been any lights in any of the houses. The Mormons had the habit of going to bed early. I arrived at Supervisor Mackay's headquarters just in time for breakfast, immediately after which I went to bed and slept until 3 o'clock.

"I stayed in Show Low two days and then hit the trail back to

Springerville, but this time I made a two days' trip of it, because a Ranger with a pack outfit came half way with me and we camped in comfort."

Probably every Forest Ranger has an unusual story to tell about being caught in a storm or having an accident while alone in the woods when he had to summon every bit of nerve and reserve stamina to make it back to help or habitation.

The late Richard H. Hanna, for many years a prominent Albuquerque attorney, served as a Ranger in his youth under Supervisor McClure and his father, I. B. Hanna, who was Superintendent of Forest Reserves for the Southwest.

In a paper he prepared many years ago, Hanna related an experience of his father's as an example of how the early Forest Officers had to be self-reliant and self-sustaining "when they traveled wild forest land and endless *mesas*, often far from any habitation."

"My father had a painful, and almost tragic experience once, on a field trip from Santa Fe," Attorney Hanna wrote. "He was riding by buckboard from Flagstaff to Lee's Ferry. He hobbled his team at night, but they slipped their hobbles and got away. He was still 30 miles from Lee's Ferry, but started there on foot. Father had a bad knee, resulting from a baseball injury in younger days, and after ten miles of walking, the pain in his knee became unbearable.

"He crawled the remaining 20 miles on his hands and knees. It was summertime, and he ran out of water, but he had a few cans of tomatoes that kept him going. When he finally reached Lee's Ferry at night, the ferry boat was tied up across the river; his shouts failed to arouse the people over there. He emptied his revolver before they heard and came after him."

CHAPTER III
Cattle, Sheep and People

Many a man who started as a $60 or $90-a-month Ranger went on to a distinguished career in the Forest Service. Generally, in reminiscent mood or writing of their experiences, they looked back with nostalgia to the early days of Forest Service employment.

Leon F. Kneipp, who held many important positions with the Forest Service and who contributed significantly to the development of the Service's grazing policies and procedures, started as a Ranger on the Prescott Forest Reserve in 1900 at $60 a month. By 1902, his salary had been raised to $90, "which put me right next to the Supervisor."

In a long letter to a friend several years ago, Kneipp described conditions and some of the duties in the Prescott Reserve in the early 1900's.

"Crown King was a hardship job because it was completely isolated from all centers of production or distribution," he wrote. "Horses had to be fed hay and rolled barley, which sometimes soared to $30 per ton and $2.75 per 70-pound sack. There were lots of vacant mining shacks, but all other items were high, so a $60-a-month Ranger salary, which had to keep a horse as well as the Ranger, had no attraction for men who could get $3.00 per 8-hour day."

The most picturesque of the early Rangers on the Prescott Reserve, he wrote, was William H. Cokely. Cokely, who served as Ranger for only a few months in 1903 and '04, "claimed a sponsor who knew where some of the residue of the Government camel herd was still running loose and had hired him to corral them."

Until his project got under way, Cokely supposedly was at loose ends and took a job with the Reserve.

"He was a superb horse-breaker and rider," Kneipp remembered, "so instead of buying horses, he talked local ranchers into turning some of their young horses over to him, later to be returned as well-broken and gentle, which they were."

In 1904, Kneipp was detailed to accompany Lou Barrett on

an inspection trip of the Prescott Reserve. When they arrived at Cokely's District, the Crown King, Kneipp introduced Barrett to Cokely.

"Hello Cokely, remember me?"

Cokely looked at him suspiciously. Barrett added, "Gut-ribber, Troop D."

Cokely lost his caution and brightened up. "Why Lou Barrett, you such-and-such so-and-so."

Cokely and Barrett had soldiered together in the Philippines, chasing Aguinaldo.

One of Cokely's duties was, of course, to notify trespassers to vacate if they built illegally on Reserve lands. In those days, as Kneipp pointed out, "whenever a considerable number of virile males was brought together by a new mining development or railroad or reservoir construction, a coterie of feminine charm was soon in nearby residence. When asked by what right they were occupying the area, the stock reply was, 'Come out and I'll show you my mining location and discovery shaft.'

"The case would be reported to the General Land Office in Washington and the consistent result was to serve a notice for vacating the area in 10 days. When nothing had happened following such service, the General Land Office was so advised and the usual instruction was to serve another 10-day notice. Some of the places had three or four such notices pasted on the bar mirrors."

Kneipp recalled that when the railroad was constructed to Crown King, a woman named Bernice established a place half way between the King and Mayer. Cokely rode over to the place to serve a second 10-day notice on her.

"The talk was pretty rough," said Kneipp. "But Cokely could be about as vitriolic as any, so that he didn't mind. However, something happened to upset him. He was riding a half-broken bronc, and he was somewhat careless in mounting him. The horse dumped him—head first into a rainwater barrel at the corner of the building.

"According to an eye-witness, he was upended in the water, and one of the male habitues declared: 'He got in by hisself, let the s.o.b. get out by hisself.' But Bernice declared she didn't want a charge of murder added to her other complications and made them haul Cokely out."

It was soon after that episode that Cokely left the Crown King District, and associates lost track of him. He was succeeded by Frank C. W. Pooler, who stayed with the Forest Service for a distinguished lifetime career.

Roscoe G. Willson, another pioneer in the Forest Service, started in the Crown King District. He had knocked around Mexico and Arizona as a prospector and miner and took a job in the Crown King, working there for five years before Ranger Frank Pooler suggested he take the examination for fireguard in December, 1905. He passed, and then in the spring of 1906 passed the examination for Ranger.

After serving on the Prescott, for a year, Willson was sent to what the Rangers in those days referred to as the "Sneeze-Cough Forest." It was composed of the Huachuca, the Tumacacori, and the Baboquivari—which is how the "Sneeze-Cough" name originated.

Reminiscing at his home in Phoenix, Willson recalled that it was on the Sneeze-Cough Forest in 1908 that he first met Will C. Barnes,* who is probably better known to the reading public as a writer than as a Forest Service official.

"He came down there to make an inspection of the Forest," Willson recalled, "and among other things I took him out to the old Tumacacori Mission. He became interested, and it was through him that they sent me an engineer to go out and survey 10 acres around the Mission and have it withdrawn as a National Monument."

Headquarters of the Forest was at Nogales, and as Willson recalled, there was no one name for the group of individual Forest Districts.

"I met with the Chamber of Commerce in Nogales and told them we wanted a name for the Forest—something that applied to the history of the region. Well, one of them suggested Padre Garces, a missionary who had been in that region quite a good deal.

"This Father Garces was the first missionary to come into Arizona after Father Kino, who had little missions at Tumacacori and where Tucson is now—San Xavier. Garces was the first priest after him. He established a mission at Yuma, and for some

---

*Will C. Barnes joined the Army in 1879 and served in the Signal Corps in Arizona, taking part in the Apache campaign of 1881, for which he received a Medal of Honor. After Army service he operated cattle ranches in New Mexico and Arizona and served in the legislatures of both states. After the reorganization of the Forest Service in 1907, Chief Forester Pinchot appointed him Assistant Forester and Chief of Grazing, and he had a distinguished career in the Forest Service until his retirement in 1928. In the 1920's he turned to writing and produced a tremendous volume of articles and books on Arizona history, personal reminiscences, and on outdoor subjects. Barnes died in 1936.

reason he aroused antagonism among the Indians and they killed him, along with a number of Spanish soldiers.

"I recommended that the new name of the Forest be Garces* National Forest, and that was done."

Willson recalled that one of his first problems was a trespass case against one of the big mining companies of the District.

"They had been cutting thousands of cords of wood," he said. "At the time I went down there, they had long stacks of it, several hundred cords piled up.

"I was instructed to start trespass proceedings against them to collect damages. It was nice live oak wood that they used in the mill in the boilers. So I started suit against them. They settled without going to court."

Another trespass case was of a different kind. The San Rafael Land Grant was owned by Colin Cameron, a brother of Senator Cameron of Pennsylvania. The grant boundaries called for six square leagues.

"He interpreted this to mean six leagues square—which made a vast difference. The cattlemen there told me that he had run his fences way outside the grant, taking in a lot of land which now was included within the Forest. So it was up to me to do something about it. I went to Mr. Cameron and got him up to the office and talked it over with him. All I could get out of Cameron was the threat that he would take my job away from me. I told him, 'Well, all right, go ahead and get my job, but you're going to have to take your fence down and put it back on the real lines of the grant, which calls for six square leagues, not six leagues square.' Well, he was going to fight it by law. He didn't do anything and finally I went out there and told him, I said, 'Now, Mr. Cameron, if you haven't started to take that fence down by Monday I'm going to come out with the Rangers and we're going to take it down.' Well, I went out on Monday and I saw he had a crew of men taking the fence down and putting it back on the line. I had a man named Fred Crater who had run the boundary and had marked it, so he was putting his fence back on the true line of the San Rafael grant. That was one of the most interesting things that happened while I was down there on the border."

In 1905, a new regulation was adopted charging a grazing fee on and after January 1, 1906, for stock ranging at large on the Reserve ranges. This provided some serious problems for the Rangers, and Willson recalled some of his experiences with this situation while he was on the Tonto National Forest.

---

*Combined with Coronado National Forest, April, 1911.

"I found that the cattlemen were not applying for anywhere near the number of cattle that they owned," he said. "The Rangers I had were mostly locals, and they knew the situation pretty well. They knew about what each individual had. I tried to raise the permits when it came time to make the grazing applications, and I didn't do very well. I couldn't get much increase out of them so I started in and organized cattle associations in each Ranger District. I got the cattlemen a little interested in getting to the meetings and I told them, I said, 'Now, you fellows get together among yourselves and decide how many cattle each of you is going to apply for.' 'Well,' they said, 'darn it, there's the county tax assessor's records; we don't want to show up too many cattle at tax time.' I said, 'Of course that's true, but you are going to have to pay the grazing fee on approximately the number of cattle you have here.'

"Well, they were in a great stew over that, having to pay the county tax fee on that basis, but I did manage to get a little raise out of them. I couldn't get them to agree to talk it over among themselves and put down how many each one would apply for. They would look at each other and say, 'Hell, I'm not going to tell how many John's got, and he's not going to tell how many I've got.' It was not a great deal of increase, although I did get some. But it was a good try; by organizing those cattle associations."

Problems with the stockmen were not to be solved overnight, and as R. A. Rogers recalls, "conditions were in a turmoil in the spring of 1908. About that time I was ordered to Nogales to relieve Roscoe G. Willson, who had been called to Washington. My first caller was Max Axford, general manager of the Green Cattle Co.

"Max did not sit down, and looked mad clear through. He said Willson had notified them that if they did not remove their cattle, he would round them up and drive 4500 of them to the Baboquivari Mountains, 75 miles or more across the desert. I told him I was the Supervisor for the time being, and if he would sit down we would go over the matter and that he would not be more fair than I would be.

"His company, or their cowboys, had torn out watering places, pried out water pipes, torn down windmills, etc. I told him there was not going to be any such thing as attempting to drive their cattle; that their status would be gone over later and a proper and fair settlement made. He agreed that the company men would repair all damaged water places and we would start over on a friendly basis.

"That night I had a telephone message from Will Barnes at

Phoenix. I met him at Lully's restaurant in the evening and after eating we went to the office where we went over the Green Cattle Company's case, which was what he had come for. After we had finished he said, 'I was sent here on this case and told to go to the range and make a personal investigation, but I am not going there. I shall report that we have a man on the ground capable of caring for the situation, and I shall leave for Washington tomorrow morning.'

"We began to try to find out how many cattle were being grazed on the Forest, which raised the antagonism to a high pitch. Robert Selkirk and John Kerr came down from the Regional Office to try to help. Kerr was the most untalkative man I ever had met. He had forgotten more about the cattle business than most stockmen had ever learned, and knew the grazing regulations absolutely. Kind, honest and considerate always, but I often thought when I heard him give a decision that he must sweat icicles.

"Cattle rustling was not legalized then, though there was little said about it, for everybody was doing it. Only when a friendless chap got caught was he taken to court. Most cases were settled on the ground at the time, and many times one man was left on the ground when the case was closed. Cattle rustling was down to a fine art with some."

Sheep were also a problem on the Tonto. While he was still on the Tonto, Willson estimated there were in the neighborhood of 100,000 sheep "that came down from the mountains and went out onto the desert. They came down here to lamb and to shear, then went back over the trail. My predecessor there, William H. Reed, had laid out a sort of trail. He and his Rangers had put posts along, laying it out, but they hadn't marked the sides or anything, and hadn't gone into it very thoroughly. One of my first jobs on the Tonto was to go out with the boys and lay out this sheep trail. One reason that it was advisable was that the year before I went there a cowman had killed a sheep man. There was a great deal of disturbance on the Tonto and the cowboys were constantly threatening the sheepherders.

"In fact I remember George Scott taking his sheep down through Johnny Tillson's ranch. A couple of men came out to stop him. Scott had his rifle across his saddle. He just turned his horse sideways so that the rifle would point right at Johnny Tillson's belly and he said: 'Now Johnny, you know we don't want to eat any more of your range than we possibly have to. I'll get the sheep out of here just as quick as we can, but we've got to get through here and there's no use in saying anything more.'

"Johnny looked at the rifle pointing at his belly and he said, 'All right, George, you get out as quick as you can.' "

There was another time when Scott was not so fortunate. The incident was recalled by Senior Forest Ranger Fred W. Croxen at the Tonto Grazing Conference in Phoenix in November, 1926:

"The sheepmen from the higher country and from New Mexico got to driving their herds into the Tonto country and on the west slope of the Mazatzals to winter on the grass and to lamb in the spring. This country had already been fully stocked by the cattlemen, and it only worked a hardship on them to have these sheep wintered on their range. A range war was about to open when the Tonto National Forest was created. . . .

"One fall, George Scott, one of the present (1926) users of the Heber-Reno Driveway, came on Hardscrabble Mesa west of Pine with four bands of sheep and heavily armed herders and tenders. Seventeen cattlemen took them unawares and disarmed the outfit, threw the bands together, shoved them off into Fossil Creek and told them not to come back. Scott had camped away from the bands . . . and could not be found by the cattlemen."

Roscoe Willson noted that those kinds of trespass cases are no problem today since "everything is clearly marked out and time-apportionment on the Forests is decided."

"The Babbitt Brothers were among the biggest sheep owners in Arizona at one time," Willson said. "I don't think they have any today. They leased out a good many of their sheep to other people, some Basques and others. Anyway, one of their outfits had been out on the desert during the winter and came back into the Forest near the Superstition Mountains and just spread out and started lambing. You know they break them up into little bunches and get extra herders when they're lambing to take care of each bunch. They put up little tents and put the lambs in with their mothers when they won't recognize each other.

"A cattleman came to me right away and said, 'Here they are camped on my range and are eating up my food and what are you going to do about it?' 'Well,' I said, 'I don't suppose I can move them if they are lambing now, but I'll go down there and try to give them a lesson anyway.'

"So I got Jim Girdner (Jim is dead now) and we went down there. I consulted the United States Attorney and he told me what to do. So Jim and I went down there and we arrested three or four different herders. We didn't take enough men away to leave the sheep neglected, you understand, so that they could not possibly bring suit for allowing their sheep to be destroyed. We took the herders down to Phoenix and had a trial in the U. S. Court. Babbitt Brothers came down there, Dave and George.

"The first man that was brought in was the foreman, Avilla, a Basque. Judge Knave, I think it was, fined him $400. We had five or six other men under arrest. I was standing at the back with Dave Babbit and he said, 'My God, are you going to soak all those fellows like that?' I said, 'Well, I don't know. That's strictly up to the Judge.' The others were just common herders, you know, and the Judge just fined them a dollar and gave them a good talking to. He told them they must pay the dollar and said that their desires couldn't come ahead of Government regulations; that they couldn't do as they pleased on the National Forest. The Babbitts were greatly relieved when they found that the other fellows were fined only a dollar each."

The extent of the permit use of the Forest grazing lands at that time is indicated by the annual report of Willard M. Drake, Supervisor of the Coconino National Forest, for 1910, which showed a total of 33,200 head of cattle and 89,550 head of sheep under permit. These figures did not include livestock not reported or trespassing on Forest lands.

Over on the Pecos River Reserve in New Mexico a new Ranger on the Reserve had a few trespass troubles early in his career. Tom Stewart, who eventually became "Mr. Pecos" to old-timers in the Forest Service, started his career on May 1, 1902, with a letter notifying him of his appointment, accompanied by a map, some stationery, and a directive to "Get busy." Stewart related the story of his early years on the Pecos to Bob Kelleher of the Regional Office Information and Education staff in 1942:

"I put in the rest of the summer of 1902 chasing trespassing herds of livestock off the Forest, fighting several small fires, trying to establish some sort of boundary on the west side of my District (that had never been surveyed), and getting acquainted with the District and the people in or near it. There were homesteads and other private land inside the Forest, just as there are today.

"To know whether logging or grazing trespass was occurring inside the eastern boundary, I finally bought a pocket compass and ran my own line over the rough country. It wouldn't stand in court, but it helped me find and report many trespass cases.

"Boundary disputes and political influence kept all but two of the cases from standing up in court. That embarrassed me, and at times I felt discouraged to the extent of giving up the job. But I liked the work and determined to stick.

"Figuring I couldn't do anything through the courts, I used an educational plan of my own. Eighty percent of the people in that locality were Spanish-American. I had a knack of making friends of them, so I attended their *fiestas* and dances, held meetings when the chance allowed, and explained the purpose of the Forest Reserves.   Before long I had the better and influential element seeing the light, and from then on my job was somewhat easier.

"That did not stop all the trespass, of course.   One case I found out about involved the taking of considerable unpurchased timber from the Reserve, by a prominent politician who had a small sawmill on the upper Gallinas River, north of Las Vegas. I'll call him Don Carlos though that isn't his name.   He claimed title to the land, but through my Supervisor I obtained General Land Office records, checked section lines on the ground, and determined the timber land involved was inside the Forest Reserve. I offered Don Carlos a chance to pay the Government for the timber he had cut.   He got mad and refused, but stopped cutting in the Reserve.   Despite his influence, he was brought to trial in Federal court at Las Vegas.   He finally settled, paying something over $1,000."

Stewart had sheep troubles too.   As Rangers had no power to make arrests, he could only drive the sheep off the Reserve.

"Some herders were bad *hombres,*" Stewart recalled, "and the life of a Ranger driving them off the Forest was not too safe. Whenever it would take several days to drive a band of sheep out to the boundary, I would pitch my camp at night two or three miles from the herders' camp, and just to make sure they wouldn't try sticking a knife in me while I slept, I would sleep several hundred yards away from my camp.

"Things changed when Rangers finally received arrest power, and I got sweet vengeance.   A band of sheep which belonged to somewhat of a politician in Rio Arriba County had been trespassing regularly in the Santa Barbara vicinity in the Forest.   It had got to be a joke among the herders because I would chase them off, and in a few days I would find them back again.   As soon as we got power to make arrests, I sent to Las Vegas for handcuffs and a padlock and ten feet of chain and started making tracks for the Santa Barbara country.   Sure enough, I found three herders (two men and a boy) with sheep and no permit.   They gave me the horse laugh, but I disclosed the joke was on them this time.   I arrested the men and sent the boy home on a burro to get other herders.

"Camping for the night, I handcuffed the prisoners to a tree. I felt certain their case would be dismissed in Santa Fe, so I decided they should get their justice on the way.   After the new herders arrived and I gave the prisoners breakfast, I handcuffed each of the two, got on my horse and marched them 25 miles on foot to Windsor's ranch.   From there we traveled by buckboard and train to Santa Fe.   Their case was dismissed but it was soon rumored around that Rangers had police powers, and the trespass troubles became less numerous."

Although Tom Stewart and some of the other early Rangers and fire guards may have started their jobs with only scanty instructions from the Supervisors, it was not long before the Forest Service had voluminous and detailed instructions covering almost every conceivable situation.

The early Use Books produced under the direction of Gifford Pinchot, Chief Forester, are now so rare as to be collector's items. The Use Book was a manual of instructions and information covering such subjects as organization, personnel, meetings, examinations, claims, various uses of the National Forests, timber sales, grazing, fire-fighting, and even such odds and ends as detailed instructions for using Rangers' card record cases and filing equipment, by drawers and sections.

It is interesting to note that in its very first sentence the Use Book expresses the philosophy that "The timber, water, pasture, minerals and other resources of the National Forests are for the use of the people."

This explains why the Forest Service dropped the name "Forest Reserves" and began to use the name "National Forests." "Reserve" was a misnomer for it was the intention to use the Forests, not reserve them.

Referring to the resources of the National Forest, the Use Book pointed out that they "may be obtained under reasonable conditions without delay.   Legitimate improvements and business enterprises are encouraged.   National Forests are open to all persons for all lawful purposes."   The purpose in creating the National Forests was summed up in this sentence:

"The National Forests are created to preserve a perpetual supply of timber for home industries, to prevent destruction of the forest cover which regulates the flow of streams, and to protect local residents from unfair competition in the use of forest and range."

While Tom Stewart was Supervisor of the Pecos National Forest, he had a young fellow in his District who had become a Ranger on January 1, 1909, and served briefly in the Jemez District.   He was to become well known later as State Game Warden of New Mexico—a position he held for many years.   His name was Elliott Barker.

"My first assignment was to headquarter at the town of Cuba in Sandoval County on the west side of Jemez Forest," Barker related.

"That was pretty rugged country in those days: I mean the people were pretty rough. There had been two Rangers—I don't recall their first names—but Brennan and Thomas, ex-Philippine campaign soldiers, had been sent over there in April, right after they had taken the examination. They had gotten into serious trouble and really got the very dickens beat out of them there one night at a saloon—where they shouldn't have been. So they quit; they had had enough. I was sent over there with A. W. Sypher, a mountain man from Arkansas, I believe it was, or maybe it was Tennessee, who knew his way around in that company. The two of us were sent.

"I was just a big overgrown 22-year-old kid, didn't have sense enough to be afraid of anything, so we went over there together. Our instructions from Ross McMillan, the Supervisor, were that we were to live together, work together, and were never to step outside of the house without our sidearms on and at the ready. We were never to ride alone anywhere and we were never to be out after dark, under any conditions. Those were our definite instructions. We were to stay out of trouble if possible and to try to tame that country.

"Now the reason that we had quite a problem was that the leaders over there, particularly one man who was very powerful politically, resented the Forest Service coming in very, very much. The common people, I don't think did, but their leaders inspired them to all kinds of devilment. The leaders resented the Forest Service coming in, prohibiting them from cutting timber how, where and when they pleased, and prohibiting them from running as many cattle or sheep on the Forests as they wanted to. They resented having to pay any grazing fee or to have to submit to any Government regulations. The going was really pretty tough. We stuck it out, though. Along in the late summer of 1909, Sypher was given another partner and they moved up to the little town of LaJara above Cuba. I was sent over to Bluebird Mesa where I joined up with Ranger W. B. Bletcher who had a little more experience as a Ranger than either Sypher or me. We worked together there until October. I may say that we stayed out of any serious trouble. I never did have to use my gun, but there were many, many times that if I hadn't had it I would have been in serious trouble; there is no question about that. On one or two occasions Bletcher did have to draw his gun but he never did use it."

In the fall of 1909, the Carson, Jemez and Santa Fe National Forests were placed under separate Supervisors. McMillan took the Carson Forest. Frank Andrews was promoted from Deputy

Supervisor on the Gila to Supervisor of the Jemez, and Tom Stewart, Deputy Supervisor of the Jemez, Pecos, and Carson was made Supervisor of the Pecos Forest. He knew of young Barker's capabilities and the fact that he was intimately acquainted with the Pecos country, and he asked Frank Andrews to allow Barker to be transferred. Andrews gave his consent, and Barker returned to the country where he had guided hunting parties and where as a youngster he had hunted predators himself for the bounty of $2.00 on bobcats and $20 on mountain lions and bears.

In his book "Beatty's Cabin,"* Barker tells a delightful story of one of his earliest assignments on the Pecos:

"I rode over to the H. S. (Steve) Arnold place on Chaparrito Creek, to take his application for a grazing permit on the National Forest for that season. I had never met the Arnold family; but at the house, Mrs. Arnold told me that Mr. Arnold and the boys were over on the Cow Creek place, three miles away, baling hay, so I rode on over there.

"It had been cold, and there was considerable snow on the ground and in fact, much of the Creek was still frozen over. When I got to the canyon, I could see the baling crew at work at a haystack a half-mile below. I noticed someone over at the creek, a hundred yards away, so I rode over there to inquire for Mr. Arnold.

"Imagine my surprise when I rode around a clump of willows and came face to face with the prettiest little sixteen-year-old girl I ever did see, standing there on the ice over a big pool in the river. The young lady was as surprised as I was, and why shouldn't she be? She was fishing for trout through the ice with a horsehair snare, which was, of course, illegal. Worse yet, it was out of season and she had no fishing license, but boy she did have a beautiful string of trout!

"It should be remembered that Forest Rangers then, as now, are required by Federal statute to cooperate in the enforcement of the state game and fish laws and, hence, they carry deputy game warden commissions. Now what would you have done had you been in my place? Chivalry was not dead; on the other hand, an oath of office in which one swears to enforce the laws of the state is not to be taken lightly. She was in a predicament, and I was facing a dilemma. She courteously directed me to her father down the canyon at the hay baler. That gave me time to think and her time to repent. What should I do?

*Published by University of New Mexico Press, Albuquerque 1953. Quoted by special permission.

"She said she didn't have the money to pay a fine, and I knew the judge would say she was too young to put in jail, so what? Well, to make a long story short, the law allows two years in which to file a complaint for a game law violation. In some devious way, within that time limitation, she was remanded to my personal custody; and in season and with proper license, she has been fishing with me ever since."

Barker and Ethel Arnold were married the next year and in the summer of 1911 were living at the Panchuela Ranger Station, 18 miles up in the mountains from the town of Pecos, when Barker got into trouble over a telephone line.

The Forest Service's Use Book had an instruction that arrangements should be made as rapidly as possible to connect the Supervisor's headquarters with the Rangers headquarters and the lookout stations, so that fires could be reported and other business managed expeditiously.

In the summer of 1912, a telephone company employee named Starkweather was sent to the Pecos Forest to experiment with different methods of stringing telephone wire quickly to get to forest fires or make connections.

"He used a very small insulated wire that was supposed to be strung out from a spool attached to the back of a saddle," Barker said.

"You know, it looked pretty ridiculous to me, and actually, it didn't work. It was an experiment that was worthy to be carried out, and I was supposed to work in cooperation with him. Well, at any rate, that kind of thing didn't appeal to me too much and I guess I just didn't cooperate like I should.

"At any rate, I got into trouble with my Supervisor and particularly with the Regional Forester. A. C. Waha was in charge of Personnel-Operation I believe they called it—and he insisted on my transfer to the Carson National Forest. In fact they talked about firing me, but finally decided to transfer me to the Carson, against my will. I didn't want to go. I didn't want to leave the Pecos country.

"However, I consented to go to the Carson, and it was the most fortunate move that was ever made by or for me. It so happened that Aldo Leopold was Supervisor of the Carson National Forest. Even then our avocations more or less coincided— our thinking on wildlife, the outdoors, recreation, that sort of thing. We hit it off wonderfully well from the very first time we met, right on through. I never had the slightest trouble up there. Leopold put me to work on things I knew how to do and could do, and I did the best I could for him. I think it was the most fortunate thing that ever happened to me to be able to work under a man like Aldo Leopold, who later became perhaps the world's greatest authority on wildlife and wildlife management."

Leopold had been made Forest Supervisor of the Carson National Forest in 1912, with headquarters at Tres Piedras.

Raymond E. Marsh, Deputy Supervisor of the Carson at the time, in a letter to Edward P. Cliff, Chief of the Forest Service, in August, 1967, related a most dramatic incident involving Leopold.

"In the latter part of March, 1913, Leopold started on a month-long horseback trip to the westernmost (Jicarilla) Division of the Forest," Marsh wrote. "He had to cross the Amarilla Division, the Tierra Amarilla Grant, and the Jicarilla Indian Reservation, a distance of about 100 miles. I remained in the office, in charge.

"The late-winter, early-spring weather was cold and wet. Conditions were not propitious for such a trip. We lost communication with Leopold. It was unusual for a Supervisor to be entirely out of touch with his office for a matter of weeks, even in those days of poor communication. Then, one forenoon, he unexpectedly walked into the office. He had left his horse in the Jicarilla country, and returned to Tres Piedras by the narrow gauge railroad that extended from Durango, Colorado, to Alamosa, with a branch line (long ago discontinued) from Antonito south through Tres Piedras to Santa Fe.

"Leopold's and my desk were back to back, mine facing the door. I clearly remember his appearance as he entered the room. His face, hands, arms and legs were badly swollen. His cowboy riding boots had been slashed so he could get them on. He emphatically insisted that nothing was seriously wrong, and seemed to think that with a few days rest he would be all right. Lee Harris, the Lands staff man, and I thought differently. We insisted that he take the next train (the following day) to Santa Fe for medical attention, which he did, reluctantly. His wife was there.

"His illness was diagnosed as acute Bright's disease. I was later told it was caused by the inclement weather of the season; that the acute form was sometimes curable, whereas the chronic form was not; that another 24-hour delay in medical attention would have been fatal. He was critically ill for many weeks. He convalesced in Santa Fe (Mrs. Leopold's home), and with relatives in Iowa. It has always been in my memory that he was on leave for 18 months. He eventually returned to duty as staff officer in the District Office."

Aldo Leopold served in a number of positions with the Forest Service from 1909 until 1924 when he left to become associate director of the Forest Products Laboratory in Madison, Wisconsin. In 1933, the University of Wisconsin created the chair of Game Management for Leopold. He gained national fame as an ecologist through his teachings and writings. Ironically, he died in 1948 while fighting a grass fire near his home in Wisconsin. In 1954, the Gila Wilderness, the first National Forest area so designated, was dedicated in tribute to his memory as a pioneer in wilderness preservation. The wilderness was established in 1924.

CHAPTER IV
New Rangers

After the Bureau of Forestry was transferred from the Department of the Interior to the Department of Agriculture in 1905 and renamed the Forest Service, applicants for Ranger jobs (who had to be between 21 and 40 years of age) were required to take an examination. The first examinations under the new regime were held on May 10 and 11, 1906, throughout the West.

One of those pioneer Rangers, Henry L. Benham, who started work in 1907, was interviewed at his home in Williams, Arizona, and was asked about those early examinations.

"Well," he said, "we had a little written test to find out what we knew about surveying, if anything, and mining. It wasn't too big a test. What they wanted to know mostly was whether a man was able to ride the range and see that the cowmen and the sheepmen stayed on their own allotments.

"I had been riding for Will C. Barnes until he sold out and moved away from New Mexico. Mr. Barnes went into the Forest Service and he wrote me and asked me why I didn't apply for a job. . . .

"They gave you a paper about the duties of a Forest Ranger, and it was a pretty good description. You had to ride and be able to take care of yourself in the open in all kinds of weather. After they gave me the written test I had to saddle a horse and ride out a certain distance in a walk, then trot over to another station, then lope back to the starting point. After punching cows for six years, I didn't have any trouble qualifying.

"Then they tested to see what you knew about handling a gun, so you didn't go out and shoot somebody with it the first day. And you had to put a pack on a horse, a bunch of cooking utensils, bedding, bedrolls, and a tarp to cover it with—and a rope to tie it on with.

"I'd learned all that before I went into the Forest Service. I didn't have much trouble. Some of the boys had an awful time, winding their ropes under the horse and around his belly.

"I took the examination in Denver, and in this class they were mostly right out of college. I remember one boy didn't get

Four Forest Rangers and three Ranger candidates on the porch of the Super
visor's Office, Apache National Forest, 1908.

Forest Ranger's Meeting, Douglas, Arizona, 1908.   1. D. D. Bronson, 2. R. E
Benedict, 3. Arthur Ringland, 4. Walter Edwards, 5. Robert J. Selkirk, 6. H. D
Burrall, 7. George Cecil, 8. Jim Westfall, 9. R. A. Rodgers, 10. Henry De Laney
11. Stewart, 12. E. H. Clapp, 13. This number not on picture, 14. Roscoe S
Willson, 15. L. F. Kneipp, 16. A. H. Zachau, 17. W. R. Mattoon, 18. Jones, 19
Bill Earle, 20. Neil Erickson, 21. T. S. Woosley, 22. Murray Averett, 23.-24
Don S. Sullivan, 25. M. W. Hockaday, 26. Frank A. Krupp, 27. R. S. Kellogg
28. Birtsall W. Jones, 29. Birdno 30. Arthur Noon, 31. Moody

through the written examination before he walked out. In the olden days they wanted cowpunchers or men who were used to being out-of-doors and knew they could get along in the open."

C. V. Shearer, of Las Vegas, New Mexico, another pioneer in the Forest Service, recalled the examination he took in 1911.

"It was a two-day affair," he said, "that is, there was a written examination and there was a field day. The written examination was not a multiple choice. You had to write things out—various questions. There were some about sawmills: how many men does it take to run a 10,000 foot mill? What are the positions of these men? What do they do? What kind of timber grows where? And, one question was, 'How would you fight a ground fire?' 'How would you fight a surface fire?' And 'How would you fight a top fire?'

"I remember one fellow taking the examination; he was just eating tobacco by the plug. He had a big spitoon by him. And he was busy writing and spitting and writing and spitting. Everything was quiet in there, not a word said. When he comes to this one about fighting forest fires, well he couldn't hold it any longer. He broke out, "How'd you fight a top fire? There's only one way; I'd run like hell and pray for rain!' "

Shearer's introduction to his new job as a Forest Ranger would have been enough to turn a young man to soda jerking or clerking or some other less-demanding job. But Shearer remained with the Forest Service for several years, then took a position as farm manager of the Los Alamos School for Boys. He later joined the Soil Conservation Service and remained with that agency until his retirement.

His appointment as an Assistant Forest Ranger on the San Antonio District of the Carson National Forest came through in November, 1911. Shearer started from his home in Las Vegas with a team and a buggy, accompanied by his mother and sister, food, bedding, two hound dogs, a cat, and a bowl of gold fish. The entourage got beyond Mora the first night, then to Black Lake the next. Between Black Lake and Taos they had to traverse a snow-covered road that was straight down the steep side of a mountain. Snow had been scooped out "higher than our heads" and it was extremely icy.

"Those two horses had to hold back," Shearer remembered. "The brakes I had on my buggy wouldn't hold anything. The wheels would just slide on the ice. We had come to this place so suddenly I wasn't able to stop and let my folks out. These horses set back in the breeching, and that buggy going down the hill—the old buggy tongue was turning into a bow. I sure thought it was going to break.   If it had, why we'd have run into the horses and been scattered all over the bare slope of that mountain.   But those horses set back and slid along, holding all they could until we got to the bottom.   What an experience."

Shearer and company got through Taos and on to Tres Piedras without more problems until they reached a point near the settlement of No Agua.

There, the temporary guard was to have met Shearer and guided him to the station.   When no guide arrived, Shearer decided to try to find the station himself.   After several false starts, when it was getting late in the day, he bedded down his mother and sister under some sagebrush beside a snowbank and set out to find the station by following a telephone line.

"I left the dogs with mother and sister, to sleep with them on the bed and keep them warm, and hoped the cat and the goldfish would live through the night.   I spent the night following the telephone line, and Lord, we got into snowbanks.   I finally came onto the road that I knew would take me to the San Antone.   So I headed back to the camp along about daylight.   The folks had spent the night in fair comfort and were all right.   They got up to get something to eat, then I had to look for my horses.   They had disappeared.   It took me till noon to find my team.   We started up to the station and finally got there before dark, about sundown.

"The snow was knee-deep and the guard wasn't around.   The door was open so I walked in.   Finally rustled up some wood, got a fire going in the little old stove in the far end of the kitchen.   We were about out of food, a few pieces of bacon, a few pieces of bread, and I think some prunes.   Maybe a can of beans and a can of sardines.   Mother started seeing what she could make out of the provisions we had, and it was enough for supper.   But it was a bleak night, I promise you that.   I looked out the window, and here comes a fellow with a pack horse.   I was getting ready to go out and hail him when he turned in.   He happened to be the fellow that took the Ranger examination same time I did.   He was Ranger on the District south, and he was out looking for horses.   Anyhow, he unloaded his pack.   He had lots of grub and set us up to a fine supper.   Next day he took me around to the sawmill and to Ortiz, where we could get some groceries.   You know, I never was so glad to see a human being in my life as I was to see him ride up that night, because we were in desperate circumstance.

"We had been there a few days when the telephone line went down, and winter really set in.   Snow drifted up over one side of the station.   When I went down to the barn to feed my horses, I had to walk the fence and beat the trail on snow three and four feet deep. "I had skis there, and I improvised a little sled. About once or twice a week I'd go to the sawmill—about five miles—on these skis. I'd throw some grub on this little sled, snowshoes would have been better, but I made out. We lived out the winter that way until it began to open up, and I could get on a horse. We didn't see a soul again that winter 'til along toward spring.

"Along toward spring I was transferred to the Las Vegas District, and they sent a man—Roland Lynch—to take my place. I worked with him about six weeks to break him in before I left.

"There were about 86,000 head of sheep permitted on the District. They had been used to running 'em free and open. They didn't like the Forest Service. It was new and they fought it every way possible. When I was trying to divide up the lambing grounds and apportion out the ranges, they told me to go to hell right along.

"There was a big politico up there—a fellow named Antonio. He went down to see our Supervisor, C. C. Hall. He went in and told Hall, 'We're tired of the Forest Service and the way the Forest Service is doing. We're tired of having your man up there telling us what to do. We want you to move him out of there. If you don't move him out, he's going out in a box.'

"Hall told him that if anything happened 'to our man up there, you fellows are not going to be able to escape the law.'

" 'The law? We're not afraid of the law,' Antonio told him. 'We'll take care of that. Just remember this, if you keep your man up there, we're gonna have trouble. It's not gonna be easy. Plenty of witnesses. Suppose your man would be able to kill a few of us, we'd have enough witnesses to hang him.'

"Hall got up from his chair and faced Antonio. 'Antonio,' he said, 'I guess we've talked it out. There's just one more thing to say: If I or any of my men ever get into trouble with you or any of your men, when we get through with you there won't be a damn witness left.'

"Well, that was the tempo of the times and the spirit of breaking in the new man.

"Another time we had a meeting in Ortiz. We were discussing grazing permits and were taking applications, when a big fight came on. Finally, a group of 'em got up and began to call us sons of bitches and all that. We just got up and left the meeting immediately.

"But I went to the village and wrote up applications, and I made a point to do it in Antonio's store. I'd stand at the counter and write 'em up. Antonio would call me names and tell me what the Government was doing to them, and I didn't know whether I was going to have a fight on my hands or not. Somehow or other things passed off without a showdown.

"There was a later showdown there in the store one time. He made some remark, called me a name I didn't like, so I went up to him and told him to apologize and say it was a slip of the tongue. He said he wouldn't. So I just reached over the counter and grabbed him by the collar and pulled him back across the counter. I had one of these old carrying cases they used to have, canvas bags in the old days. Mine was loaded with books. I got him across the counter and I come down with that and I give him a rap on the butt with that thing as hard as I could. I turned him loose, and I said, 'Now, be more careful of your language after this,' and I walked out. I saw him after that but it was never mentioned. Never another showdown. Just an incident that passed by. But that was the way we had to get along in those days."

Although Elliott Barker also served as Ranger on the Carson, he did not encounter too many problems in carrying out his assignments, and he recalls that because he could speak Spanish it contributed greatly to whatever success he enjoyed on the Carson. About four-fifths of the people he dealt with were Spanish-speaking.

"I was a Ranger at Servietta that first winter (1912), a little place 12 miles south of Tres Piedras on the D. & R. G. Railroad," he said. "We had no water there except what the railroad company hauled down in water cars. They had a tank car and we had to water horses from that. In the spring of 1913, I was moved to the Cow Creek Ranger Station, eight miles west of Tres Piedras. There we were very happy. Our oldest son was a year old. We had a three-room cabin that was quite comfortable in the summertime, but the chinking wasn't very good and the floor consisted of just 12-inch board with cracks about a quarter of an inch wide.

"We got an old carpet to put down on the floor so we could put Roy down and let him crawl around a little bit but when the wind would blow it would hump up like he had an elephant under him. But at any rate we got along. There was no inside plumbing at all. When I had to be gone for several days, as I frequently did on my Ranger District work, my wife had to draw water from the well and carry it to the house. She had to feed the horses, the extra horses, and she had to milk the cow and take care of everything around. Sometimes that country gets really cold, down to around 20 or 30 degrees below zero in the wintertime, but we got along fine and had no trouble at all. We were very happy there.

"Our big job at that time, in addition to handling two or three timber sales that we had going on, and the usual routine from free use permits and all that sort of thing, was managing the grazing.   There was a lot of stock on the Carson Forest at that time.   Far more than there should have been.   As a matter of fact, during 1913-14, three-tenths of one percent of all the sheep in the United States summered on the Carson Forest for a period of three to four months.

"Naturally we were having to initiate programs to put into effect programs of reduction of stock to the carrying capacity of the range.   That wasn't easy to do.   It caused a lot of resentment from the permittees.   While we were there, conditions were not what we could call really rugged or rough, as they had been at Cuba; still there was a pretty salty element to contend with.

"Not only that, but politicians were always on your neck whenever you tried to do anything about it.   I think they are to some extent the same today toward the Forest Service when needed reductions are insisted upon.   We had the political pressure on us all the way.   At any rate, that was the program that Leopold had started.   Supervisor Raymond E. Marsh succeeded him in, I think it was the latter part of 1913.   Leopold had become ill and took a couple of years' leave.   We were trying our very best to get the stock reduced down to a lower number and we were making a little headway."

Barker became Supervisor after Raymond Marsh was transferred to the Coconino in July, 1917, and remembers that World War I "disrupted a great many plans and programs, took lots of men from the Forest Service.

"I lost several Rangers," Barker said, "and the worst thing that happened to us was that we got orders from Washington to take care of just as many additional livestock as was applied for to aid the war effort—to produce meat, to produce more meat. Well, it was a short-sighted policy because it didn't actually aid the war effort.   By the time they got around to producing more meat the war was over.   Human nature being what it is, people wanted to take advantage of getting their stock on the Forest and keeping it there.   So, at the end of the war we had more stock on than we had back when Leopold tried to start to reduce it—and that was a very bad situation.   Some of our areas had become badly overgrazed.   Then the stock market bottom dropped out and there was no market where people could sell their sheep or their cattle.

"You told them they had to get off the Forest, and they said, where the heck would they put them, where could they go?   Many

of them went broke.   One of the biggest sheep permittees I had—
I think he had 23,000 head on the Carson—went around back of
his newly-built garage and blew his brains out. . . .   There were
many others who went broke, and we caught the blame for a lot
of it by having to reduce the number on the Forest.

"It went that way through the war period.   We had to do
double duty and it was pretty tough going.   The toughest situation
that we had came in the fall of 1918 when that terrible epidemic of
influenza hit the country.   Taos, it was said at that time, was the
hardest hit of any community in the United States.   I was chairman
of the Red Cross for Taos County and therefore shouldered a great
deal of work in connection with the influenza epidemic.   We
turned the church and the schools into hospitals.   We got six
doctors and nine nurses from St. Louis to help us out, but they
were virtually helpless as to what they could do for the people.

"I closed the Forest Office for something over 30 days.   We
didn't even open the door, didn't answer any mail, didn't get our
mail.   I lost my chief clerk and janitress; others were very ill
with the flu.   I got by until November 9.   Nearly everyone else
either had it and had died or was getting well and over it.   I
came home one night at midnight from one of the outlying communities we were trying to help out.   About 2 o'clock I woke up
as sick as I ever was in my life.   I was unconscious for nine days.
I didn't know for two weeks afterwards that the Armistice had
been signed.

"I was supposed to die, but I didn't.   They pulled me through
somehow."

Barker recalls that the illness left him depressed and discon-
tented, and in the spring of 1919—against the advice of Regional
Forester Paul Redington, he resigned to go back into ranching
and eventually into the State Department of Game and Fish
where he achieved a national reputation for his work as State
Game Warden.

CHAPTER V
Fire!

When the Forest Reserves were created, the most responsible work of the early Forest Rangers was undoubtedly fire fighting and fire protection. Before the creation of the Forest Service little organized effort was undertaken to fight fires.

There had been many bad fires in the Southwest that had devastated thousands of acres. On the mountains above Santa Fe a fire had raged for weeks in the 1880's. Nothing was done to fight the fire; it was allowed to burn itself out, destroying tremendous acreage of natural resources. Today the snags of that old fire and burned-over areas may still be seen on the high mountain side.

The principal instruction given to new Rangers was to patrol their District and watch for smokes. The Use Book (the manual of instructions) directed that "Officers of the Forest Service, especially Forest Rangers, have no duty more important than protecting the Reserves from forest fire."

"Generally the best tools for fighting fire are a shovel, mattock and ax," the Use Book pointed out. "The Ranger should always carry at least an ax during all the dangerous season."

The Use Book listed these general principles for fire fighting:

"Protect the valuable timber rather than the brush or waste.

"Never leave a fire, unless driven away, until it is entirely out.

"Young saplings suffer more than old mature timber.

"A surface fire in open woods, though not dangerous to old timber, does great harm by killing seedlings.

"A fire rushes uphill, crosses crest slowly, and is more or less checked in traveling down. Therefore, if possible, use the crest of the ridge and the bottom as lines of attack.

"A good trail, a road, a stream, an open park check the fire. Use them whenever possible.

"Damp or even dry sand or earth thrown on a fire is usually as effective as water and easier to get."

On the day that Tom Stewart started his assignment on the Pecos Reserve in 1903, he rode to the top of the mountains to look at his District. The first thing he saw was smoke from two forest fires.

"I scratched my head and cussed," Stewart said, "and decided to handle them one at a time."

For help on one, in the Sapello District, he rode fast to Rociada. Ranchers there had seen the smoke and were already gathering tools when he arrived, so they hit for the Sapello. The fire was controlled by next morning.

Without any sleep, Stewart then rode to the other fire, about two miles from the village of Agua Negra.

Stewart rode into the *placita,* sought out the *alcalde* (justice of the peace) and asked for his help to get men to fight the fire. The *alcalde* at first was curt and brushed off the request: "I don't give a damn if the whole Forest burns up."

Stewart let loose a stream of fluent Spanish, telling him that the people of the village were users of the Forest, that they would be hurting themselves to let the Forest burn, and that it was their duty to help put out the fire. He finally convinced the *alcalde,* who then got on his horse and began to round up volunteers. In no time he had collected 15 or 20 men.

"We worked from about 3 p.m. to 3 a.m.," Stewart said, "and we got that fire under control. The *alcalde* agreed to stay in charge of the men. And you know, after that he was the best cooperator I had in my District, right up to the day of his death."

Roscoe Willson used to enjoy telling about how he had seen Halley's Comet while he was fire fighting.

"We had a big fire up under the Mogollon Rim above Pleasant Valley," Willson recounted. "That was in 1910. I went up there from Roosevelt and got the boys. We got some cowboys too. It was mostly a ground fire. I remember fighting the fire there with the boys. They were keeping it under control, so I took an old quilt and rolled up and laid down. I looked up and could see this Halley's Comet just as plain. It was streaking the whole sky."

Edward G. Miller, who made a life-long career of the Forest Service until his retirement as Chief of the Division of Lands of the Regional Office, reminiscing about his early years in the Service, recalled some incidents of fire fighting.

"When he was Ranger on the Flagstaff District, Ed Oldham had complete fire crews organized from settlers," Miller related. "I can still see George Moore, with a plow in his wagon, driving his team on a long trot toward a forest fire. You didn't have to send for him; he watched for smokes and was on the way as soon as he saw one. The same was true of a lot of those *per diem* guards, men who were not part of the regular firemen's or lookouts' organizations. They were appointed as supplementary guards to

A monkey would have felt at home on early-day National Forest fire lookout towers.

go to fires when they saw one, or when called upon by the Ranger or his assistant. We used some Indians back in those days, but crews hadn't been organized as they are today at the various Indian pueblos, on the Navajo Reservation, and in some of the Spanish settlements. We depended largely upon the work crews at the lumber camps. All the brush crew were trained in fire fighting. Also a lot of the men around the sawmills had fought fires so often and so much, they were first class hands."

The early fire guards had very little equipment to work with in fighting fires. Henry Woodrow, long-time Ranger on the McKenna District of the Gila National Forest, remembered that when he was first assigned as fire guard in 1909 "all the instruction I had was to go up there and look out for fires—and put them out."

"I packed my outfit, which consisted of chuck and bed, on one horse," Woodrow recounted. "No tools were furnished me. I took my axe and a shovel—all the equipment I had with which to fight fires. No tent was furnished. The first fire I had occurred on the West Fork of the Gila above the mouth of Turkey Feather Canyon. I rode to the fire and found an old prospector camped near there by the name of Beauchamp. He was an old timer in the country, and he already had part of a fire line started around the fire, which by this time was burning half way up the side of Turkey Feather Mountain.

"Later in the evening Robert Munro, who had just started work as forest guard, and a Ranger by the name of Shanks from the Datil Forest, arrived. At that time there were no telephone lines in the mountains so we had to rely on a messenger to carry the news and gather up men. Some time during the night Ranger Stockbridge with two firemen from Apache Cabin came to the fire. Next day Forest Ranger Herbert Fay from Mogollon with a bunch of men, Bob Reid from Alma Ranger Station, Fred Smith from Gila Station, Frank Andrews, Deputy Supervisor from Silver City, all were there. By this time the hard wind had carried the fire all over the south side of Turkey Feather Mountain and was finally corraled along the top of the ridge.

"When this fire was under control, another was discovered in McKenna Park which I, with three other Forest Officers, soon got out. Then another was discovered at Pryor and one on Little Creek south of E-E Corral. The one at Pryor was soon put out—about 100 acres. The one at Little Creek burned over about a section. Forest Ranger B. H. Cross, from Pinos Altos Ranger Station, came to this fire with several men and cowboys from the Heart Bar Ranch. Other Forest Officers on this fire were Deputy Supervisor Frank Andrews, Rangers Bob Reid, Robert Munro.

"When this fire was controlled still another fire was discovered on head of Mogollon Creek where the trail now crosses to Sycamore and Big Turkey Creek. We went to this fire, that is, Frank Andrews, Bob Reid, Robert Munro, Fred Smith and I. Later in the evening Rangers Stockbridge and Fay, and two fire guards came and we started work on the fire during the night. Next day several cowboys came in from Cliff but the fire kept traveling southwest at a rapid rate. We kept it from going north across Mogollon Creek. Finally, on July 4 a light rain came and checked the fire. Next day all the men went out except one fireman and me. In a day or two he went out and left me to patrol. I kept patrol around the fire and kept it from breaking out. I kept this up until July 23 when a general rain came and put it all out. This fire burned over approximately five sections."

When the call comes for fire duty, it takes precedence over everything else—even a dish of long-awaited, mouth-watering ice cream.

That was the experience of Edward Ancona, another career man in the Forest Service, now retired. He was telling about the time he was serving as Ranger on the Crown King. It was hot there in the summer time. The only way they had to keep things cold was to hang them down the well. Ice was almost unheard of. But one hot summer, arrangements were made to ship in some ice.

"That was the only time I ever got mad, really sore at my job," Ancona said. "An old fellow had some cows there in the Basin, and he had saved the cream for about a week or two to make ice cream. The shipment of ice arrived, and the ice cream was made, and we were all at this party. We were just about ready to serve the ice cream when a fellow rode up outside and knocked on the door. 'Is the Ranger here?' he called out. I scringed down in my chair, but somebody answered, 'He's over there.' He looked over at me. 'Well, you've got a fire up on the ridge up above here. Lightning just struck a big pine. I can see it from my place.'

"The call of duty was stronger than that of the ice cream. I had to leave—and that's one of the big regrets of my life. I went out and sat by that burning tree all night while my friends were eating up the little ice cream that there was—the only ice cream in Crown King in two years.

"But I put the fire out, by golly. I sat by it until there was nothing left of it."

Over on the Catalina District, Stanley Wilson was building a log fire-lookout on Mt. Bigelow. It was a pretty rugged job,

putting up the poles and an eight-foot platform forty feet up. So
when Wilson and Frank Howe came in tired on Saturday night,
they were saying how glad they were next day was a holiday.

"If there's a fire, I wouldn't go to it," Wilson said.

"Wouldn't you really, Stan?" Howe questioned.

"Of course not. Tomorrow's a holiday."

Then Wilson remembers that when they got to the cabin,
word came that there was a fire.

"So, of course, we started off to that fire. It was a little different from what you start with now. We started to the fire,
myself and Frank Howe, and a kid named Pick and an old fellow
by the name of Henry Hiller.

"We started afoot down the ridge on the back side of Bigelow,
which was pretty rough country, carryin' shovels. Pick was a big
awkward kid, and every once in a while he'd lose his shovel, and
Frank Howe would say, 'Stan, Pick's lost his shovel.' We'd stop
and dig up his shovel for him. Well, finally we got to this fire—
it was between Edgar and Alder Canyons—on the east side of the
Catalinas, and we started at the top of the ridge between 'em.
I said, 'Frank, you and Pick take one side and Henry and I will
take the other.' Well, actually we were whippin' with pine boughs,
not usin' our shovels. The last thing I heard of Frank Howe and
Pick, Frank said, 'Stan, Pick's lost his shovel, so how the devil
do we fight the fire?' I said, 'Go ahead and fight the fire.' So
we fought that thing and we were doin' pretty well 'til about 10
o'clock in the morning when the wind began to whip up. Well,
Henry Hiller was quite an old man, and he slipped and slid down
the side of the hill. A little tongue of fire got away from him,
and that was that. It went then for another week and burned
5,000 acres. There were many, many people on it before it was
finally put out. Now that's particularly interesting to me because
later on when I was in the Regional Office, we had a quota out
here of 7,000 acres for the whole Region—and I had burned most
of that quota in one fire in my day!"

Paul Roberts remembers that when he was Supervisor of
the Sitgreaves National Forest there were a few incendiary fires
on the Lakeside District. Clarence Shumway was the Ranger
there.

"Everybody knew him, so I figured that he'd have a hard
time detecting the culprit," Roberts said. "I had Bill Freeman,
who was a resident of Snowflake, and Bill always liked to work for
different Federal agencies, so I had Bill play detective and go up
there and see if he could find, or apprehend, the incendiary.

"Bill went up and spent about a week up there, and thought

that he had discovered the culprit. He went to McNary where the JP was located then, to make arrangements to bring the fellow into the JP and have a hearing. Well, while Bill was tellin' the JP about the case, the JP became very interested in it and after a while he said to Bill, 'Well, how much shall we fine him?' Bill said, 'We haven't found him guilty yet.' And the JP said, 'Oh, Hell, he's guilty all right. It's just a question of how much we'll fine him.' So Bill took him in the next day, I think and the JP fined him $25 and costs. Well, $25 happened to be all the money the fellow had and of course that didn't leave the JP anything, so he rescinded the $25 and fined the fellow $22.50, plus $2.50 court costs!"

Another problem Roberts recalled was the danger of fire from some of the farmers who would want to smoke out bees in a bee-tree.

"We had one case on the Pinedale District where a fellow smoked out the bees, but he hadn't put his fire out and the fire spread a little bit. Dolph Slosser, who was a pretty good detective, went over and saw horse tracks. Dolph could read horse tracks as well as he could read writing. He started sleuthin' around to find out who'd been up there. He was sittin' on the corral one day talkin' to this fellow. He denied that he had anything to do with the fire. Dolph looked down at a horse track and recognized it as one of the horses that had been tied up there near the fire. He said, 'Well, Bill, (or whatever this fellow's name was) that horse track is the same track that was up there at that bee tree.' So the fellow admitted. 'Well, that's mine all right.' He hesitated, then he says, 'There ain't no law against lyin' a little to keep out of trouble, is there?' "

When O. Fred Arthur* was Supervisor of the Lincoln National Forest he had an incendiary fire that had tragic consequences.

There had been two incendiary fires on the Lincoln in March, 1927, and on March 15 another was reported in the Capitan area. Ranger Willard Bond left Baca Ranger Station for the fire and took with him A. R. Dean and Lloyd Taylor, Dean's son-in-law and foreman of the Block Cattle Company, whose range extended over the fire area.

Dean offered to drive them in his car, which they loaded with supplies, including also a rifle and six-shooter. In Capitan, they met Ranger Lee Beall from the Mesa District with some firefighters.

*O. Fred Arthur started as a Forest guard in 1907 on the Prescott National Forest. He retired in 1947 as Supervisor of the Cibola National Forest.

The two groups drove up into the mountains, stopping at a closed gate in front of the T. H. Shoemaker house. They left the cars parked near the fence and went on afoot across the hills to the fire.   Later in the day a fire camp was established, and about 2 a.m. Ranger Bond walked back to Ranger Beall's car to move it to the fire camp, about two miles farther east.   Then along toward morning Lloyd Taylor, accompanied by a couple firefighters, Charles Pepper and Apoliano Romero, returned to Dean's car to pick up additional supplies that had been loaded in it at Capitan.

Pepper was carrying a lantern, standing at the rear of the car. Taylor was getting some things from the front seat when two shots were fired from the vicinity of the nearby Shoemaker house. Pepper felt a sting in the back of the neck.   Later they decided it was a sliver from a piece of rock, struck by one of the bullets. Pepper immediately dashed out the lantern and all three ran for the brush.   A bit later, Taylor quietly made his way back to the car to get the equipment, then they returned to the fire and reported the incident.

After daylight, Taylor and Dean returned to the car to move it to the fire camp, and they discovered that the rifle and six-shooter that were in the car had disappeared.   They discovered also that the car had two bullet holes.   One had entered through a front curtain, passing through the back cushions.   The other had hit the running board, damaging wiring directly underneath the car.   Both bullets had narrowly missed Taylor, one apparently went a few inches above his body and the other a few inches below as he stooped to get something from the front seat.

Later on in the morning, the Rangers sent word to Supervisor Arthur at Alamogordo that some shots had been fired at the firefighters, supposedly by Shoemaker in front of whose house the cars were parked.

In his report to the Regional Forester later, Arthur wrote that he had been advised that "a little evidence had been collected already identifying Shoemaker with this fire."

"I then called Mr. French, Assistant Solicitor at Albuquerque, and told him in a general way what had happened and requested that he come down and assist in the collection of additional evidence and prosecution of the case in event such action proved warranted."

Arthur decided to go to the fire and left about 1 p.m. in a Forest Service truck and took with him W. C. White, executive assistant, who had previously served as Ranger in that District. That night they met Solicitor French in Capitan, and drove out to the fire area at daybreak to interview the parties concerned with the shooting.   Pepper, who had been nicked by the sliver of rock, did not want to press any charges, and evidence regarding the incendiary fire was insufficient for a government case.

"Mr. French and I decided that in the event complaints were made and search warrants issued for the stolen firearms, the matter could be turned over to the local authorities, which would provide sufficient time for the government to go ahead in the collection of evidence," Arthur wrote in his report.

"Ranger Bond said he was anxious to recover his rifle, and stated on his own responsibility he would make a complaint and request a search of Shoemaker's premises.

"We therefore left with him and drove to Carrizozo, reaching there about 6 p.m. and talked the matter over with the justice of the peace and Sheriff Sam Kelsey.   A search warrant was issued, which Mr. Kelsey said would be served the following day."

Before they left the office, Arthur got word that Lloyd Taylor, Dean, and Pepper were coming to Carrizozo and to await their arrival.   It turned out that Dean was pretty much upset when he returned from the fire to find his car damaged and the guns stolen and talking it over with Taylor and Pepper, they decided on their own initiative to make the necessary complaints.   So an additional warrant was issued, charging assault with deadly weapons.

The following morning Sheriff Kelsey and his deputy, Pete Johnson, arrived in Capitan and a strategy meeting was held with the Forest Service officials.

It was decided that the Sheriff and Dean would first go to the Dixon Ranch, because Dixon was supposed to be on friendly terms with Shoemaker and they would try to persuade him to intercede with Shoemaker to give himself up to avoid bloodshed. The deputy sheriff and Forest Rangers and ranchers were deputized and assigned to designated places to determine primarily the whereabouts of Shoemaker so that if Dixon could not get him to surrender, the Sheriff and Dean would make the arrest.

Arthur and Deputy Johnson were assigned to the nearby Koprian Ranch, and at the fire camp they picked up White, Arthur's assistant, and a pickup truck which White drove.   White and Deputy Johnson sat in front, both with rifles, and Arthur sat on a spare tire in the back of the truck.

"Reaching the highway about a mile and a half away we turned west toward Encinosa," Arthur said in his report.   "As we rode down a hill, at the bottom of which a side road leads down from the Shoemaker Ranch and passing the Hipp Ranch joins the highway, I looked ahead and saw two horses at the mail box, on one of which was a woman.   I do not recall seeing anyone else, but the thought occurred to me that possibly the other horse belonged to Shoemaker. Because of their position and, also, because of mine in the rear of the car, we drove past them before I noticed the other party, who proved to be Shoemaker. He was standing alongside his horse, near the butt end of his rifle which was in a scabbard hanging on the left side of the saddle, the butt in a forward position. Going about 100 or 150 feet, the car stopped and Johnson got out and started walking back on my left side; my back being toward the front end of the car. My attention was concentrated on Shoemaker to see that he did not make any movement. I cannot say exactly how far Johnson had gotten when Shoemaker reached for his rifle. Johnson whirled and started back. I then noticed that he carried no firearms. He said, 'Look out, he is going to shoot.' My gun was on the bottom of the car at my side. I grabbed it and jumped out on the right hand side and ran around in front of the car. White remained in the seat. Shoemaker started shooting. I fired also. Johnson grabbed his rifle quickly, took his position on his knee in front and at the left hand side of the car. I recall his saying, 'Throw up your hands, Shoemaker.'

"Johnson was directly in my line of fire at Shoemaker. I could not do much shooting without exposing my entire person, while Johnson remained in a way protected. I did not fire over three shots if that many, Shoemaker was firing rapidly. My time was spent trying to shoot from underneath the car. During this time my attention was distracted from our main purpose twice; once seeing White slip down into the seat, and it occurred to me that he was shot. Immediately afterward I decided that he was slipping down out of the way of the bullets; the other time was when he pitched forward on his face in the rut of the road directly in front of the car. I further noticed during that time that the woman on horseback had pulled out to the north side of the road, sitting on her horse and viewing the entire scene. The firing stopped and I saw Shoemaker laying face downward on the ground. Johnson started toward him, I returned to White. Immediately upon going back I saw Shoemaker crawling for his rifle. Johnson hurried back and asked if I had any shells left in my gun. I replied there was, he said, 'Give it to me,' which I did. He ran back and when about halfway, Shoemaker was within five or six inches of his rifle and reaching for it. Johnson fired a shot which ended Shoemaker's life. The saddle horse had been shot and was staggering around on the north side of the road. Johnson went over and finished him.

"Johnson came back and we gave our attention to White. His face was terribly mutilated, and I saw no hopes for him. Johnson said we would put him in the truck and rush him to Ft. Stanton, 25 miles distant. I replied that there was no use, that the radiator had been shot to pieces and that we could not go over a mile, but for him to remain there and I would rush back to camp and get another car. Before leaving I went over to the woman and asked her to please ride to the Hipp Ranch and tell them to come down. I got out and started running to camp when I met French and Strickland and others who had not left the camp. We got in French's car and went to the shooting and found that Johnson had left with White in the mail car which had passed along directly after I left. Newt Kemp was at the scene. We let out one or two parties and Strickland, Boone, French and I drove on. . . .

"An inquest was held over Shoemaker's body, at which time the woman's testimony was secured. She proved to be the wife of Mr. Guy Hix, a Block cowpuncher. I was not present at this hearing, but my testimony and that of Mr. Johnson was taken that night before the coroner's jury.

"In closing I might add that the guns covered by the search warrant were afterwards found in the Shoemaker house."

White died at 9:30 p.m. on Friday, March 18. Ironically, when he was a Ranger on that District he had been threatened several times by Shoemaker. Whether Shoemaker knew that White was in the cab of the pickup is not known, of course. Shoemaker may have been merely firing blind at the back of the truck. Newspaper reports of that day said five slugs of soft nose bullets had pierced the rear, and it was regarded as a miracle that Arthur and Johnson had escaped.

The Associated Press reported that Shoemaker was alleged to have refused to make payments to the Forest Service on his land, that he generally opposed the Forest Service and had boasted that he set fires in 1925 and 1926 as well as the fire then raging, which required about 75 men to control.

Forest fires have plagued the Forest Service since the inception of the organization—but constant vigilance has resulted in a splendid record of fire protection.

After he became District Forester in 1908, Arthur C. Ringland began to plan a program of increased fire protection for the Southwestern Region.

"The logical way to bring this about," Ringland wrote to his Supervisors in Region 3, "is by a careful study of the conditions on the Forests and the adoption and use of a definite fire plan."

Among the suggestions Ringland made were construction of lookout stations on high peaks, construction of telephone lines

Arthur C. Ringland, first Southwestern District (Regional) Forester (1908-1916) pioneered fire planning.

Ringland and Southwestern Regional Forester Wm. D. Hurst, Regional Office, Albuquerque, New Mexico, May 15, 1972.

from lookout stations to Ranger's or Supervisor's headquarters, construction of trails for fire patrol and roads for rapid transfer of firefighting forces, placing in strategic locations tool boxes and firefighting tools, and provision for volunteer and hired firefighters.

And as a closing note, Ringland wrote that "I feel that it is an important part of good administration to make Rangers, who bear the brunt of the hard work in firefighting, feel an intense interest in the preparation of the plan under which this fighting must be done."

Ringland had been a Ranger,* so he knew the job from the Ranger's viewpoint. The Forest Service's long-standing policy of promotion from within the organization, which resulted in so many early Supervisor appointments from the ranks accounted for the close-knit spirit of teamwork that marked the early years of the Forest Service.

Paul Roberts who had worked as a grazing inspector and as Supervisor of the Sitgreaves National Forest in the 1920's, put it this way: "It was a period of tremendous crusading spirit; I don't know whether the Forest Service could ever get that same type of thing going again or not, because a lot of those fellows that had the crusading spirit didn't know anything about forestry.   They were ex-cowboys and lumberjacks and all that sort of thing, but they believed in it.   Most of 'em went into it because of the spirit of adventure and because it was something worthwhile.   It took a hardy breed to do the job and they did it.   Whatever their faults and failures, they still did a tremendous job of getting the Forests established and going."

Today the Forest Service has a couple other rugged breeds of fellows working for them and fighting fires.   These are the professional smokejumpers and the Indian and Spanish-American villagers who have been organized into professional year around firefighting groups, on call at the sound of the telephone ring any time of day or night.

---

*Ringland was one of the original group of students recruited by Gifford Pinchot at the turn of the century, and in 1905 when he graduated from the Yale School of Forestry, he became a charter member of the Forest Service. He began his career as a Ranger on the Lincoln National Forest and was appointed District Forester, with headquarters in Albuquerque, effective Dec. 1, 1908, serving in that capacity for eight years.   He went on to an important career in the Federal government after service in the AEF during World War I, then in charge of mass feeding of children of Czechoslovakia by the American Relief Administration, directed by Herbert Hoover, and the relief and evacuation of White Russian refugees in Constantinople in cooperation with the League of Nations, 1922-23.   In succeeding years he held numerous high government appointments in the Department of Agriculture, the World War II Relife Control Board, and the Department of State, retiring from that agency in 1952.   At the time of this writing (1972) he was living in Washington, D. C.

The organized "Southwestern Firefighters" are famous for "hitting 'em fast and hard" throughout the western states.

The Forest Service discovered years ago that an organized crew was much more efficient in fighting fire than a pick up crew of volunteers or hired labor.   Indians are particularly suited for this work since they are used to rugged country, hard manual labor, and working as a crew.   Since others in their pueblos or reservations can take over their labors at home, they can leave at any time.   And they may be gone anywhere from a couple days to two months.

Each of the Indian or Spanish-American groups has its own distinctive hardhat decoration and name.   The first of these was the Mescalero "Red Hats" organized in 1948.   Now there are picturesque designs on hats for groups from the Rio Grande pueblos, from the Arizona pueblos and reservations, and from the Spanish-American villages of northern New Mexico.

The hardhat fighters must be between the ages of 18 and 60 in good physical health, determined by periodic medical examinations.

In 1971 more than 3,000 trained firefighters, organized into 20-man crews, were available to the land managing agencies.   Since the first call from outside the Southwestern Region came from California in 1950, these elite troops have battled wildfire throughout the western states.

A couple dozen smokejumpers in the Southwest operate from Silver City, close to the Gila National Forest which has a high incidence of fire over the years.   Much of the National Forest and Gila Wilderness can be reached only on foot or horseback, and the use of aerial firefighters makes fire suppression quickly available.

Besides the twin-engined planes which fly the smokejumpers to the fires, aerial tankers are also used to carry multi-ton loads of slurry, a fire-retardant mixture of chemicals and water.   Helicopters are used both to carry firefighters and to retrieve them and their equipment.

Gilbert Sykes, of Tucson, a long-time Ranger on three Districts of the Coronado National Forest, believes that one of the first uses of an airplane in connection with a forest fire was in 1921.

"We had a big fire in the Catalinas back in 1921, nearly 10,000 acres," Sykes said.   "It came up out of the Canyon del Oro and topped out along the ridge to Summerhaven and right up to the top of Mount Lemmon and out on the San Diego Ridge.   The Bureau of Public Roads had just completed a new road up the side of the mountain and we used that.   Some of the fire lines stopped going around the mountain north and east, and this road made a pretty good line. Fire spilled over in a few places but the road held it in the real dangerous, deep canyons there on that side.

"Hugh Calkins was then our Forest Supervisor on the Coronado in Tucson. He managed to get an army airplane from Fort Bliss to do some scouting. I think it was one of the first times a plane had been used for aerial work on a fire—at least down in this area. Hugh made several flights over the fire. . . . He said he got a lot of good information from this aerial scouting, but the pilot flew pretty high.

"We started probably one of the first attempts at parachute dropping of supplies. It was about 1936 on the Chiricahuas. I was Ranger at Portal at the time. Charlie Mayes was an old pilot who had flown everything since about 1912. Fred Winn got him to make some tests down at Douglas. He was running a little field in Douglas at that time, out east of town. We made several drops, test drops, and decided we were pretty good. Fred Winn got the bunch up at Rustler Park to try some dropping up in the timber there at the top of the mountain.

"Fred would take a friend of his on 'show-me' trips—oh, about once a month, on the Chiricahuas. That was one of Fred's favorite retreats to get away from it all on weekends. They would stay up at Cima Park, there in the old cabin. They would take 2 or 3 horses up and would spend the weekend, he and Mrs. Winn and Johnny Ball, from Bisbee. Johnny Ball was quite a photographer. Fred wanted this officially recorded, this dropping, so he could show the boys here and there, and maybe back in Albuquerque, how good it was: Charley Mayes came over about the scheduled time and made some nice drops. We had just got some new radios at the time and we dropped one of those to see how it came down.

"It came down in good shape and we dropped a case of eggs and it came down and only a few of them broke. Johnny Ball was busily photographing each drop as it came down. One almost hit him, he was so enthusiastic, it plunked right down beside him. When he got all through Fred came over and said, 'Well, John, did you get some good shots of that?' 'I believe so,' he said, and he started to put his camera away. Then he said, 'Oh, my God, look—I forgot to take the cap off my lens.'

"So all these drops were duds—all these photographs. We didn't try it again that time. The next year we made several drops down around the Santa Rita Range Reserve trying the various size loads. The pilot and some of the boys got together and when he had made about his last drop, all of a sudden a man came out of the plane and he fell and fell and fell and his 'chute didn't open, and he plunked down about two or three hundred yards from the bunch.   Everyone started running over there except two or three of us who happened to be in the know. It was a dummy they had thrown out, but it gave them quite a thrill anyway."

Improved efficiency and modern firefighting techniques have steadily diminished losses from fire, even though the number of fires has increased.

Recalling a series of fires, Robert Diggs, of Williams, Arizona, a long-time Forest Service career man, commenting on firefighting, related that "it was in 1956 that we had the Dudley Fire.   Then after we got the Dudley Fire controlled—it was about 17,000 acres —we looked across to Mingus Mountain, and there she was blowing up right on Mingus Mountain.   They just put the whole shooting match into a DC-3 plane and took them right on into Prescott. They took the same organization right off the Dudley Fire and put them on the Mingus Fire.   That was 15,000 acres, and we nailed that one.   We got home in time for a Fourth of July rest, then went right back to Safford on the Outlaw Fire.

"It is remarkable the way Forest Service crews can adapt themselves to a situation; to different Forests and different terrain, and different organizations, so to speak.   They just click.

"Of course, you've got the Indian crews, and boy—those crews are fine!   I don't know what we would do without them, how we would get the job done, whether it's Hopi No. 8 or Santo Domingo No. 2 or any of the others.

"Now we have the slurry planes.   Those slurry planes are good.   We used them on the Hell's Canyon Fire down here.   We had a 500-acre fire south of Bill Williams.   It could have been one of the largest in the history of the Forest Service if it had come across Bill Williams, but we nailed it."

C. A. (Heinie) Merker, of Santa Fe, a career man in Region 3 since 1923, recalled the 1954 fire on the Los Alamos Reservation as one of the most unusual he had been involved with.   At the time Los Alamos was still a "secret city."

"The fire wasn't so big, but was it made into a big thing," he said.   "I first saw the fire from my backyard here in Santa Fe when it started.   Immediately I recognized that we were in trouble —or could be—when we found out it was on Los Alamos land.

"I sent Leon Hill over to advise them.   Well, he spent the afternoon advising them.   All the time they were trying to put the thing out and didn't know how to go about it.   Finally, I went over.   Just about the time I landed there, they came to the conclusion they had a bull by the tail.   In the meantime, stories got out that the town was threatened. That got back to the Washington office of the Atomic Energy Commission, and they established a 'hot line' between Washington and Los Alamos. Then Albuquerque got word of it and they sent a whole staff up from down there. Toward evening, the powers-that-be at Los Alamos came to me and said, 'Now look, we don't know how to fight forest fires. How about you taking over?' I said, 'Who's going to pay the bill?' They said, 'Oh, don't worry about that, we'll pay the bills. Just put the fire out.'

"I got hold of Otto Lindh (Regional Forester) on the phone and told him about it. He hotfooted it up there, and Mayhew Davis (Chief of Operations) came up. Oh, everybody came up. They even drew up a written agreement as to who was going to pay for what.

"The head of technical services there, Norris Bradbury (the director of the Los Alamos Scientific Laboratory) stayed up the whole night. About every half hour he would come up to our headquarters wanting to know for sure that the fire wasn't going to get across the highway that runs north and south. He didn't explain what was on the other side of the highway, but every time a spark would go over there, everything was turned loose to get on that spot fire. I found out later it was some sort of explosive stuff down there. What it was I still don't know. But he was sure concerned that the fire was going to get across the highway and get into the technical area. I guess all hell would have broken loose if it had.

"We finally got the fire under control the next afternoon. Everybody and his dog were up there, including all sorts of Indians. Everybody who had come in through the gate, including the firefighters and the Indians, were registered and their names taken and they were given a badge. There was one person who got in that did not have one of those things. How he got in nobody could ever find out, but he had a devil of a time getting out. They had no record of him. He had no badge. It was Dahl Kirkpatrick, Chief of Timber Management!"

Merker said that an interesting thing about the fire was, who started it? It was learned that the sponsors of the Boy Scout camp (one of them was the fire chief) was clearing the site of old slabs and set fire to it.

"They set it off in the evening and they stayed all night watching it burn. When morning came it was pretty well burned up, and they left one man and a boy to watch it. They went to the spring there to get some water. When they got back the wind had come up and it threw a spark out, and away she'd gone.

Well, the fire chief and the manager of the city had set the thing off. Boy, were their faces red!"

About nine-tenths of the forest fires nation-wide are man-caused, from cigarettes thrown from cars, camp fires left unattended, failure to put out fires when leaving camp or dropping lighted smokes or matches on the ground. Years ago the Forest Service began a continuing campaign to get the cooperation of the public in preventing forest fires.

Their star salesman in this campaign is Smokey. Although a fictitious Smokey preceded him, there has been a real Smokey since June, 1950. In the man-caused Capitan fire on the Lincoln National Forest in May, when 17,000 acres of forest land were destroyed, the men on the fire line discovered a cub bear that had been severely burned about the feet and was near death from shock, burns and hunger. Ray Bell, chief field man of the New Mexico Department of Game and Fish, volunteered to take the cub to Santa Fe to a veterinarian to see if its life could be saved. After emergency treatment, Bell kept the cub at his home for several weeks until it was completely recovered. It was named Smokey for the poster bear of the Forest Service, State Foresters, and The Advertising Council. Then the cub was flown to Washington and presented by the Forest Service to the Washington Zoo to aid in the campaign for prevention of forest fires and conservation of wildlife.

Smokey has become an eloquent and living symbol of the need for fire prevention. Pictures of the tiny cub taken during his convalescence were used extensively in publicity, and the appealing little fellow found a place in the hearts of America's children and grownups alike.

J. Morgan Smith, who was Assistant Director of the Smokey campaign, is now Assistant Regional Forester, Division of Information and Education, with offices in Albuquerque. His collection of Smokey pictures, clippings and other material includes a number of letters addressed to Smokey.

A North Dakota girl wrote, "I read in our 'Young Citizen' that it cost billions of dollars every year to pay for the damage done by fires, so I am contributing five cents to help pay for the damage." A Burbank, California mother wrote to say that Smokey was her five-year-old son's "very best friend." "No one would dare throw a lighted match or cigarette out in the forest or mountains when he is in range," she wrote.

Another California mother wrote to Smokey to say that her son was seven years of age "and practically stands at attention when you talk on television. There is never a cigarette thrown from our car any more. We really get told!"

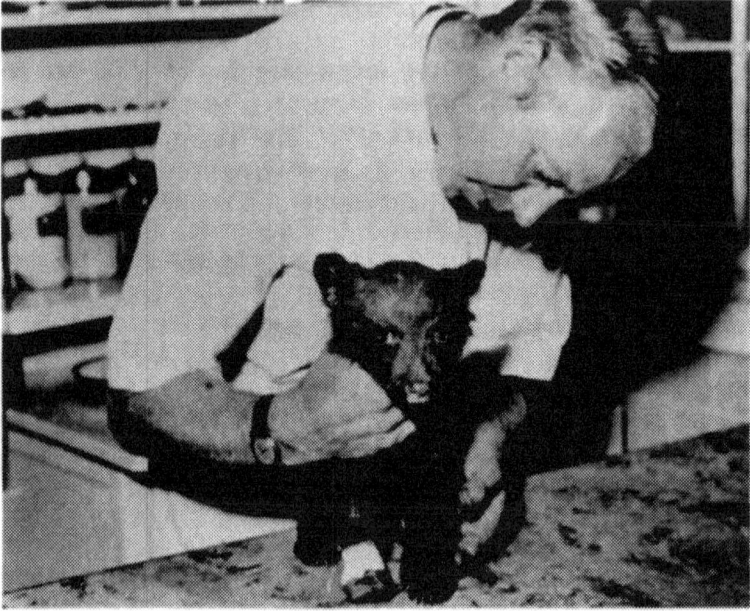

The story of the live Smokey Bear began when a burned, frightened cub was rescued from a man-caused forest fire on the Lincoln National Forest in 1950.

Smokey, who makes his home at the National Zoo, Washington, D.C., is visited by people from all over the world who know his story.

Today, fully grown, Smokey lives in the Washington Zoo and still attracts thousands of visitors. The story of his rescue from a tragic fire in New Mexico has been told and re-told in publicity stories, magazine articles, TV and radio programs and in cartoons. Forest Service officials regard the Smokey campaign as the most powerful single force in preventing wildfires in the United States today.

CHAPTER VI
Wild Times and Wild Horses

The early days of the Forest Service coincided to some extent with the heyday of the big ranches in the Southwest, and, of course, the "big men" who ran them. One of the most picturesque was Ray Morley, of Datil, whose ranch in west central New Mexico spread over an area of hundreds of sections of range and forest land. Morley, according to his sister, Agnes Morley Cleaveland, owned two hundred 640-acre sections, controlled several times that number because of control of watering places, and additional sections under Forest Service permits.

Forest Service regulations required grazing permits under an allotment system to prevent overgrazing by unauthorized livestock.

Morley had been an All-American and captain of the Columbia football team in 1900-01 and was a man of tremendous physique and physical strength. His sister described him as "just under six feet, with broad shoulders, bewhiskered and suntanned."

Writing in the December 1941, issue of New Mexico Magazine, Mrs. Cleaveland described him as "an amazing combination of gentleness and rugged strength. . . . He was as tenderhearted as a child and as implacable as a granite cliff when he thought he was right."

Morley had many a run-in with the Forest Service before he finally came to an acceptance—though not always agreement—of the Forest Service philosophy and regulations.

"Nor was he always wrong," Mrs. Cleaveland wrote. "Typical was Ray's threat to take his grievance to the Board of Health when an over-officious young Ranger was slow in marking logs for a new bathroom."*

Long-time career man Stanley Wilson, who retired in Phoenix, had worked in the Magdalena office of the Datil Forest as Deputy Supervisor in the early twenties, and has a fund of Morley stories.

---

*"No Life for a Lady," by Agnes Morley Cleaveland, Houghton Mifflin Co.

Wilson recalled a case where the Forest Service Regional Office had written Morley a series of three letters asking for his side of reports from the Datil office that he was in trespass violation with a band of sheep.

"Ray had an interesting way of letting his mail pile up and then he'd read it all at once," Wilson said.   "He came into the office one day when I happened to be Acting Supervisor."

"Wilson," Ray said, "I've got notices from the Regional Office to give my side of the three trespass cases you've reported on. What am I gonna tell 'em, Wilson?"

"Well, Ray, that's up to you," Wilson replied.

"I can tell 'em. . . ." and Ray went on with what Wilson described as a "string of stuff."

"Don't tell them that," Wilson told him, "because we can prove that it isn't true."

Wilson recalled that Ray then tried a different tack, but Wilson interrupted, "No don't tell them that either."

"Oh," Ray said, "I've got something.   Did you know this Watson, the man that looks after my sheep is sick with stomach trouble and he's been in Albuquerque.   They've been putting barium in him and takin' X-ray to see what's wrong with him. So my sheep were neglected while he was in there."

"Ray," Wilson said, "that's new material, that's something you can tell them."

"Let me borrow a stenographer, will you Wilson?"

Wilson said, "Sure," and Ray sat down and wrote three replies to the Regional Office, answering the three letters.

"He got out of all three of them, just like that," Wilson commented.

When Morley operated Navajo Lodge for travelers going through on U.S. 60, he gained wide fame for the tall tales that he told the travelers.

"I got in there one night with a nephew of mine," Wilson remembered.   "Ray was there, and I thought, gee, this kid has a chance to hear something he'll remember all his life."

Wilson was talking to Ray, and he said, "Ray, I've been hearing some stories about you.   Are they true?"

"Well, it depends on what you were hearing, Wilson.   What'd you hear?"

"That story about you killing a lion by holding his head under snow water."

"Oh yes; yes, that's true," he said, "I was riding up in White Horse Canyon.   There'd been an early snow, or a late snow— I'd have to figure out which time the fawns come.   I saw a fawn behind a down log and I figured I'd get off my horse and sneak around until I was behind that log and then I'd make a flying leap over the log, catch this fawn and take it home for a pet. I went around a circuitous way, and I peeped over the log and I saw a tiny thing there, and I made a big jump over the log and unfortunately I came up with a full-grown mountain lion. Well, there was a pine tree between it and me, and I had it by the scruff of the neck with my left hand and it was around the tree and I had its tail in my right hand, and it kept comin' after me, and I kept backin' up, and my boot heels got hot and melted the snow, and pretty soon I got enough water so I held his head under and drowned it."

By the time Ray launched into his story there were nearly two dozen people in the lounge, and Wilson said they accepted the yarn without a quibble. In fact, one of them asked, "Is this the skin here, Mr. Morley?"

"No," he told them, straight-faced, "it's the one in the other room. But I'll tell you about this one. This one jumped on the running board of my car, and I killed it by sticking it in the eye with a hat pin."

Wilson remembers that he went on telling stories and finally told one "that I knew to be absolutely true."

"He said that in the early days he had to make a trip to Magdalena," Wilson related. "That was 34 miles away, and he decided he was going to make it in two hours. It had never been made in two hours before."

"Morley had in the car John Kerr, Assistant District Forester in the Grazing Division, and a couple other men.

"They started out," Wilson said, "and when they passed a teamster, Morley hollered at him they were going to set a record and get to Magdalena in two hours. About that time Morley wasn't watching where he was going, and he turned the car over. Nobody was hurt. The teamster came up and helped them to put it together again, and Morley turns around and says, 'We can still make it in two hours,' and he started again. Then, 'We got to the Continental Divide, 12 miles out of Magdalena, and we hit a rock that musta been fastened in the center of the earth. We turned over again and that time I thought I was dead. They couldn't hear me; they thought I must be dead, but I was crowded under the front seat of the car and couldn't do anything. When they rolled the car off of me I wasn't hurt but John Kerr had a broken shoulder.'"

According to Wilson that was true. "John Kerr did get a broken shoulder. He was always uneasy riding fast with people

after that. When Morley finished his story, one of the Oklaho-
mans in the room told him, 'Mr. Morley, that's one I don't believe.' So I said to Morley, 'Ray, that's a story I personally know
to be absolutely true, and it's the only one you tell that anybody
doubts."

Frederic Winn, who was Supervisor of the Coronado National
Forest when he retired, spent a couple years as a Ranger in the
Datil Forest, and was a close friend of Ray Morley's. Winn had
first come to New Mexico as a cowboy-artist. He had attended
Princeton, and had lost his hearing in an ice-boat accident on one
of the lakes outside Madison, Wis.

Stanley Wilson tells this story about Ray Morley at the time
Fred Winn was staying at his place:

"There was a young fellow that Ray met down at the Post
Office. Lots of people came out here to the Southwest for their
health in those days, and this young fellow asked Mr. Morley if
he could give him a job. Ray said, 'Well, you come up to my
place and you keep the woodbox filled and do odd jobs, and it'll
be worth your board, and I'll pay you a little money. If you're
worth anything, I'll take you on.' Well, he was in the negative
category; he wasn't worth anything. So they arranged that they
would pull a game on him. There was a fellow named Johnny
Payne; they called him Bow-legs because he was bow-legged. I
can't think of the other men. They arranged that they would
stage a fight. Fred Winn was there but being deaf couldn't hear
the plans. They took the bullets out of their cartridges to make
them blanks when they got ready to go on this thing, and Johnny
Payne brought his dog in the house and the other fellow took a
kick at it. Johnny says, 'You can't kick my dog,'—and he pulled
his gun. The boy started trying to get out the door; the other
fellow grabbed him and held him so he couldn't get to the door.
They exchanged shots and finally Ray Morley fell over on his
back, apparently dead. Fred Winn had jumped up on something
that put him so high up he had to stoop against the ceiling. He
thought this was real, you see. He was looking down at what was
going on. Ray Morley looked up and winked at him, and Fred
was mad. He was really mad.

"They decided that this boy would probably go over to Mrs.
Cleaveland's and she would be worried to hear that Ray was dead.
Johnny says, "Well, I'll saddle my horse and lope over there and
tell her that this was a joke.' So he did, and as he was coming
back he remembered that he had used all his cartridges. He got
out his six-shooter and started to load it as he was going over a
little bridge. This young fellow was hiding under that bridge.
He came out and says, 'Please don't shoot me.'

Johnny says, 'Now look, you're in a tough situation, Ray Morley's dead and I know you didn't kill him, but that other fellow's gonna say you did, so the only thing I can think of for you to do is just get out of here.'   So the boy left the area.   Later on, Ray used to go back and ride in parades and things back East. One time he saw this young fellow and the fellow told him, 'Mr. Morley, you missed your calling.   You should've been an actor!' ''

One time when Morley had been gone from Datil for awhile, Fred Winn was in Baldwin's store and saw a new buckboard and team.   He asked whose it was and was told Ray Morley had come home.

Morley had come home with a new wife, but they hadn't told Fred that, Wilson remembers.

"They told Fred, 'Ray's in such and such a room.'   Fred went in and knocked on the door.   Ray tried to tell Fred his wife was in there with him and he couldn't let him in.   Fred couldn't hear him.   So Fred went around to a window, and he pried the window open.   There was a trunk there under the window and he came in on his hands and knees over this trunk.   When he got in, there was Morley's wife, sitting up in bed, with a blanket wrapped around her and screaming bloody murder.   Fred, of course, backed out.   Being shy, it almost killed him."

Some of the stories involving Morley included as a participant Steve Garst, who was a Ranger of the Datil Forest for more than 20 years.   Garst was a big man, weighed in the neighborhood of 250 pounds, and was the son of a retired Navy admiral.   He was the kind of man who could get along with Ray Morley.

Steve Garst early discovered that Ray was running some loose cattle on the Forest that he had no permit for.   Wilson related that Garst got hold of Ray and told him that he had found some trespass cattle on Morley's range.

"Why, gee, Steve, that's bad," Ray said.   "We ought to get rid of them.   Whose are they?"

Steve said, "Well, I just don't know.   I haven't found out yet, but they're branded so-and-so."

They were Ray's, of course, and he just said, "Oh, heck. . . ."

When they opened the Black Canyon Refuge to hunting, Wilson related that Morley went down there with a wagon and came back with six deer over the limit.

"When he came up to the head of Railroad Canyon," Wilson said, officers met him and they took him over to Dub Evans, the JP.   Dub fined him $50 for each extra deer—$300.   Ray said, 'Now, Dub, and you fellows, now that's perfectly all right.   I took a chance and I'm perfectly willin' to pay my money, but for God's sake, don't ever tell Steve Garst about this because I'll never hear the last of it.' Dub Evans said, 'Ray, who do you think tipped us off? It was Steve Garst!' "

Over in the Apache National Forest, the Rangers were holding a meeting* to discuss a variety of problems including trespass, reconnaisance, timber sales, and even wild horses.

"A wild horse is a pest and ought to be gotten rid of," spoke up M. L. Nichols, Ranger on the Metcalf District.

"I don't know of any feasible way of catching wild horses," Ranger Chapin, of Murioso, told the group.

J. H. Sizer, of Eagle, didn't agree. "At least three or four Rangers ought to start out and gather up every horse they could find—and go it alone if they could not get any stockmen to go along with them."

Jim Reagan shook his head. "It would take three or four years to round them up."

It did, in fact, take many years to solve the wild horse problem.

Telling of wild horses on the Apache National Forest in the 1920's, Jesse Fears recalled that the Forest was overrun with "unpermitted horses," as he referred to them rather than as wild horses:

"I first notified these people and tried to get 'em to get rid of their horses, and they laughed at me. Said if they had trespass horses, why didn't I get 'em for trespass, and I said, 'I will when I get to it.' Then Roy Swapp and I threw in together and the first winter we gathered—before they knew it we had 'em gathered down on Campbell Blue—over 800 horses in one bunch. Then I actually gathered 2600 head of unpermitted horses on the Greer District. They were tallied and a record made of 'em before I killed a horse. We threw them out on the public domain. Loco weed got a lot of 'em."

Fears told of another bunch of horses he rounded up and advertised for sale when possible owners made no claim after 60 days.

"Nobody bid on 'em except Melvin Swapp," Fears said. "He bid on a mare that was unbranded. When nobody else would bid on them, I said, 'Well, I'll just keep 'em and see what I can do with 'em.' I turned them back out in the pasture. So when things quieted down I got a permittee and a fellow working for me and we went up there and rounded 'em up and we shot 'em.

"We left the best looking ones out there. Well, it was a month or two before they discovered those dead horses, and then the fat

---

*Rangers meeting, September 8-14, 1910, at Springerville, Ariz.

was in the fire. A lawyer got hold of it, and he agreed to prosecute me through the courts for $300 if they would put up the money and he'd be deputized. They dug up the money for him. The sheriff I knew well. I told him, 'Any time you get a warrant for me, just call me up. I'll come down. You won't need to come up and serve it.'

"So he called me, and I went down to St. Johns."

Fears told of the court routine and the delays due to attorneys' arguments, and the judge's final decision to give the opposing attorneys 10 days in which to submit briefs.

E. S. French, the Forest Service law officer, submitted his brief in 24 hours, since it had already been prepared.

"The funny thing was," Fears remembered, "they didn't have anybody there who could write shorthand. They could write a few words of the testimony, then they just put a lot of lines out there. French got hold of the clerk and said, "Don't you remember asking this and him saying that?" So the clerk put those words in afterwards—different things that weren't in the shorthand notes.

Fears recalls the case went on for quite awhile. There were letters back and forth about the prosecution briefs which were not filed or copies sent to French, and finally the Forest Service attorney demanded a speedy trial. So the judge set a date for the hearing—and found Fears guilty.

"He had the decision already written up," Fears related, "because he said there would be a few minutes recess, and we didn't get out of the courtroom until he called us back. He had it already typed up, and he read it. He said he couldn't see where Regulation T-12 of the Department of Agriculture had any effect in law. Therefore he would find me guilty and would fine me $1.00. Then French got up and said, 'Your honor, my client refuses to pay the $1.00 fine. What will be the alternative?' The judge turned to the sheriff and told him to levy on any property I had for that $1.00 fine. French immediately filed notice of an appeal to the State Supreme Court.

"After they had studied it, they sent it back and said that everyone knows that Federal laws are paramount to state laws. Therefore they had no right to arrest me when I was carrying out the instructions given me by the Secretary of Agriculture and they should throw out the charges against me and refund my bonds. It was a year before we got a release on the bonds."

The government attorneys next enjoined the county and state officials from interfering with the carrying out of Forest

In the early 1900's, bands of unpermitted horses multiplied unchecked on many western ranges and competed with domestic livestock for forage.

Service regulations and the case went to Federal court in Los Angeles and after a delay to the Federal Court in San Francisco, where a decision was handed down in favor of the Forest Service and helped to establish the precedent for disposing of unpermitted horses.

Paul Roberts, talking one time about the wild horses on the Sitgreaves National Forest, said, "Well, we could never get rid of them. We'd impound them, and they would come and get them and take them home, and then in a little while they'd be back on the Forest."

"We rounded up some," he went on, "and we had some horses that you couldn't round up. We rounded up the east end of the Forest one time and we put these horses all in a pasture near Show Low. Then we put a guard on the pasture so they couldn't get them out of there while we went farther back and rounded them up.

"We went still farther east and rounded them up and brought them back. When we got back with this outfit from the east end of the Forest, we'd been gone about a couple of days. Well, by gosh, you'd of thought Coxie's army was camped on that flat. There were just bed rolls all over the place. We had only one corral and we had to rope them out of there for those who were claiming them.

"Old Captain Hale was helping. He was an old cow hand just off the Forest. I guess Cap musta been about 70 at that time. Well, by golly, he and I roped horses out of that corral all

day long.   I was riding a great big gray horse, one of Clyde Shumway's—he was big and stout to rope on.   You know that was the
only time in my life I ever pulled the cinch rings oblong on a
saddle.   But that night my cinch rings were just pulled out oblong—roping those horses and dragging them out of there."

Another time, Roberts recalled, they ran into a problem because of shooting wild horses.   "Those fellows that owned horses
would go out in the spring when the colts were weak, and they'd
rope and branded them.   Then they might never see those horses
again.   In shooting horses, Dolph Slosser (then Ranger at Pinedale) and his assistant, Bill Porter, shot a couple of branded
horses.   The outfit that owned them beat up on Porter and put
him in the hospital for a while.   They tried to get old Dolph, but
someway they didn't do it.   I was up in Denver and I got a wire
to come back home quick.'   Slosser and Porter had been arrested.

"My wife met me at the train and took me up to Taylor.
They guarded me going into the JP's office there . . . anyway,
they bound these two fellows over to the Superior Court.   In the
meantime, we went down to Phoenix and applied for an injunction in Federal Court, enjoining the county from interfering with
us in shooting these branded horses.   The case didn't look very
good for us for awhile either.

"Well, that day we were eating breakfast in the cafe and in
came all these fellows that were prosecuting the case.   They all
filed by me and they all spoke to me, 'Hello, Paul,' and smiled.
They figured they had an open-and-shut case.   Old Dooley
McCauley was county attorney.   The sheriff (Navajo County) was
sitting beside me, and he says, 'Paul, I think we're gonna lose
this case.'   And he was the one that was bringing the case
against us.   He wanted to be enjoined.   He thought the Forest
Service was going to lose.   Anyway the thing went on for quite
a while.   The judge called a recess and went back in his chambers
and came out.   He was only gone for about five minutes.   He
came back and he gave us an injunction.

"That night I was sitting in the same cafe and these guys
all came in to eat supper, and there wasn't a damn one of them
that would speak to me.   But we won that case.

"I don't know whether this is true or not, but I think it was
French who told me that the judge looked up the definition of a
wild horse in the dictionary and it said that any horse on the
range that had the appearance of being wild was a wild horse.

"That was the case that cracked the Secretary's shooting order, wild horse shooting order.   I don't think there was ever
much difficulty about it afterwards.   We removed horses on the

Chevelon District that were wearing brands that hadn't been run for 20 years. It's a wonder that there was any range left. That took a big load off of the range."

The injunction referred to by Paul Roberts was issued by Judge F. C. Jacobs in Federal Court in Phoenix on April 9, 1931, in the case of the U. S. vs. C. D. McCauley, county attorney, and L. D. Divelbess, the sheriff of Navajo County.

In a memorandum to Forest Officers, Quincy Randles, then Acting Regional Forester, pointed out that the case was of much importance to the Forest Service in carrying out its policy of ridding the range of wild horses.

The injunction authorized the Forest Service to "dispose of, by shooting if necessary, any wild horse of unknown ownership, as herein defined, whether branded or not, found in trespass on the National Forest running at large on the Forest after said range has been closed by the Secretary of Agriculture to the grazing of wild horses of unknown ownership as herein described and reasonable notice has been given thereof."

Commenting on the injunction, Quincy Randles wrote the Rangers that "It is realized that where wild and gentle horses are mixed on the same range, it is rather difficult to distinguish the gentle horses from the wild ones, consequently a gentle horse may be killed accidentally, in which case the Service would be criticized, but if reasonable diligence is used to determine whether the horse is wild or gentle and notice of the time set for shooting the wild horses is given to the local stockmen, it is felt the closing order procedure will be supported by the Federal courts and by public sentiment."

Most of the old-time Rangers can recount unique experiences in trying to rid their districts of wild horses. Bob Ground, who was a Ranger on the Carson and Santa Fe Forests for 34 years, told of men coming into the Jicarilla District of the Carson National Forest to try to round up some of the wild horses.

"They'd run and kill a good horse to get a poor one," is the way Ground put it. "A lot of people seemed to get a lot of sport out of that—runnin' wild horses."

By the time Stanley Wilson was appointed Supervisor of the Carson National Forest in 1924, the wild horse problem had become particularly vexing.

"In 1925," Wilson recalled, "we issued notices that the trespass horses on the Canjilon District of the Carson would be rounded up, and that permittees could redeem their stock caught in the roundup by paying the cost per head of the roundup, and the rest of the stock would be sold at auction. We rounded up

1200 head of wild horses. Very peculiarly, when you looked at them in the bunch it looked like there were some pretty good horses, but actually when you got among 'em, they were all small, so one that was a little bigger kind of stood out. Well, I figured that the cost per head was $3, so we let people redeem their stock at $3 a head. Some were redeemed, but not a great many. Then we started letting people go in and pick out some they wanted and pay $3. Well, that wasn't good because we were creaming our bunch. So then we offered to sell the whole outfit at auction, and that didn't work. We had no bidders. Then we decided we could sell them by private contract. I think the first sale we made—there were three young fellows from Colorado who had worked on some of the Forests on fires up there and had some government checks. They said they were willing to spend them on horses if we didn't charge too much. We asked them how many they wanted, and, as I remember, they said they would take a couple of hundred head. We said we'd sell them for 50c apiece and throw in the colts. Also we would let them have a 5% cut on horses they didn't want. So we started counting out their horses. We came to one with a hip knocked down and the fellows said, 'Well, we don't want that one.'

"L. L. Feight, who was the District Ranger, said, 'That's all right; take that one and we'll give you an extra one for him.' We let them take whatever it was, a couple hundred head I think, and then we gave them additionally for the ones they complained of. What we wanted to do was get rid of horses. Well, we sold some to the local people. Frank Andrews later griped about it because he said that one fellow took the horses from our Forest and came down and turned them loose on the Santa Fe, where he was Supervisor.

"Those three boys from Colorado kind of got cold feet on their deal so they started selling these horses to people who came around. So one of them said, 'Well, I'll tell you, we'll sell enough horses to get our money back and we'll turn the rest of them loose.'

"Ranger Locke Feight happens to be a very ingenious fellow. It was a little difficult branding all those horses. Locke made up some stamp branding irons so we could just hit them once instead of doing it the hard way. We had a chute and we put them in there and we branded them. When we were pretty near through, I said to one of these fellows who was figuring on turning these horses loose, 'You know, when we have a lot of horses belonging to many owners, it's very difficult for us to do anything, because you can't make 50 trespass cases against 50 owners for $3 head apiece. But, when we've got one owner that has an appreciable number of horses, why we can go to court and make it stick.'

" 'Furthermore,' I said, 'if you're worrying about the difficulty of driving your horses back into Colorado, we'll lend you a couple of Rangers to help you get over across the line.'   So we actually did get rid of them 1200 horses OK."

Perl Charles, who also served on the Carson, remembers that when he was a Ranger on the Jemez River District, he started rounding up horses in the early 30's after the Forest boundaries were fenced.

"We took over 1500 head of horses off that one District," he said.

When the Rangers started removing horses on the Carson, some cattlemen began killing wild horses on their own.   "Of course, we got blamed for it," Perl Charles said.   "We had some pretty close shaves with those fellows.   There was nothing we could do but try to talk them out of it.   Personally, I had a lot of experience with that.   I couldn't run very fast, and I wasn't big enough to fight, so I had to talk them out of it."

Once when Charles was rounding up a bunch of horses on the Rock Creek area of the Carson, he found a local rancher, a fellow named Manuel, in the horse corral.   Manuel had once been in the penitentiary for killing a man.

"What are you doing in there?"   Charles demanded.

"Gonna get my horses."

"You can't take them," Charles warned him.

"I am."

The Ranger then walked into the corral, with a dozen of Manuel's *compadres* standing around the corral, some of them armed with weapons of one sort or another.   Charles recalls that he must have stood there in the corral for as long as two hours, just arguing with Manuel.

"There was just nothing for me to do but talk them out of it," he said.

Finally, to settle the matter, he told Manuel: "You can take your horses, the horses you want.   They'll be $3.00 apiece."

"I don't have three dollars."

"O.K. I'll give you a job and we can work it out."

And that's the way it was settled.   "I gave him a job in camp," Charles said.   "He didn't do anything but stayed around long enough to work it out."

Another time Charles and Ranger Joe Rodriguez were rounding up horses in the San Pedro Park district and then the Baca Location for a total of about 400 horses.

"Fellows had been coming up there and buying those horses for a dollar or two a head," Charles said.   "They didn't have much interest in them. They'd get loose and come back again. So this time I told them we'd start the sale at $10. If they were interested enough in them to pay $10, why they could buy them individually. Otherwise we'd sell them in a bunch and take them off the Forest. They told me I couldn't do that. Then they called the old man, Frank Andrews (the Supervisor)."

The conversation went something like this:

"This fellow down here, he's not doing this according to law. We're pretty mad."

"All right. All right," Supervisor Andrews said. "I'll be out."

"You'd better get here pretty quick."

"What time is he going to sell them?" Andrews asked.

"About 9 o'clock in the morning."

Nine o'clock came. No Supervisor. The sale started. Ten o'clock. Still no Supervisor. The sale neared its end.

Finally Andrews arrived.

"He was just as apologetic as he could be," Charles said. "He said he had a breakdown—car trouble or got stuck or something. I wondered if he ever intended to be there at 9 o'clock. These fellows who had called him told him the sale was illegal. The old man told them, 'Well, it's done now. There's nothing we can do about it.'

"Years later he told me he hadn't been too anxious to get there too early!"

CHAPTER VII
What the Well Dressed Ranger Should Wear

The subject of uniforms was always a volatile one in the early days of the Forest Service. All it took to get an argument started at Ranger meetings was to mention uniforms. In the 1905-06 era, the usual field clothing consisted of a pair of Levis—Levi Strausses, they called them then—a work shirt of almost any kind, with a short blue denim jacket and a wide-brimmed Stetson.

When the Ranger was working in brushy country, he added chaps to his wardrobe. Most of the early Rangers also wore a gun belt and six-shooter. Supervisor McClure still wore his Prince Albert.

A. O. Waha, who was one of the first of the technically-educated foresters to be assigned to the Southwestern Region, discovered on his arrival in New Mexico in July, 1905, that his favorite riding habit was not quite in style in the Southwest.

"While still at New Haven, I had made a very attractive riding suit of brown-flecked corduroy," Waha has written. "I realized immediately after noting the characteristic dress of the he-men of the southwest that my riding clothes were quite out of keeping and would make me entirely too conspicuous. While I didn't go as far as to adopt the Levi Strausses, I did use khaki trousers for about the first season, and subsequently khaki riding breeches, and while I found the latter much more comfortable for riding and just as comfortable as trousers for walking provided they were not too tight in the knees, I must admit that considerable intestinal fortitude was required to wear them.

"However, I had a little support due to the fact that we had some ranchers from the East who on occasions wore riding breeches, and then there were several English 'remittance men' who sometimes wore the choke bores; as they were called by the Rangers and cowhands, but for the most part they were so anxious to 'do as the Romans do' that they wore the most disreputable looking clothes they would find and largely forgot about their 'bawths.' It was always a matter of wonderment to me how these supposedly wellbred Englishmen could go from one extreme to the other in so short a time.

"Many were the arguments I had with the Rangers regarding superiority of riding breeches, but I knew they would not be convinced unless they actually gave them a trial. After Ranger Goodard, who had been a top cow hand, bought a pair and liked them, others followed suit. But as long as I was assigned to the Gila, choke bores were anathema to the resident stockmen and cowpunchers."

An attempt had been made as far back as 1903 to get the few scattered Rangers into uniforms, and a paper in the Fred Winn collection reveals that the order to get into uniforms "was not accepted with any degree of enthusiasm, for they were well aware that the people with whom they had to deal were not the type who would be awed by a uniformed official representing the Federal government."

The Rangers "ordered their uniforms and then conveniently hid them away and went on about their work in the garb that was current in the neighborhood."

In 1908 a Forest Service uniform was adopted based on the design of the German foresters, with a tight-fitting collar. The Rangers soon began calling it the "German Crown Prince" uniform.

Waha recalled that because of poor fittings the Rangers were getting by mail order purchases, "some of the men wearing them looked more like pictures of German soldier prisoners during the World War.

"At some hotels," Waha recounted, "the bellboys were wearing uniforms of about the same design and color. Arthur Ringland, who was short of stature and rather boyish looking, was made painfully aware of this when we were staying at the Gadsden Hotel in Douglas, Arizona at the time we were having a Ranger meeting there in 1908. Ringland had his uniform on and was walking bareheaded across the lobby when a guest approached him with a letter, saying, 'Boy mail this letter.' Ringland, who was always a strong advocate of uniform clothing for Forest Officers, did not allow his enthusiasm to be dampened by this incident, but for a time his face was red and of course the story went the rounds."

It was difficult to "sell" Rangers on uniforms. At the 1909 meeting of Rangers at Springerville the subject was discussed several times.

"I always got a perfect fit, but the goods are absolutely worthless," J. C. Wheatley spoke up. "They won't stand rough usage."

D. C. Martin affirmed the judgment, "The suits are o.k. except when they are worn in brushy country."

1910   1971

The well-dressed Forest Ranger

Aldo Leopold commented that he found the uniforms satisfactory, "except for the fit." "The point is," he said, "whether we expect to get some kind of goods that will stand the roughest kind of wear, and high in price, or whether we want a uniform that we can wear only in office work and when we come to town—and pay a comparatively small price for it. They ought to put more wool in the shirts and charge a little more."

"The trousers wear slick and look more or less like a spotted cow," Ranger Wheatley put in.

The Rangers at the meeting voted compulsory wearing of uniforms and the resolution was approved with a couple of dissenting votes.

Arthur Ringland suggested that since a coat was hardly ever worn, a gray shirt with a green tree embroidered on the points of the collar be used as a suitable insignia. No action was taken on the suggestion.

For years it was not compulsory to wear uniforms and many Rangers wore them only at Ranger meetings.

On August 1, 1910, A. F. Potter, Associate Forester in Washington headquarters, sent a memorandum to all Forest Service Officers urging them to order uniforms.

"While the use of Service uniforms is not at present compulsory, it tends toward economy, efficiency, and the dignity of the Service," Potter said in his memorandum. "The uniforms are cheaper than other suitable clothing and are adapted to the needs of the work. Moreover, they distinguish Forest Officers from civilians and awaken in the public a proper respect for the Service and its organization. The Forester heartily approves of them. It is hoped that they will be generally worn."

With the memo were price lists and a descriptive folder showing styles of worsted, olive green uniforms, Mackinaws and overcoats that today are as out of style in their design as hoop skirts and bustles are for the ladies. Only the hat would get by even the un-style-conscious Rangers of today. The hat was a light drab Stetson with four-inch crown and three-inch brim. Trousers were cavalry style riding breeches with laces at ankle and puttee leggins—or if preferred, straight cut long trousers with or without a double seat. There were many supplementals: cap, sweater, reefer, denim jacket and overalls.

The prices offered by the uniform company, the Fechheimer Bros. of Cincinnati certainly would be welcomed by Rangers today: coats, from $7.55 to $9.70; trousers, from $4.45 to $5.90; hats, $3.45 to $4.50; denim coat, $1.10; denim trousers, 90 cents.

A. O. Waha reported that "it was a sad day when they had

to give up wearing their Stetsons.   Having had my fling with this type of hat for years, I personally had no objection to the changed type which is really a more comfortable hat for general wear. In the horseback days, however, I am thankful that sombreros were recognized as the hat the well-dressed Forest Officers should wear.   As a memento of those days, I still have the Mexican hand-carved leather hat band which I used to make my hat, shall I say, somewhat distinctive."

In 1918, Waha was an inspector in the Division of Operations in the Washington office, and was designated a committee of one to design a new uniform.   The English army officer's uniform with its open collar and large bellows-type pockets furnished ideas for the 1918 uniform.   The arrangement of pockets was changed, according to Waha, and a sewed on belt was added.

"This style," he said, "was effective until about 1934 when a Service-wide committee designed the present day uniform, which retains the best features of the one I had designed and, unfortunately, some that are longer so good."

CHAPTER VIII
Six-Guns and Sons o' Guns

The well-equipped Ranger of the 1900-1910 period would hardly consider riding out over his District without his rifle and six-shooter. The guns were as necessary a part of his equipment as his tools for firefighting.

When the technically trained foresters began to come into the Service from the East, they were usually less inclined to carry guns—and, in fact, some had never before handled weapons.

As Bob Ground, longtime cowboy Ranger on the Santa Fe and Carson National Forests, put it, "People around here, everybody carried a gun, and everybody that rode much always carried guns on their saddles. I did just like they did, I got guns and carried a gun, too."

Ground said he never did use the gun on anybody, but once "scared a man down there pretty bad. There was this fellow that was supposed to be a bad man, a horsethief—run him out of the country once. I just scared the life out of him. I rode down around his place on a barefoot horse after a rain. He saw my tracks."

An undated paper in the files of the Magdalena District of the Datil National Forest discussing the history of the District for the 1910-13 period reported that "frontier conditions obtained throughout the Forest in 1910, and the residents of one of the principal creeks were said by one of the Washington inspectors to be as hard a lot as existed on any Forest in the Nation."

The report went on to note that "while conditions in Magdalena at this time were not quite as lively as they were in the old days when the cowboys were said to have run their horses up and down the board sidewalks of the main street and jumped them off the high end near the Santa Fe branch railway station, occasionally shooting into the air, or perhaps putting bullets through the walls of the few houses that bordered the street . . . still, in the fall when some 100,000 head of cattle and sheep were handled through the corrals, things were decidedly brisk, and the saloons and brothels did a heavy business."

Two Rangers in the Magdalena district unfortunately were

involved in a killing that resulted when they were deputized by the Sheriff to assist in trailing a rustler.

Assistant Rangers J. D. Jones and Clinton Hodges and a rancher, J. W. Medley, owner of one of the big ranch outfits, came upon the suspected rustler in the act of burning the offal from a carcass of a cow belonging to Medley. The Rangers, both armed with 30-30's approached the man and were within a few feet of him when he reached for his six-shooter. The gun was out of the holster when both Rangers fired. The rustler's gun fell from his hand as he dropped to the ground without firing, dying instantly. The Rangers were exonerated after a hearing.

When Stanley Wilson was Deputy Supervisor on the Datil National Forest a few years later the Rangers were having trespass troubles because certain ranchers were running unpermitted cattle on the Forest. It was decided to have a roundup.

"These are dangerous people," Supervisor Douglas told his Rangers. "You'd better all wear guns."

To Stan Wilson it seemed ridiculous because as he put it, "I would have been of no use in a gunfight because I wouldn't have known when to start. I mean somebody could have killed me three times before I ever pulled my gun."

Wilson said that he figured the only fellow who showed real sense in the situation was Garvin Smith, a Ranger from Chloride.*

"I'm not wearing a gun," Smith told Wilson. "It's not my game and I'm not wearing a gun for anybody."

Wilson said the group had started for the roundup without telling any of the ranchers about it, and when they got to the roundup area, Supervisor Douglas sent Wilson and Garvin Smith to the headquarters of the ranch that was in the trespass.

"I had an army gun on my hip," Wilson said. "I tried to hide it under my sweater, but it didn't work very well. We got down to B's place. He took one look at us and went in and came out with a rifle. I told him we were rounding up his stock. We had a little conversation about it.

"Then we started picking up his stock right there at his ranch and driving them. Boy, I didn't feel happy about that because we were turning our backs on people and we didn't know what they would do.

"The interesting thing was, it was a foggy morning and they thought they could get in there and run their cattle off the Forest. Instead of bothering with us, as soon as we were out of sight, he and his two sons saddled up and went up into the Forest. Well,

---

*Father of Zane Smith, a second generation Ranger, who began his career in the Forest Service in 1937.

as it happened, we had quite a few people. When the ranchers went along the ridge, they met two of our men. When they went somewhere else, they met two more. So they decided it wasn't lucky. They threw in with us, but tried to beat us as much as they could. It was a very unhappy time. I remember I was riding a little gray horse. I was punching some cattle on top of a canyon, and there was kind of a steep edge. I heard B. say, 'Well, I don't wish that gray horse any ill luck, but I wish he'd go over the cliff. There'd be one less so-and-so.' "

Fred Croxen was the Ranger on the Bly District of the Coconino National Forest in 1921 and had the misfortune to have on his District an ex-convict, who was on parole from the State prison at Florence, and who had the reputation of being a boastful bad man.

This fellow—we'll call him Bird, though it wasn't his name— had made trouble for Ranger Croxen and had made threats against him to people down in the desert country. They had passed along the word to Croxen as a friendly warning. Croxen had passed the information along to the Supervisor, Ed Miller, and also to Sheriff Bill Campbell, who had been a former Ranger on the Coconino. So they were pretty familiar with the situation. But when Miller was away, Bob Rinehart was acting as Supervisor, and he knew nothing about the trouble between Bird and Croxen. Rhinehart sent a letter to Croxen telling him that Bird wanted to trim some limbs of pinyon pine trees in his forest pasture so the grass would grow better and that the matter needed to be checked.

Croxen's first thought was that it was a put-up job by Bird to get him down there.

"I studied over it for two or three days and didn't sleep much those two or three nights," Croxen recounted. "Finally I decided, 'I will be considered a coward if I don't go down. I might just as well quit if I'm a coward.'

"So I went down but couldn't do any business with him. He wanted to do business directly with the Forest Office. I went over about a quarter of a mile to a brother of his. They hadn't been on speaking terms for about a couple of years until just before that. So I went down to his place, and he said he was gonna do all his business with the Forest Office, too. I said, 'That's all right.'

"I had to come back by this Charlie's place. I heard a rifle shot over by the house. I looked over, and he had tried out his rifle out on a bucket hanging on a post about 75 yards from the house. He shoved the rifle in the scabbard of his saddle; he had saddled this mare of his and he'd shoved the rifle in there.

"Farmer-like, instead of getting on his horse and riding around, he led her by the bit, and she hung back—fortunately for me. I had to go through his gate because I wasn't gonna go turn back to old Arthur's place, because he'd probably have his .30-gun out there laying for me, too. (I found out later that he didn't carry fire-arms at all.) Well, Charlie had gone around to his barn and had mounted his mare. In the meantime I had opened this gate, and he came out and spotted me. He rode over and said, 'You've trespassed me three times and I'm gonna make you stop it, understand?' He dropped his hand down to his right trouser pocket. I knew he had a .380 Savage automatic, and that was where he always carried it. I had my pistol stuck in my belt—and I out with it, and I never saw a man move so quick in my life. I shot right where his heart ought to have been and he went off the right-hand side of his horse. That darned bullet just creased him right across the top of the head. My horse jumped, I'd never shot off this horse before, it was little horse of my wife's. Charlie jumped up just right, and I shot him again. It went clear through him, and he just reached up and took about a foot and a half shorter grasp on the bridle reins. Then I shot him in the head. The bullet broke his neck, right at the base of the brain. He went down.

"I rode to the Ranger Station and called Ed Miller and told him, then I said, 'You get C. B. Wilson.' C. B. Wilson was our family attorney as well as the owner of the building that the Forest Office was in at the time. I asked Miller to notify Sheriff Campbell, too. C. B. Wilson was in Phoenix, and Sheriff Campbell was at Grand Canyon. They both got there as quick as they could. Well, Campbell impaneled a coroner's jury. They came out from Winslow and met me on the way in to Winslow. I had a Model T. Ford, and the front wheels were shimmying, so I went on into town along with the Sheriff. I turned over my six-shooter to Sheriff Campbell and kept my .30 gun. When we got into Winslow we walked up the street, with me still wearing my .30 gun, to the Palace Hotel and secured a room. When we got into that room he handed me his six-shooter and says, 'Here, you take this. If any of those fellows try to break in here, let 'em have it.' Well, I took it, and thought, 'Well, this won't do,' so I gave it back to him, and thanked him.

"The next day we went out to where this shooting happened. I showed them about it, and then we went into Winslow, and then from Winslow to Flagstaff. Next day I told my story before the coroner's jury there. The coroner's jury brought in a verdict of justifiable homicide. Along sometime in February we had a preliminary hearing and the Judge said, 'After listening to all this testimony, and in view of the verdict of the coroner's jury, I can't find any grounds for further court action.' And the case was dismissed right there. While we were there, Mrs. Bird was there, and she came over to my wife and put her arm around her and she said, "I'm glad he got it instead of your . . . husband."

One of the fabulous cowmen of an earlier generation in New Mexico was Cole Railston. He earned a niche in history as one of the great pioneers of the range. Eugene Manlove Rhodes used him to portray some of his fictional characters in his *Saturday Evening Post* stories of the 1920's, and he is among these that Agnes Morley Cleaveland portrayed in *No Life for a Lady.*

Samuel R. Servis who was a Ranger in the Magdalena District in the thirties became well acquainted with Railston in connection with his official duties and collected many stories about the great old cowman.

"Railston was 78 when I knew him. He went to a dance one night in Magdalena, got to dancing with Mrs. Gibson, the wife of another Ranger there at Magdalena. They got to cutting up. Cole was so deaf, he couldn't hear the music, but he would get behind somebody and follow them. Apparently he got behind some high-stepper, for suddenly down went Mrs. Gib and ol' Cole. He broke her finger and she kicked out two of his ribs!"

Servis said he believed Cole Railston was probably one of the best managers of a range that he'd ever been around. "He knew range management from the word go. He knew so much about grazing that it was interesting to ride with him, and he had a reason for everything. He and an old sheepman up north—I think he was in Region 2—were the two people that the Forest Service first visited when they made the grazing policy and regulations in the Forest Service. Our grazing policy today is exactly as Cole dictated it to the Forest Service except for two things: the distribution policy which he never agreed with, and the free-use policy which allowed the homesteaders to come in. It was made for the homesteaders, and he had no use for the homesteaders."

Servis told a story that was current at the time about a homesteader and his family and their cattle and horses who came by the headquarters ranch of the V-Cross-T in those days. The homesteader asked Cole where he could get a little water. Cole said: "You can fill your quart jar up at the well outside here, and then go on—but you aren't to stop on my range."

Servis remembered with delight that he rode for a week with Cole. "He had an allotment out on the range—East Berley, I believe it was. He was extremely interesting. We would get up at 3 o'clock in the morning and work like the deuce and make our breakfast right quick, then ride until about 3 o'clock. We would come in and make biscuits and visit and play coon can until midnight. Then we'd sleep until 3 o'clock and get up and run like fools until 3, and then eat hurriedly and play coon can and visit."

Talking about the homesteaders, Servis told how Railston had paid his cowboys 50 cents a corner to ride all over the country and pick up section corners and turn them over. "When the homesteaders came in and endeavored to locate a piece of land, which they had to do, and it had to be surveyed, they couldn't find any corner. Cole would always say, 'Well, the country is not surveyed. You better go on about your business.' So they didn't settle there. This also happened with the outfit that was down on the Gila River. They did the same thing when the homesteaders came in. They shoved them all through to Arizona and elsewhere. That's one reason there weren't many old ranches along the Gila River on the New Mexico side. That's also the reason why the water of the Gila all goes to Arizona. It was settled prior to the time that New Mexico settled along the rivers. Our old-time stockmen pushed them out of this country and shoved them right on down the Gila River into the desert around Safford and Coolidge and so forth. That's how all the water got to Arizona. They established use rights that way along the river."

Servis said that Cole had eight or ten of the top gunmen of the West riding his west line.

"Those people came in to homestead or to hide out from the law. They endeavored to raise a few crops along the rivers, along the Middle Fork and the East Fork, and couldn't do it. So they naturally went to preying on the adjoining large stockmen. They started butchering beef and jerking it and taking it to the miners at Mogollon and Georgetown and Santa Rita and everywhere else they could peddle the jerk-meat."

The V-Cross-T was a big outfit and Servis described it as extending from the Gila River to Apache Creek, bordered on the west by the Negrito, on the east by the Rio Grande and on the north by the mountains beyond Red Lake.

"They had a light year when they branded 10,000 calves," Servis said.

He noted that Cole Railston was responsible for the Forest Service's salting policy, which was established after Talbot came out from Washington and talked to him.

Talbot asked Cole how he was salting livestock. "Why, away from water, Mr. Talbot, away from water, of course."

Servis said Cole's policy was to salt on feed most of the year but he salted on water two months of the year when he wanted the cows bred, then the rest of the time salted on feed, away from water. "And he moved the salt where the feed was quite continually," Servis said. "In fact, he carried a burlap sack to pick up salt and pack it around with him as he went around the range."

So when Talbot visited Cole and asked how he salted his range, and Cole told him "away from water," Talbot told him he'd have to prove it. So Talbot got on a horse and they rode out on a long ridge toward Magdalena. Salt was scattered up and down the ridge for about six miles. There was no water on either side.

Servis said that what Cole didn't tell Talbot was how the salt got there in the first place.

"It seems," Servis related, "that a cowboy was sent out to scatter a wagonload of salt along the range and was told where to put it.

"It was toward the end of the week, and he was going to a dance in Magdalena, so he hid his saddle under the tarp. When he got out on the range, he decided he wouldn't go around the regular trail or wagon roads to scatter the salt, but that he would cross the ridge. It was springtime, and when he brought the wagon out on top of the ridge, he got bogged down and couldn't get out. He unhooked the team and put the harnesses in under the tarp and sent one horse back to the ranch; just turned him loose and, of course, he went back to the ranch. He climbed aboard the other horse and rode to Magdalena for a big shindig on the town, and a dance and a drink. Well, he came back to the ranch the following week and ol' Cole was madder than a wet hen, and he said, 'Well, where's the wagon and where did you put the salt?' The cowboy said, 'I bogged the wagon down.' So Cole said, 'You go on up the ridge and get the wagon out and scatter the salt up and down the ridge, and don't go any farther.'

"Well, it was just about two weeks later that here came Talbot. Cole took him out and spent two days on that ridge with a big story telling Talbot just how to do it. But he actually did salt like that and he actually believed in it. Except at breeding time for the cows, and then he salted on water so that the bulls wouldn't have to walk too far to find the cows. He would always try to keep some waters closed up during the breeding time so that he could keep the cows pretty well gathered around for a couple of months, and the salt and bulls were kept on water.

"Now when you were riding with him and he found a cow that was bulling, he'd take off and spend the rest of the time hunting a bull and take her right to the bull, because it was too hard on the bull to get up there.   But he sure would drive that old cow up to the bull.   Another thing, he'd come along and a fence was down, boy, he'd stop everything right then and there and patch it up.   Even though he carried a little sack full of new staples, he'd hunt up the old staples.   As he pointed out, that was what made money in the cow business—instead of using something new all the time, instead of coming back with the work crew and fixing the fence—you fixed it as you went by, you did everything as you saw it.   When you needed more salt, you went and found a salt ground that had salt on it, and moved it, and tried to determine why the cows didn't come to that particular neck of the woods and use the salt.   That was the way to manage range and, of course, you had to ride everyday.   You couldn't go to the bar and stand your foot up on the rail, so forth and so on.   No, Cole knew, within a few cents, exactly what he paid for prunes, horseshoe nails, or horse-shoes, by months, by the year.   He had a tremendous mind and was quite a stockman, in my opinion."

Besides rustling there was also bootlegging down in the Gila country.   During prohibition days, Federal officers made numerous attempts to dry up the source of the southwestern mountain version of "Taos Lightning."

When G. Lee Wang was a Ranger on the Mimbres District, he was almost arrested himself as a bootlegger.

It has been the custom of the State Game and Fish Department to stock the mountain streams, even the ones almost impossible to reach except on horseback.   Wang would help out by leading a pack outfit of mules with fish for planting up the head waters of the Mimbres.

"I packed ten or eleven mules, two cans to a mule," Wang said, "and took them up the Mimbres.   On the way down again, it got dark, and I hadn't tied these cans on particularly tight. Here was a string of mules, ten or eleven of them, with loose cans, jogging along.   All of a sudden a couple of fellows came out there and stopped us."

One of the men said, "You're under arrest."

"For what?"

"For transporting white mule whiskey."

Wang was a bit flabbergasted.   "Do you know who I am or what I had in these cans?"

"Well, I don't know, but you're under arrest."

Wang remembers that the revenuers really thought they had made a big haul.

"If you'll look in those cans," he told then, "you'll see that they are empty.   This afternoon, they did have fish in them.   I packed fish up to the head of the river."

So the prohibition agents had to look elsewhere for the source of the white mule that was coming out of the Gila.

There was probably a still in many of the southwestern mountains in those days.

Ed Groesbeck, who was a Ranger on the Sitgreaves and the Carson back in the twenties and thirties remembered that a cache of whiskey gave Bootlegger Hill, near Flagstaff, its name.

"When they were cutting timber in that area," he explained, "they piled brush along the road. It laid there most of the summer. That fall Bob Rinehart and his crew started out one day to burn brush. They had just started to light these piles when down the road came a car hell-bent for election. It went through and around this crew and got to about three or four piles ahead of them. A guy got out of the car and run over to the pile and got a jug and put it in the back of the car. He went on and stopped at every three or four piles and must of got four or five jugs out finally. His bootleg whiskey was hidden in that brush and Bob was about to burn it up. So they called the darned place Bootlegger Hill after that."

Rangers have a variety of stories of wrecked stills and ruins where stills were operated that they have come across in their patrols.

Lee Wang recalled that in McKnight Canyon there was a still about half a mile above an old sawmill camp. "I was coming up the canyon one morning on horseback," he said. "The prohibition boys had been there and wrecked the still. This must have been just the day before. They'd tipped over some of the barrels and some of them were still standing, full of mash.

"The chipmunks were in there—50 to 75 of them, I'd say. And the drunkest things you ever saw in your life. They'd eaten that mash, and they'd just almost fight you. It must have been good fightin' whiskey because those little devils would stand up there, straight up, just looking at you and cussing you out— drunker'n all get-out."

There was a lot of violence in the Gila country during—and before—the early years of the Forest Service. Ben Kemp who grew up in the Forest and worked as a cowboy, lawman, and Ranger, knew the Gila country like the back of his hand. He had wanted to be a Ranger ever since he was a kid when Fred Winn was the first Ranger in the District where he lived, about 1908.

Kemp said the naming of Dead Man Spring was a result of a gun fight between three cowboys that started over a snide remark about one cowboy's sister. He mentioned also a bunch of graves in a horse pasture at Negrito, where Victorio and his Apaches had killed nine of Solomon Luna's sheepherders in the 1880's.

"They killed the sheepherders and turned all the sheep loose on the range," Kemp said. "Sheep were running all over that country. Some sheepmen around Aragon got their start from those loose sheep. Two V-Cross cowboys were riding the range out there about a year later and they ran onto nearly 2,000 head of sheep. A couple of dogs were herding those sheep. They were trained to take care of sheep and that was a year or better after the Indians had killed the sheepherders.

"The dogs wouldn't let the cowboys come up to the herd. They'd charge 'em every time the cowboys got close. Those fellows killed the two dogs. Dad always said it was something pretty bad for them to kill the dogs after they had guarded their sheep for better than a year."

Later on Solomon Luna had the rock monuments set up in the pasture—one for each sheepherder killed—and a priest held a service there, blessing the *campo santo,* although actually there were no bodies. The bodies had never been found, although Bob Lewis, Marshall of Magdalena, later found several skeletons.

Indian raids were frequent in the Gila country until the late 1880's. Probably the last Indian marauder to live in the Gila area was the Apache Kid, as he was called, though he was not the same person as the Apache Kid of Arizona.

The Kid stole a horse that had once belonged to Ben Kemp's father. The horse was one of a band of wild horses that the elder Kemp and others had "walked down" from the high country in many days of running them tender-footed until they could be corraled. The horse* that the Apache Kid finally stole was just a colt then, a brown blaze-faced colt, with stocking legs. The Kemps named him Baldy Socks.

"That colt," said Ben Kemp, "made one of the best cuttin' horses in the Southwest."

The elder Kemp sold the horse to Charlie Anderson in 1900.

"That horse was the cause of two different men gettin' killed. One of them was the Apache Kid who stole him. A posse eventually trailed him to the top of the San Mateos.

"By the time they got up on Blue Mountain side there it was dark, or almost dark. They could see fire-light right down ahead, in one of the deep saddles. They tried to get down there but couldn't make it. They found it too rough, and got off on the wrong point and went down the wrong way and had to back track.

---

*The horse was stolen a second time and resulted in an argument between the horse thief and a man who was going to report it, resulting in the latter being killed. Then the horse was killed and buried to destroy the evidence, according to Kemp.

By the time they got back on top it was nearly daylight. As soon as it got daylight they could see tracks going down this ridge. They went down the ridge and got down on the side of the slope into this saddle, and they run into horses grazing on the side of the hill. So of course Billy knew this horse of his Dad's as soon as he saw him.

"They just got off their horses and laid down in the grass among the logs and rooks, and waited amongst the horses. Along about daylight—the sun was just comin' up—the Apache Kid come up there to get the horses. Bill Kiehne said he walked up to within 16 feet of them. They had all agreed to shoot at once, and boy, they let 'im have it. He was carrying a rifle across his arm. They said he jumped as high as he could go, nearly, and went right over backwards and threw his rifle—he had a .30-.40 and they said he threw that rifle down the side of that hill about 30 steps.* There was another Indian with him and when they started shootin' at him he run off down through the saddle—and they never did find his body. But there was blood spattered on the rocks just like you'd shot a deer through the heart. So they figured he didn't get away."

Henry Woodrow, who spent his entire career as a Ranger in one District of the Gila National Forest—the McKenna Park District—is another one of the authorities on events and people of the great Gila National Forest country.

In 1912 he was assigned to handle the count of sheep (nearly 20,000) to be grazed on the McKenna District.

At that time there were three big outfits on the District: the Bergere Estate, Frank A. Hubbell, and Solomon Luna, who also looked after the Bergere interests.

Woodrow had been warned by well-meaning friends that it would be a hard job and that he would have a difficult time trying to get along with Solomon Luna.

"I told them that I had been around Spanish-American people most of my life and that I thought I could get along with them," Woodrow related. "I met Mr. Luna and found him to be very agreeable, also his nephews, Ed and Manuel Otero, whom I met a great many times later on the sheep range.

"After I got the sheep counted that were to go on my District, Mr. Luna called all his foremen and herders together and made a talk to them. Instructed them to cooperate with me in

---

*A story of horse and wife stealing by Apache Kid, by Eugene Manlove Rhodes appears in the January, 1928 issue of New Mexico Highway Journal (now New Mexico Magazine).

every way they could in the way of keeping down fires and handling sheep, as I would direct them on the range, and to let me count any herds at any time and to keep off the cattle ranges. So I had no trouble to speak of from then on. Very few fires ever occurred on this District from sheep camps."

Old time cattlemen in the Gila country were Ab Alexander and Buck Powell. Henry Woodrow recalled that Powell was involved in a killing in E E Canyon in the 90s, as result of a feud between homesteaders.

"James Huffman was a homesteader on a piece of land on Middle Fork near the mouth, which is now part of the Heart Bar Ranch," Woodrow said. "Jordan Rodgers also had a homestead, which is part of the Heart Bar, and had a bunch of cattle on the West Fork in the Prior country, running with Jim Huffman's cattle.

"Huffman had threatened Rodgers' life and Rodgers was afraid to go up there and work his cattle. One day Rodgers and Buck Powell rode up EE Canyon and they met James Huffman and started a row. Buck Powell shot Huffman once, and Rodgers, thinking he was not dead, rode up and fired several shots into him. Rodgers stood trial and came clear. Huffman was buried beside William Grudging, killed by Tom Wood, just south of the Grudging cabin.

"Buck Powell was later killed at the little mining town of Fairview."

Ranger Ben Kemp was also familiar with the story of Buck Powell and remembered the details of his death.

"Some fellow by the name of Allen killed him," Kemp said. I suppose there was some kind of feud. Buck had come in the bar at Fairview. Old Man Marks was running the bar. Buck was standin' up at the bar and he had a pocket knife in his hand and was pecking on the bar—just standin' there absent-mindedly turning the knife over and letting it drop on the bar. Old Man Marks said, 'Buck, don't do that. The boys have beat it with six-shooters and one thing and another and dented it already. The old bar's already in bad shape.' Buck said, 'Yes, all right,' and just stuck the knife in his pocket.

"This Allen just jerked out his six-shooter and shot him from the hip and hit him right between the eyes and killed him instantly. They never did know what the trouble was. They sent Allen to the penitentiary for 50 years, I think it was, and he died in the penitentiary."

In later years, Ab Alexander, mentioned as an associate of Powell's, was a permittee on the Gila and ran some cattle from the N Bar Ranch on the Forest.

When A. O. Waha was working out of Silver City in McClure's time back in 1906-07, he used to stop over with Ab Alexander and Shack Simmons at the N Bar when on patrol.

"Ab owned cattle and Shack worked for him," Waha related. "They were bachelors and lived very simply. Their log cabin was very comfortable. The meals, usually comprising yearling beef cooked in a dutch oven in deep fat, sourdough biscuits, potatoes and thick canned milk gravy and coffee, were just what an outdoor man required and liked, and there was always plenty of horse feed, so I never passed up an opportunity of stopping with them. Besides they were good company.

"Ab was quiet and reserved, while Shack was inclined to be outspoken. His language was most picturesque. A forest guard had stayed with them at the ranch for awhile whom Shack did not like. It seemed that he bragged too much—and in other respects showed he was not the kind of man to be admired by a man of Shack's temperament. So when Shack was later telling me about this guard, he said, 'Hell, he hadn't enough brains to grease a gimlet. You can knock the pith out of a horse hair and put his brains in and they would rattle like a peanut in a boxcar.' "

Sam Sowell, who was Ranger on the Araviapa District of the Crook National Forest in the twenties, found in that isolated District that law and order were very limited even in those years of the late twenties.

"Over the years, it was the scene of many gun battles," Sowell related in a paper describing his assignment in the District. "In the early days, the Galiuro Mountains was a hideout for the tough element around Tombstone and Charlestown."

In those days, Safford and Wilcox were the nearest shopping centers and the Ranger usually made a trip once a month for supplies. Mail service was limited to three days a week. There were no telephones and no radio communication on the District.

"As late as 1925 to 1930, during my assignment on this District," Sowell wrote, "range disputes and murder continued. During this time there were thirteen cold-blooded murders committed, and only one man paid the penalty for his acts—he committed suicide.

"In the earlier days, it was the custom for Forest Rangers to carry guns, but I soon learned that was a sure way to get into trouble, and discontinued this practice.

"In June 1930, we were having Sunday dinner with my wife's family and someone called to me from the front of the Ranger Station. As I reached the door he called again and at that time I saw him fall from his horse. This was a young man about 25, and our nearest neighbor. I could readily see that he was badly hurt, with his clothing saturated with blood. Although shot through the body with a Winchester carbine he was able to relate the entire story to us and remained conscious for 45 minutes. Within a matter of minutes the assailant and his son drove up in a car, got out with gun in hand, walked over to the dying man, looked the crowd over and left.

"This shooting had happened approximately one mile below the Ranger Station, along the stream bed of the Aravaipa, and he rode his horse across country through a dense stand of mesquite to the Ranger Station. The assailant was following him by car, but had to go around the mesquite thicket to the highway, which took him a few minutes longer to reach the Station. It was assumed he was following him to finish the job as he was not aware he was mortally wounded until he saw he was shot through the body and dying at the time. Within a matter of only a few hours the entire community arrived at the scene, besides the tourists passing, and a very large crowd assembled. The victim was very popular in the community and the citizens were worked up to a point of a lynching party. A posse was quickly formed and organized to prevent the culprit's escape. Had he been encountered the results would, no doubt, have been serious. He no doubt realized the situation and drove direct to Safford, the county seat, and reported the killing. Self-defense, of course. But the young man was at the Station before and after the incident, and was not armed. The assailant and his son were placed in the county jail and during the night he committed suicide by cutting his throat with a dull pocket knife."

Ranger Sowell recalled another incident of a shooting in 1927 when a rancher named Clayton was riding his horse toward home from a cattle drive and was waylaid and shot from his horse.

The killing was not discovered for several days, then it was determined that Clayton's body had been dragged by horseback several miles into the Galiuro Mountains and left in a deep *arroyo*. The sheriff formed a posse, and Ranger Sowell was sworn in as a member. Indian trailers were employed from the San Carlos Reservation, but due to heavy rains the trail could not be followed. A hat and spurs were found, however.

Circumstantial evidence pointed toward a neighbor, who was arrested and brought to trial. All indications were that a conviction was evident, Sowell recalled.

However, on the night of the last day of the trial, Ranger Sowell discovered from his diary that the man was innocent.

He rode into Klondyke, where the trial was being held, and showed his diary to officials. On the day that the accused was charged with killing Clayton, the diary showed that he was making a range inspection in company with the Ranger!

Sowell testified to the diary evidence, and the jury brought in a verdict of "not guilty."

Clayton's killer was never discovered.

When Zane Smith, the second generation forester, was just a boy, his father Garvin Smith was District Ranger at Mayhill, east of Cloudcroft.

"The country was pretty wide open," Zane Smith recalled. "There weren't very many fences, and one of the big problems confronting the Rangers was getting livestock numbers under control. Trespass was a tremendous problem. The National Forests hadn't been in existence long enough to be very well accepted. The established ranchers in the country included many individuals who had grown up and gotten established in the days of the open public domain, and they didn't like to have somebody come along and tell them how many head of cattle they could run, or where they could run them, or what season of the year they could run them, on public lands.

"I remember dad had quite a hassle with one of the early-day pioneer families that lived down on the Penasco about 12 or 15 miles below Mayhill. I won't mention their names because probably some of their descendants are living and they might not see the funny side to it. Dad had made a trespass on them and given notice to round up and remove many head of cattle. I remember old Mr. Mayhill, for whom the little town of Mayhill was named, and who was quite friendly with the Forest Service and particularly with my father, came and told him that this family had gotten all the sons and brothers, everybody, together, and that they were going to refuse to move their stock. They were all armed, and he advised my father not to press his luck and, if he did go, to try to get someone from the sheriff's office, or other Forest Service personnel, to go with him, because he was afraid there might be violence.

"I remember my father refused, and decided not to go armed, because he was afraid if he did, that could in itself bring about some shooting or violence. He showed up unarmed and I think it so shocked the whole group that it threw them off-balance. Simply by standing up to the 10 or 12 people that were there, unarmed, he talked them into moving the livestock off. I've thought back about the early-day Forest Rangers, and some of the things they had to do, and I've known of other Forest Rangers who were doing similar things, coming up against similar bad situations.

Zane Smith recalled another incident involving his father in the Sacramento Mountains at the head of the Agua Chiquita.

"Dad was running a trapline at that time and I was stringing along with him. We were riding down a little drainage and saw a man walking along up towards us with his rifle over his shoulder. That didn't attract any particular attention because everybody more or less carried rifles in those days. In fact, my father had a .30-30 rifle in its scabbard, hung on his saddle, and he also had a pistol that he carried on his belt and it stuck down in one of his hip pockets. Well, we pulled up to stop and visit, as most people did in the country back in those days. A few words were spoken and this fellow suddenly raised his rifle and pointed it at my father. 'You're another one of these Forest Rangers that was sent in here, I guess,' he said. 'You know I run the last three Forest Rangers out, an' you're gonna be the fourth.' He accused my father of a lot of things that was new to both him and me and knowing my father, I could see him beginning to smoke quite a bit under the collar, and getting pretty mad.

"The fellow looked him over after he had cussed him out, and he seemed to run down with what he had to say—looked him over and decided that all he had was a rifle in the scabbard. So he set his own rifle down and leaned it against his side, and got out his Bull Durham and rolled a cigarette. When he stuck his head down to light his cigarette, my father pulled his revolver out of his hip pocket and when the guy looked up he was looking into this revolver, I remember his mouth came open and his cigarette fell to the ground. I thought my father was going to shoot him, he was so darned mad, but he didn't. He finally told him to drop his rifle and beat it down the trail, and if he ever saw him again he was going to shoot him.

"We went on down the trail a little ways and then my father got to wondering what this was all about. We had a dog with us, so we started making some circles in there and the dog located a badly wounded doe that had recently been shot. Apparently this was the reason for this man having tried to run us off with his rifle—he figured my father would prosecute him."

CHAPTER IX
Grazing Problems

Ranger Henry Woodrow offered a simple solution for Rangers who had problems with grazing permittees—if they were widows, that is.

"There happened to be a widow on this part of the District (the McKenna Park District of the Gila National Forest) with a grazing permit on the Forest and a ranch near the Gila Ranger Station," Woodrow said. "So I married her. . . . Later I heard of Rangers on other Forests and Districts having quite a bit of trouble with widow permittees.

"I would suggest that the Forest Service put a single man for a Ranger there, and probably he would marry her and stop all the trouble."

Unfortunately for single Rangers elsewhere, many of their problems were with male permittees.

Edward G. Miller had hardly moved into his new position as Supervisor of the Prescott National Forest in April 1917 than he was faced with the problem of handling a "hot potato."

Early one morning a man appeared in the Prescott office, introduced himself and was all smiles for a few minutes. It was not his name, but we'll call him Mr. Perry.

Without any preliminary warning he addressed the new Supervisor, "Young man, you bear a wonderfully fine reputation, but if things don't change you're going to be fired."

Then Mr. Perry went on to spell out the doleful things that had happened to a U. S. judge who had found him guilty of land fraud and sentenced him to Federal prison, and what had happened to one or two others. All had suffered injuries or afflictions of some kind that were imposed by the Almighty due to the fact they had been "unkind and unjust in their dealings" with Mr. Perry.

Then Mr. Perry got down to the business of the day. He had bought around a thousand head of drouth-stricken cattle in southwestern New Mexico and he proposed to graze them on the Walnut Creek District of the Prescott National Forest. He claimed title to forty-acres on which a spring was located and felt that since he owned that water, he should be allowed to bring cattle on the District, even though it was already fully stocked—in fact, parts of the District badly overstocked.

Supervisor Miller, unimpressed by the story of the dire consequences of opposing him, informed Mr. Perry that there was absolutely no chance of his getting a permit to graze a thousand head of stock—or even a fraction of that number—on an already overstocked range.

Mr. Perry then announced that he would "appeal on up the line," and was advised that was quite satisfactory with the Supervisor.

A short time later, Regional Forester Paul Redington, accompanied by the Chief of Grazing and one of the grazing men from the Washington office, arrived by train at Ash Fork and were met by the Supervisor and Ranger Fred Haworth of the Walnut Creek District. They visited the range with Perry, then went to Seligman and sat down and argued the case for a day.

"Of course Mr. Perry did not get his grazing permit," Miller said. "Regional Forester Redington had sized up the situation almost exactly as did the Ranger and Supervisor."

Talking about the history of grazing in the Coconino district where he was Supervisor for sixteen years, Miller said that in the late 1880's and 1890's when Camp Verde was still occupied by the U.S. Cavalry, "too many cattle were brought into the country."

Miller went on, "Jerry Sullivan and George Hance, who were soldiers and later became stockmen, told me that several times the number that the ranges would carry were brought in. No one knew about carrying capacities then. They were brought into that country because of the mild winter climate, and because they figured with the troops there, their cattle would not be molested by the Apache Indians. While the troops were there, Indians with hoes would go out and cut the grass, particularly the fine grasses like Porter's muhlenbergia, locally called Black Grama. The sod was practically killed over a large area. Those Indians would cut the grass, dry it, and sell it for hay to the troops, to the United States Government. The big drouth came on and, according to both Hance and Jerry Sullivan, you could ride anywhere out from Camp Verde, particularly to the east, and be in sight of dead or dying cattle continuously. I thought, after going over that range in 1919, that it would be possible to bring a lot of that country back within 25 years. After spending 16 years on the Coconino, it seemed safe to predict that several decades, maybe a hundred years or longer, will be required to bring the ranges back to the conditions that existed when the white man first came in with his cattle and sheep.

"One of the first moves that I think helped the country east of the Verde River was to divide the cattle ranges into summer and winter allotments.   Those winter allotments had the summer growing season with very little stock to eat the grass.   We thought that in a short period of four or five years, that we could see considerable improvement."

Miller noted that another grazing problem on the Coconino that developed in the 1920's was control of damage by livestock to yellow pine reproduction.   Miller said, "There were millions upon millions of little pine seedlings.   Research men were keeping a close watch to see what happened, and some of the boys felt that by 1923 excessive damage was being done by sheep to the little trees.   One or two of the researchers openly recommended exclusion of sheep from the yellow pine country, at least on the cut-over areas, until the pine seedlings reached a height where sheep damage would be negligible.

"So-called individual sheep allotments had been in existence for a number of years, but unfortunately cattle were not excluded.   Actually those allotments were dual-use allotments.   We proposed to separate the two industries, cattle and sheep.   Col. Greeley, with his chief of Grazing, along with the Regional Forester and our Chief of Grazing, came out and we held meetings at Flagstaff during the early summer of 1925.   The sheepmen agreed to have the Forest Service fence National Forest boundaries and to help build the interior fences that would divide cattle and sheep."

Miller said that the group argued over sheep reduction and decided that it would be unfair to make heavy reductions overnight.   The thing to do, it was argued, was to divide the ranges on an individual basis as far as practicable, then allow each permittee to see what numbers he could graze without serious damage to yellow pine reproduction.

"Local Forest Officers had spent a lot of time following sheep and cattle around," Miller recounted.   "They found that under certain conditions in June, particularly where water was scarce, old cows, and some younger animals, did a lot of damage to reproduction.   So did deer; so did antelope.   Squirrels liked the tender seedling buds; so did mice.   Within a few years we found that the sheep ranges were making much more rapid recovery than were the cattle ranges, because the sheep could be controlled more easily.   They were constantly under the control of the herder.   Some reductions were made in both cattle and sheep numbers, but unfortunately old Mother Nature had a way of stepping in.   We had an exceedingly dry year over parts of the Forest in '26, even in some of those plots that were fenced in 1912. Considerable grass sod dried out due to drouth below.

"Cooperrider and other research men found that in several plots that had been under fence for a good many years, death from drouth, mice and other rodents, was almost equal to the damage outside of the plots. Of course when the big drouth of '34 came on, hundreds and hundreds of cattle were shipped out of Flagstaff and other shipping points. A lot of 'em came up from the Tonto. Poor wobbly old cows. Even the stockmen who had claimed that this grass would be all right if it ever rained had to admit that animals had to be moved or they would die just as cattle had died back in the nineties."

Jesse Nelson, who was the first Ranger on the Yellowstone Forest Reserve, later became Inspector of Grazing in the Washington office and served as an Inspector of Grazing in Region 3. With the help of Will C. Barnes and Leon Kneipp, he was instrumental in putting across the grazing regulations with livestock men in the Southwest, according to Paul Roberts.

Roberts attributed some of the grazing problems of the 1920's to the extra burden put on the ranges during World War I and immediately after when the livestock industry hit a depression. Ranges were overstocked and cattlemen could not sell their livestock.

After a reconnaissance on the Sitgreaves National Forest in 1916, Roberts devised a program for a grazing plan for each individual allotment. That system was later adopted.

Discussing the problem of cattle and sheep on the same range, Roberts said it did not cause as much conflict in the Southwest as in the northern areas.

"They had some sheep and cattle war-type incidents," Nelson said, "but they never had the intense sheep and cattle wars in New Mexico and Arizona that they did in Montana and Wyoming and a part of Western Colorado where the sheep moved in. Up there the sheep moved in on an established industry. But down here, sheep were in New Mexico long before cattle."

Another of the men who were influential in establishing the grazing program was John Kerr, the old-time cowman, who had served as a Ranger, Inspector of Grazing and Chief of the Grazing Division of Region 3. "The stockmen all liked John Kerr," Roberts said. "John was very fair. It was an inter-developmental time, and nobody knew anything about the grazing capacity of the ranges. The first job was to really make some kind of reasonably fair distribution of the range on the Forests between the old prior users, and get them located on allotments. But sheep

Closely-herded sheep quickly damaged already marginal range——1914.

Longhorn cattle were a familiar sight in the Southwest in the early 1900's

—sheep went everywhere. They didn't have any allotments. They had to get them tied down some way, and that was the big job for a good many years. As a matter of fact, they didn't establish allotments in a lot of places for several years after the Forests were established. Permits were just issued on a numbers basis. They established the number as best they could by prior use, by what people had run there before. That was pretty feeble in many cases. The numbers we could establish any prior use for were far beyond any reasonable carrying capacity of the range.

"I can remember we were having a big fight over the seedling damage, and it was really tough. We were under a tremendous amount of pressure. H. H. Chapman was taking a year's sabbatical leave from Yale. He was Chief of Silverculture, they called it then, in Albuquerque that year. I remember one afternoon he came in and was talking to John about sheep damage, and of course Chapman was hell-bent on getting rid of all the sheep. Old John would never talk during the day, but along about 4 o'clock, when we quit in those days, John would lean back and he'd philosophize to me. Chapman had been there all afternoon. I was sitting across the desk working, not paying too much attention to what they were saying. But after Chapman left, and 4 o'clock came along John leaned back and said, 'Paul, that man Chapman has got a good education hasn't he?' And I said, 'Yeah, John, I guess he has.' Then he said, 'That's the only thing he's got that I'd want.' He and Chapman didn't get along; they tangled over this grazing business all the time.

"John Kerr was criticized. I think all of those old timers were criticized later on for not doing more to reduce the numbers of stock, but they were handicapped. Nobody had the knowledge of what the capacity was. They actually did a tremendous job of getting any kind of compliance and they made a lot of friends among the stockmen. There was a lot of cooperation in those days. In Arizona, the attitude of the sheepgrowers is mighty good now."

Roberts attributed much of the cooperation between the sheepmen and the Forest Service in Arizona to the influence of Harry Emsbach, the first paid secretary of the Arizona Woolgrowers, who went to work for the organization in 1923.

"He was instrumental in dividing up the range," Roberts said. "He was always cooperative in working with the Forest Service. There isn't any doubt that he had a tremendous influence on the attitude of the Arizona Woolgrowers Association. Of course, in those days we had almost a million sheep. Now we have a hundred thousand or something like that."

Regulation No. 64 in the first Use Book (1906) provided that "persons wishing to drive stock across any part of a Forest Reserve must make application to the Supervisor, either by letter or on regular grazing application form" and must have a permit from the Supervisor before entering the reserve.

Old time cowmen resented or ignored the regulation, and provided problems of trespass for the Rangers. The *Gila Monster,* the District publication issued from time to time by the people of the Gila National Forest, related this story of a trespass:

". . . An old-time cowman was trailing a bunch of four or five hundred head of cattle through a recently established Forest Reserve. On being asked for his crossing permit, he significantly tapped the six-shooter on his hip and said, "Here is my crossing permit."

The *Gila Monster* for March, 1920, pointed out that "Twelve or fifteen years ago the members of the Forest Service were facing a united opposition to the entire Forest Service policy. Forest Officers knew at the time that the policy was sound; that they were engaged in a great public service which would benefit not only the present generation but future generations as well. With this knowledge back of them, the incentive to see it through in the face of all opposition and abuse was instilled into every member of the Service. . . .

"The Service policy is a recognized fact and has the support of practically all of the western people. The old-time spirit is still there, but is dormant because of the lack of opposition."

Sheep crossing cattle ranges was always a hot issue. In 1922 it was decided to establish a sheep driveway from the Salt River Valley to the White Mountains in Arizona. The driveway would have to cross cattle range. The cowmen came to the party with guns. The sheepmen did not show up. The driveway was not established.

Henry L. Benham, who started his career on the Black Mesa Forest (later divided among other National Forests) remembers no real range war on his District, but recalled that "sheepmen and cattlemen were pretty mad at each other."

Benham said that sometimes sheep from outside the Forest would be slipped in to get water. "They would slip in to Garland Lake from out north of the Forest, if we weren't watching. Or sheep would come in on another sheep rancher's territory and get water from their stock tanks or water holes.

"Cowman out north—I won't mention any names—I remember he shot and killed a sheepherder. He kept threatening and warning the sheepherder away from the water hole. He went down to the water hole and there was the sheepherder, and the sheepherder took a shot at him. He had his rifle and he fired back and killed the herder."

In contrast to grazing problems with non-cooperative ranchers, Gilbert Sykes, of Tucson, who was a Ranger on the Nogales District from 1952 to 1962, discussed harmonious conditions that existed there.

"That strip from Sasabe to Douglas, right parallel with the border and maybe not going over 30 to 35 miles north, the high rainfall comes in the summer months, just when you need it," Sykes said. "About 60 percent of the rainfall in the summer time in that strip, and about 40 percent in the winter. So we get a big growth during the growing season because of the extra moisture. There is lots of cover except in a few little isolated areas. There is a remarkably small amount of erosion. We have managed to keep the grazing load down to about where it belongs, by and large. While I was down there, and I think the boys that followed me have done the same—I had excellent cooperation from the stockmen. I've had several of the cattlemen time and time again come around and say, 'Hey, you know this season looks kind of tough. I took a hundred off the other day. To heck with it, I'm gonna lighten up.' They'd voluntarily do that. They played ball with us fine. You get that sort of cooperation, you don't have to go after too many range transects or anything else if they are willing to realize their responsibilities and try to stock pretty much accordingly."

Jesse Bushnell, who had been a Ranger at Munds Park and Sedona, was transferred in 1928 to Mesa, about the time the sheep were starting to come down the Heber-Reno Trail for the winter.

Supervisor Theodore Swift assigned Bushnell to "get up there and watch that trail. We had 75 trespasses in there last year, between Long Valley and Sugarloaf."

"I got up there," Bushnell said, "and the first band of sheep to come down was one of Scott's, and I helped. Those sheep had come all the way from Tonto Creek to Sycamore Creek at Round Valley. That was about a 5- or 6- day drive, and no water—no water. The sheep were heavy with lambs and they were almost famished for water. They'd come in there to Sycamore Creek and filled up with water. The trail was laid out so that when they crossed Sycamore they had to climb right up Herder Mountain where they'd been trespassin' the year before. When they'd watered at Sycamore just below Round Valley, they'd cut down to Sugarloaf on the east side of Herder Mountain, and it made the drive a day shorter and they didn't have to climb that high mountain. The trail come down like this, and then climbed the mountain and made this big elbow up there, right up over the mountain. So I told the rest of the sheepmen, 'Don't you pay any attention to the trail in there. Just go on the east side of Herder Mountain. Don't try to climb it after your sheep have been without water for almost a week.'

"So when I went to town I told Supervisor Swift, 'That's a dirty shame to try to force them sheep to climb Herder Mountain after they've been so long without water, and heavy with lamb.' 'Well,' he says, 'You try to get the sheepmen and cattlemen together and get 'em to widen the trail.' So I did. And there was no objection to it at all. By George, they agreed to it, and there they'd been fightin' each other for years, gettin' out there with guns, and everything like that. The cattlemen agreed to have the trail widened out, and they widened it out, and there never was any more trespassing. Now, sheepmen lost 300 sheep from Tonto Creek to Sugarloaf that fall, just died along the trail. We went over the trail and pulled the dead sheep up in a pile and set fire to them and burned 'em up. So next fall Mr. Swift gave me an allotment to build a tank up there at Round Valley, and we built the tank. So that put water in there for the sheep."

When, early in his career as Chief Forester, Gifford Pinchot visited Arizona he was particularly disturbed at the overgrazing of sheep and the damage this did to the Forests. In his book, *Breaking New Ground,* Pinchot reported that "not only do sheep eat young seedlings, as I proved to my full satisfaction, but their innumerable hoofs also break and trample seedlings into the ground. John Muir called them hoofed locusts, and he was right."

Soon after the Forests were created there was a movement to exclude all sheep. As Ed Miller recalls, "it required several years of hard work by men like Bert Potter and Lee Kneipp from Washington, and a lot of work on the part of the local Forest men to convince the Forester and the Secretary's office that sheep, as well as cattle, could be grazed within the ponderosa pine belt with proper handling."

When Alva A. Simpson was transferred to Region 3 in 1937 he became Chief of Range Management after a short period in Personnel Management. "I think I sensed a change in the attitude of stockmen commencing about 1930, possibly a few years before that, right after World War I," Simpson said in discussing conditions in the 30's. "Here in Region 3, I think there was very little change because the cattle industry in particular was based on yearlong grazing. It was based on numbers, and the use of browse to a great extent rather than grasses. Any interference in the way of regulation was not appreciated by the vast majority of stockmen. It was almost impossible to correct the condition because of the terrain and the type of country in which the cattle were grazing or were using."

Simpson said that as Chief of Range Management he stiffened up on trespass. "I decided that I would do the same down here in Region 3 that I had done in Region 1. If a person trespassed, he had to pay the penalty. And that penalty was going to be a pretty stiff cut on his preference. That commenced to stop the trespass pretty fast. We encouraged roundups, as far as we could finance them, and we commenced picking up this trespass which had been a problem in the Region for thirty or forty years—and gradually we commenced getting control. Now, of course, the big thing that has happened, to my mind, to conservation of the range resources and conservation as a whole, is the changed attitude of the public in looking at conservation as a national necessity, and the changed attitude of the press, of the recreation people and things of that sort."

He said he thinks the new generation, many of whom are graduates of agricultural colleges, "have been exposed to conservation practice and conservation knowledge, and have changed their ideas."

"I think you'll find not only better cattle, but better-conditioned cattle, few losses, and bigger calf crops today than you did 15 or 20 years ago," he said.

Simpson said he believed that there is a change in the attitude of stockmen themselves. "After a long period of time, they have come to the conclusion that there's more money to be made in having a productive range than there ever was in running a bunch of low-bred cattle, in scare-crow condition, just in order to get numbers."

In the 1920's, range surveys were taking on new or added importance as a means of developing long-term range management planning.

W. G. Koogler was for several years chief of party for range reconnaissance and part of the program was training Rangers and staff men.

"This first large scale program of Ranger training was followed by the influx of a steadily increasing number of technically trained men from the colleges," Koogler wrote in a report on range reconnaissance.

"Throughout the 1930s, increasing amounts of money became

available to employ technicians for carrying on the CCC program, and this large influx of technicians along with the added force and emphasis given to conservation under the various emergency programs of the Roosevelt administration ushered in the beginning of a new era in range administration. By the start of World War II, most of the range staff jobs and a high percentage of the Region 3 Ranger Districts were manned by technicians. Keeping pace with the changes in personnel was the change-over from horseback to automobile travel."

Roger Morris worked as range examiner in the 1920's and described how the survey operated: "We were doing horseback surveys and we would just travel through the country and make notes on forage conditions, kinds of vegetation, herbage, topography and anything else that would be pertinent. We entered our data on maps. Then in winter we would go into the Regional Office in Albuquerque and work up our data and work up allotment management plans for the Ranger Districts in cooperation with the local men."

Morris remembered that when he was working up carrying capacity figures on a couple of sheep allotments on the Tusayan, the allotments were higher than the stocking that was actually on them at the time—a rather unusual situation. "The fellow in charge . . . his stocking figures were under my capacities," Morris said. "I happened to be up at his headquarters, up toward Grand Canyon, on the flats there, and I saw him one day and he said, 'Hell, the trouble with most of these cowboys around here, they don't know range. They don't know what a range is.' "

C. A. (Heinie) Merker believed the range policies of the Forest Service had improved tremendously.

"There was a time," he said, "when both our policies and our approach to range management were pretty sorry. The big improvement came when the biologists, let me put it that way, took over from the mathematicians. If you recall the old range reconnaissance system, I don't know how the formula went— multiply acreage by density by palatability, divided by forage-acre requirements, whatever the formula was. There was a time when the forestry people took that as Bible, you know. That was it. You stuck to that figure regardless of what the country looked like. Then they began to realize that it was less important to determine what the carrying capacity of the range was than the potential capacity, if it were given reasonable range management. That's when the big improvement started."

Merker cited as an example the area along the road from Grand Canyon to Cameron, along the Rim.

"In the early twenties I went through there," he said, "and the Grand Canyon Cattle Company was running cattle in there, and literally, it looked as if a fire had gone through there—wasn't a blade of grass, wasn't an oak leaf in reach of a cow, not one. It was just as though you had gone through with a blow torch and burned every leaf off of every tree, every oak tree in reach of a cow. Well, it doesn't look that way now. The range mostly is in good shape."

Roger Morris recalls that the first palatability figures that were used "we got more or less out of thin air."

"Those early figures proved to be very high as far as palatability was concerned," he said.

The figures were refined by trial and error, but the weakness was that in most cases stocking was not reduced to the extent the figures said they should be.

Morris said that while he was on the Tusayan National Forest he worked over old range surveys and made new ones and reworked the management plan set up for the Forest.

"We were never able to get the stocking down to the figures it looked like we ought to," Morris said. "It just wasn't administratively feasible at the time. I worked on some of that stuff on the Verde District. Well, when the Supervisor saw my figures for that, he almost turned pale. He was always pretty pale anyway. He said, 'My God, I know we can't. That's what we ought to do if we could do it, but we can't do that. It will be a long while before we ever get down to those figures.'"

When Fred Miller was working on the Carson Forest he walked as much as 50 miles a day when he was making a management plan. His widow, Mrs. Louise Miller, of Taos, recalls that Fred was away from home on one trip for about a month and that for most of the month his diet consisted of canned cherries and crackers. He had found a store that for some reason or other was out of everything but canned cherries and crackers.

"I met him at the Long John Dunne bridge over the Rio Grande," Mrs. Miller said, "and I had prepared fried chicken and all the trimmings. I never in my life saw a man so hungry or wolf so much food as Fred did that day."

CHAPTER X
Reconnaissance

Raymond E. Marsh, a Yale Forest School senior, was completing his field work in Louisiana in the spring of 1910 when he decided to take the Civil Service examination for Forest Assistant in the Forest Service.

Notice of appointment came through in June after, as he put it, he had fled to Illinois "to escape the enervating heat of Louisiana."

"As a northern boy, I had not become inured to it, nor to the rampant ticks, chiggers, and water moccasins, to which one living in camp and working in the woods was especially exposed," Marsh wrote in some memoirs* recently.

His appointment as Forest Assistant, effective July 1, 1910, instructed him to report to the Headquarters of Region 3 at Albuquerque. He had been attracted to Montana and asked to be assigned there, but the assignment was to the Southwest. Although he had not been pleased with the location of the assignment, he accepted and "became very fond of the Southwest." He did not leave until 1926, and then "with some regret."

When Marsh arrived at the Albuquerque office of the Region 3, he met a group of men who were destined to become important figures in the U. S. Forest Service. A. C. Ringland, the Regional Forester, went on to a distinguished career in Washington. So, too, did Associate Regional Forester Earle H. Clapp who became Acting Chief Forester (1939-1943). T. S. Woolsey, Jr.,** scion of a noted Yale family and himself a Yale Forest School graduate, was Assistant Regional Forester for Forest Management, and his assistant was A. B. Recknagel.

"Recknagel informed me that I was to join the timber reconnaissance parties already at work on the Apache National Forest," Marsh*** recounted.

*For the Oral History Office of the Bancroft Library, University of California, Berkeley, California. At the time he prepared these notes he was living in retirement in Washington, D. C.

**Woolsey left the Forest Service a few years later and had a tragic death, as a suicide, according to Marsh.

***Marsh, too, had a distinguished career, going up through the ranks to the position of Assistant Chief Forester.

After a journey by train to Holbrook, then a two-day trip by stage and transfer to a light spring rig, Marsh reached Springerville, only to transfer again to a freighter wagon headed for the camp of the reconnaissance party more than 40 miles farther south in the Black River watershed.

Aldo Leopold was chief of the reconnaissance party, succeeding J. Howard Allison (now Professor Emeritus, University of Minnesota.)   A year or two previously, a systematic program of taking inventory of timber resources had been started on the National Forests.   Called timber reconnaissance, the purpose was to obtain information for timber management and sale policies. The first party in Region 3 began work on the Coconino, the most important timber sale Forest, in April 1908.   Allison was the only technical forester on this reconnaissance, and served under Frank Vogel, "a well-known, tough, able woodsman, who had gained an enviable reputation as a timber cruiser," according to Marsh. When Vogel was transferred to Colorado, Allison took over and soon was made technically responsible for the work in the Region.

Marsh described a typical field party as including the party chief, usually a graduate forester, Forest Assistants, forest school students, an occasional lumberman or Forest Ranger, a cook, and a horse wrangler—10 or 12 men in all.   Later some parties also included a draftsman to make preliminary maps and sketches.

Members of the party enjoyed the luxury of sleeping on army cots, for the parties were moved by wagon every few days, and double and single tents and a large cook-eating tent were set up.

The work of the cruisers included estimating the volume of timber and describing its character on each 40-acre block, with sketches to show natural feature, culture, forest type boundaries, and topography.   Elevations were obtained with an aneroid barometer.

"Each cruiser worked alone," Marsh related.   "He carried a Jacob's staff, the staff compass on his belt, an aneroid barometer, and a hand counter for counting paces.   He carried a light lunch in a large handkerchief fastened to his belt, and in dry localities a canteen with drinking water slung over his shoulder."

In making his reconnaissance, the cruiser started from a known section corner, and getting his direction from the compass and the distances by pacing, "he walked through the three-mile row of outer forty acre areas, tying in at each mile with a section corner."   He then turned around and came back through the center of the adjacent row of 40-acre blocks.   This was equivalent to six miles of cruising line, or one and one-half sections for the day.

Timber reconnaissance party in camp, Apache National Forest, July 26, 1910. Left to right: Lonnie Prammel, R. E. Marsh, H. H. Greenamayer, J. H. Allison, C. W. McKibbin, G. H. Collingwood, R. E. Hopson, H. B. Wales, J. W. Hough, Aldo Leopold, and John D. Guthrie.

The timber reconnaissance party figuratively buried the cook, whose biscuits were heavy, with flowers and exaggerated humor. Left to right: Aldo Leopold, Harris Collingwood, Hopson, McKibbon, O. F. Bishop, J. W. Hough, Basil Wales, J. H. Allison.

"The cruiser estimated the volume of sawtimber on a 40 by the (Frank) Vogel method," Marsh said. "This was to calculate the volume on one or more sample acres or fractions, expanding this to a full acre, and in turn to the 40."

Marsh reports that there was little opportunity for recreation, though some camps were near a trout stream, and game was plentiful.

"We tried to inject a bit of humor by pretending to bury the cook, whose biscuits we thought were too heavy," Marsh related. "This was done with much ceremony—the grave marked with stones and many flowers, and the mourners lined up beside it, registering internal discomfort."

Another interesting highlight was an overnight visit from Deputy Supervisor Fred Winn and his new bride "a concert or opera singer of high repute in Paris," Marsh said. "They were a gifted and entertaining couple. For years afterward, Mrs. Winn sang on many important occasions in the Southwest. Fred pretended not to like being called Mr. Ada Pierce Winn."

After a couple months of reconnaissance, Aldo Leopold took the technical members of his party to the Apache Rangers Meeting at Springerville, September 8-14, 1910.

During one of the sessions, Leopold made a talk on reconnaissance, describing in detail how his party operated.

"The area covered last year was 65,000 acres," Leopold reported. "The area covered to date is 170,000 acres. Two hundred thousand acres remain uncovered. Cost of the work last year was four cents per acre—this year one and two-thirds cents, and at the rate we are going, by the time the work is finished, the cost of the work may be reduced to one and one-half cents."

Leopold also told the Rangers of "the fine crew of men" working for him during the summer—Yale and Michigan men, some graduates.

"By the reconnaissance system, a green man can do surprisingly accurate cruising," he said, and went on to explain the method of training the men to do accurate pacing in measuring distance.

Leopold's party continued the reconnaissance on the Apache National Forest until driven out by snow in November. After an assignment on the Lincoln National Forest (then called the Alamo), Marsh was assigned to another reconnaissance party on the Carson National Forest for the summers of 1911 and 1912. The reconnaissance party and operations were typical of the Apache cruisers. One of the cruisers on the Carson was Harvey Fergusson, who in later years became a famous southwestern novelist. He was then a student at the University of New Mexico, working at a summer job between semesters.

Marsh related that later on when he was Forest Assistant on the Carson, Earl Loveridge was assigned to do a one-man timber reconnaissance of two months duration of the distant Jicarilla Division.

"He was his own cook and camp mover," Marsh recounted. "His camp was broken into, robbed and food stolen, and he worked under much difficulty. He went without mail for five weeks. This assignment would not be considered reasonable under the criteria of later years. As Forest Supervisor, I, no doubt, shared with the Regional Office responsibility for it. Loveridge did the job. He displayed boundless energy and devotion to duty that characterized his Forest Service career, the last twenty years of which he was Assistant Chief for Administration."*

Reconnaissance was difficult and often disagreeable work, as were other phases of forest activities in the early years.

Ray Kallus likes to tell this story about Ralph Hussey and Landis (Pink) Arnold:

They were making a land classification on the Santa Fe National Forest in the early days. They ate their meals at the Harvey House, and had some kind of a shack that they rented in town and were sleeping there. They spent their time, of course, in the field. One morning Huss got up and put on his clothes and shook Arnold, but didn't say anything, just made him think it was time to get up. As he walked to the door, Pink wasn't ready yet, hadn't got his clothes on, and Huss said, 'Well, Pink, you're just too slow, I can't wait for you.' So he went on out the door and in a few minutes, Pink came out. Huss went on around the house, came on back in and went to bed. Pink went on down to the Harvey House ready for breakfast. He ate breakfast, drank a cup of coffee, and was wondering where the heck Huss had gone to. He ordered another cup of coffee and, finally, with his third cup of coffee he looked up at the clock and saw the time—2:30 a.m. That Hussey was always pulling stunts like that."

---

*When Loveridge died, he was cremated and his ashes were scattered over the Pecos Wilderness—"the wild and beautiful land he loved."

CHAPTER XI
Timbe-r-r-r!

Quincy Randles, armed with a master's degree in forestry from the University of Michigan, walked into the Flagstaff office of Willard M. Drake, Supervisor of the Coconino National Forest, one morning in July, 1911, to report for assignment.

Drake was rather short shrift. He dismissed the new forester quickly. "You're going out to the A. L. & T," he said, and went back to his paper work.

Randles turned and walked out into the street. "I didn't know where the A. L. & T. was—or what it was," he recalled. "I ran into some lumberjacks that I knew from up in Michigan. They told me what the A. L. & T. was. (Arizona Lumber and Timber Co.) They told me where to catch the log run, and I went out to the camp. The man that was there when I got there left in about a day and turned it over to me. That was all the instruction I had as to what it was all about. I talked to the foreman and the lumberjacks and a few others and got the lay of the land."

Randles was doing the marking of timber to be cut and such scaling (estimating the amount of lumber in logs or standing timber) as he had time to do.

"We didn't have any scaling manual in those days and no recognized marking rules for ponderosa pine," he said. "You just had to figure out how you thought it ought to be. Of course, I knew something about scaling and that sort of thing. Anyhow, we went on that way. I rotated from camp to camp, doing the marking."

Such was Quincy Randles' introduction to a Forest Service career and long years as Assistant Regional Forester in charge of the Division of Timber Management.

After a short stint in Arkansas, Randles was assigned back to New Mexico in 1913 and while en route visited Juarez, Mexico, just when Pancho Villa captured the town. "We went to the races and had seats about 15 feet from Villa and his staff," Randles said. "Villa was dressed in cowboy hat, no coat and an army khaki shirt. The staff was all dressed up in gold braid. The soldiers, many of them, were barefooted—but all of them were equipped with extra good guns, and a couple of straps of ammunition. Some of them had straw hats, some didn't have hats. They quartered their horses, the cavalry horses, in the stands over there where they used to collect customs, and when they peeled the saddles off of them, the hide slipped with it. There were dead horses all over town. . . .

"I was supposed to stop at Silver City on my way back to Albuquerque and check on a sawmill up on the Black Range. I met Case, the Forest Assistant at Silver City, and we got a car and went to the mouth of East Canyon, and the car broke down. Case and I walked, and got up to Tom O'Brien's sawmill at midnight. We had a piano box to sleep in, back in the backyard. Got up the next morning at daylight and started up to see this sawmill. As I went out the kitchen door, I felt something go 'whoof' in my ear—and I made a valiant leap. It was Tom's pet bear, but I didn't know he was a pet—and the noise didn't sound like a pet!"

After his inspection, Randles went back to Albuquerque to work in the office.

Timber business had picked up immensely, Randles said. "We hadn't any volume tables," he explained, "so I was detailed to measure a bunch of yellow pines and blackjacks and try to get the material for a volume table, which I did. They probably have a better one now, but that was in use when I retired. In the meantime, the appraisal work in the Region was kind of touch-and-go, and they put me on that along with other stuff. There again we had to more or less feel our way because there wasn't any Appraisal Manual at the start.

"In those days, the companies weren't very anxious to turn loose any figures at all, but we finally come out with some stuff. It's rather interesting, in those days the average mill-run selling price of ponderosa pine, which included all grades, No. 3, common, and better, the selling price at the big mills was about $13.50, $14.50 a thousand. I haven't seen a figure showing what it is lately, but it must be $70 or $80. Lumberjacks' wages in those days; the best men got $3 a day; the worst of them got a little less than that. But they were good men. All the logging was horse logging, big wheels, and skidding teamsters to bunch logs for the wheels. The logs were taken into the landing and laid out in wonderful shape for scaling. They were picked up with a steam loader, and outside of that, it was just about the same as today."

Discussing the marking of timber to be cut, Randles said the absence of sound marking rules made it rather difficult to get uniform results.

"And we had one other additional problem," he went on. "The railroads were depended upon for transportation from the woods to the mill, and railroads cost considerable money.   So the contracts in those days were based on two-thirds cut.   Sometimes in the marking we would leave a little more than that, which brought on a considerable squawk from the company, which was logical.

"It was only later that we were required to check certain sections to see whether or not we were holding up our end of the contract by leaving only one-third.   The same with the scaling. As I say, we had no scaling manual, and everybody had more or less his own system.   But through rather frequent check-scaling we came out with a pretty close result.   The logs were laid out on the landing and they were clean on the ends . . . you could see what was going on and our scaling was, I think, as sound as was possible to get it.   The company was running scalers all the time to check on the output of saw crews, and they didn't hesitate to check us once in a while.   Then this office did some checking.

"Of course, with the collection of the volume of table material we finally got a volume table, which permitted us to do a little better job on cruising of cutover stands than we were able to do before.   I'll admit that it always cramped your style a little bit when the published manuals came out, if they varied from what you'd been doing.   The result of course was good because it was possible to put on some untrained men, and not rely on somebody who had been trained some place else.   In the early days, practically all of our timber sale force were former lumberjacks, and until about 1911 there were no technical men in the woods on sale work.   And after 1911 we began to get a few.   None of them were very anxious to go into the sales business because it was pretty rough and rugged stuff in those days.

"We had to board at the camps, which was a lucky thing because they had good eats.   Sometimes we had to put up tents in the camps because we had no cabins of our own.   Finally we got cabins, and the company of course when they moved camp would pick ours up along with the rest.   About the only equipment in those cabins, even when we had them, was a little old tin stove, and a water bucket which, of course, we had to furnish, and a washpan and our own beds.   Everybody carried his own bed; he didn't take any chances with anything else."

Randles related the details of log drives—or rather tie

drives—in dry New Mexico, when ties were floated down the Rio Pueblo and Rio Grande:

"The Forest Service entered into a cooperative arrangement to exchange timber lands for timber," he said. "The lands and timber were in the Zuni Mountains and the timber to pay for that land was on what is now the Carson National Forest. Cutting the timber was the Santa Barbara Tie and Pole Company, which cut ties and banked them on the Rio Pueblo and drove them down the Embudo and rafted them at the mouth of the Embudo until the flash floods came on the Rio Grande. Then they were driven down to the Santo Domingo boom where they were taken out and loaded on a spur, then taken to the Albuquerque Tie Fitting plant.

"In 1912 I was sent to the cutting. In those days we had to go by narrow gauge railroad to Embudo, where I was met by a log wagon at 6 o'clock in the evening. The Company took me over Penasco Hill up to the Santa Barbara Tie & Pole Company headquarters, which was east of Penasco several miles. We got in around midnight. The next morning we got horses and rode over to the top of U.S. Hill, where the company was cutting ties. The Ranger in charge of the sale was Wayne Russell. He had to handle some hundred men cutting ties and, to say the least, he had more than his hands full. As soon as I got back, I recommended that we send a couple of men up, at least one, to help out. George Kimball was unlucky enough to get elected to the job, and had to work on that sale during the summer. One other recommendation I made, was that the contract with the Santa Barbara Tie & Pole Company was not being fulfilled, in that they were limiting their cuts to ties, whereas the contract called for the removal of sawlogs. As a result of that recommendation, I was *persona non grata* to the then Supervisor."

Randles noted that logging today is entirely different, with tractor logging and trucking, and conditions for the scaler are much different than in former years.

Probably one of the earliest large offerings of timber for sale in this region was that for 90 million feet of ponderosa pine on the San Francisco Mountain Reserve, now the Coconino National Forest, in 1907.

The file of records on the sale revealed the many problems that confronted personnel in connection with initiating such a large sale without the benefit of previous knowledge of how such stands of ponderosa pine should be cut.

The policy which was to be followed was written by Gifford Pinchot while he was Chief Forester, and was outlined in a letter to T. S. Woolsey, Supervisor, in November, 1906. The letter noted that the aim of marking is to leave enough trees standing to fully seed the ground after logging. Mature timber was to be removed unless needed for seed, and young, fast-growing trees reserved for more profitable later cut.

When Edward G. Miller was Supervisor of the Coconino National Forest the office ran an appraisal of lumber prices around 1920.

"As I recall, the average mill-run selling price was $23 and some cents," Miller said. "The average stumpage price on the Coconino was around $2.00 to $2.50 per thousand board feet. The highest price that any timber brought under bid on the Coconino was on a State sale covering Section 6, south of Flagstaff, 20 north, 6 west—that timber brought $4.00 a thousand. I imagine the boys today would wonder what was wrong, but you could build a very good house back in those days for $2,000. The average wage for lumberjacks in the Zuni Mountains and at the mills on the Coconino was about $4.00 a day and board."

The logging operations in those days were mostly by railroad, and Miller recalled that the bigger operations "like American Lumber Co. in the Zunis, the Greenlaw, Flagstaff Lumber Co. and the Arizona Lumber and Timber Co. at Flagstaff and Saginaw at Williams were all railroad operations." "They used big wheels most of the time in summer," Miller said, "in winter, on snow, they used what they called drays, which were big sleds. Instead of calling them sleds, a lot of the lumberjacks called them drays. Some of the Mormons brought in wagons. The first I saw were, I believe, in 1912 or '13, in the Zunis. Those were contract loggers. The contract loggers and the Flagstaff Company began to use 4-wheel trucks, but those first 8-wheelers seemed to be able to operate on wet ground where some of the 4-wheelers would bog down. Later, outfits like the Arizona Lumber and Timber Company, and the Saginaw, operated their own switch crews, but some outlying tracts they would let to these little contractors. Some people we knew made a living for years by contract logging. Along in the late twenties, about 1927, the successors to the Flagstaff Lumber Company brought in some tractors. The Katy Lumber Company from the South had moved in and taken over the operation. That was the first tractor operation we ever saw. They weren't as successful in the wintertime as the old horses and drays."

"Those early-day operations had some fine teamsters," Miller related. "Most of 'em had handlers, and gradually some of them worked in to be sawyers. They'd fell trees and buck 'em up.

Pemberton's Tie Camp, Pecos River Forest Reserve, 1900.

Before the day of the bulldozer, logs were skidded by horses

Four-wheel and eight-wheel wagons were used in hauling logs, 1924.

Big Wheels" ready to haul a 16-foot log scaling 1590 board feet to the railroad.

Unloading "big wheels" at a railroad landing.

In the early days, railroads played an important part in the harvesting of timber from the Southwestern National Forests.

Saginaw and Manistee Lumber Company's sawmill at Williams, Arizona, had a capacity of 200,000 board feet per day.   Photo taken in August 1919.

Portable schoolhouse at the Greenlaw Company's logging camp, Coconino National Forest, July 7, 1920.

Some of them got to be pretty good men and could take contracts for cutting timber. They got about a dollar a thousand. Some of them, a crew of Spanish-Americans could probably average about $10 a day; they'd cut about 10,000 board-feet. Those northern teamsters were proud of those big teams; they babied 'em, curried them twice a day, and made sure they had water morning, noon, and evening. And in the wintertime when it was cold, they had nice warm barns.

"Incidentally, in those days the farmers in the Zuni Mountains and at Flagstaff depended very largely on the logging companies. I can remember when we first moved to Flagstaff in 1919, those spud-raisers were prosperous. The men who raised oat hay did fairly well. The same applied in the Zuni Mountains. But after the coming of the cat, and the cats made good, the little farmer who depended upon the sale of hay was just about finished. Then came the long shutdowns, due to panics, and even The Arizona Lumber and Timber had to close for a time there at Flagstaff. There just wasn't any sale for lumber. In the good days, in the days when much of the lumber from the Flagstaff-Williams area went into Chicago and that part of the country, it was nothing to see 10 or 15 cars loaded out of one of those towns in a day. Fifteen to twenty thousand board-feet on a car, sometimes heavier timbers would go on flatcars."

When Fred Merkle, now retired in Phoenix, went to work for the Forest Service, he was assigned to work with Ed Miller, who was then the District Ranger at Guam in 1913, and also assisted Bob Moke who was in charge of the McGaffey timber sale in the Zuni Mountains.

"It developed into quite a sale," Merkle remembers. "They were cutting 25,000 or 30,000 feet of lumber a day."

In 1916, Merkle was put in charge of the sale and moved to the McGaffey mill. "I stayed there at McGaffey until 1918, when I was transferred up to the Santa Fe Forest, to work on the New Mexico Lumber Company timber sale," Merkle said. "That was out on the Coyote District of the Santa Fe Forest. I think that was the year the war was in progress. I was up there alone on that sale—well, I had a scaler. He was a French-Canadian, an old lumberjack—Charles Laller. Of course I had all the marking to do, marking all the timber. They were cutting about 100,000 feet a day. It was at El Vado, out from Durango, Colorado. The company was located in Denver—the New Mexico Lumber Company.

"It was on that narrow-gauge D & RG. It was pretty rough going and it was snowed in part of the winter and they couldn't keep the track open. It connected at Antonito and ran up to Alamosa, Colorado, where it connected with the wide-gauge tracks on into Denver. That year I lived in scaler shacks, they called them. They moved them along the railroad tracks, you know; just picked up the whole rig, family, furniture and all, loaded onto a railroad car. Our living quarters were built for easy transportation—had big old log skids under them.

"That was strictly a horse-logging operation up there. It was different from McGaffey. McGaffey had been using sleds. They used high wheels in the summertime. But the snow was so bad it was difficult in winter, and they used a sledding operation, the front runners of a bobsled. They loaded the front end of the logs on the sled runners and the rear of the logs would drag. On a regular bobsled operation, they would have four runners on the sled—load them up by crosshaul in the woods and drag them in. Now this operation at El Vado was a sleigh operation. They had 120 horses in the barn up there.

"In the spring of 1920, I was moved down to the Pecos, still on the Sante Fe. I had charge of the timber sales there. Had some prop sales for local mining, and two pretty good-sized saw-mills up there. H. K. Leonard outfit was up in the mountains cutting up there. I lived at Pecos. I had some mules up on the mountain, across the mountains from Las Vegas—government mules. It was 15 miles from my station to that sawmill, and I'd ride a mule over, get started about 6 o'clock in the morning and cross the Pecos River, ride over the mountains, scale logs, and get back that night. No place to stay there, just an old logging outfit. That's a pretty good day's work. I remember one day I scaled up 350 logs that day. Went over there in the morning and got back rather late that night, around 10 o'clock.

When Edward Ancona was on the Supervisor's staff at Taos before World War I, he used to help out on the big Hallack and Howard Lumber Co. operation in the Carson Forest.

"We had a big railroad operation, something you don't see much of any more," Ancona said. "La Madera had a big mill over there. I guess it was big. It looked big to me in those days. It was a sizeable mill."

Hallack and Howard logged over a hundred thousand acres over a period of eight or 10 years, with limitations on cut and under Forest Service supervision.

Ancona put his finger on the merit of the Forest Service regulations regarding logging when he said that today you can hardly find where they cut:

"I've been there only once since then, three or four years ago, and I went to places where I thought, 'Well, this is where we had a big logging camp.' There was no trace of it, and the timber has grown up and it's hard to see where that big operation was carried on—which I think is a good sample of what you can consider conservative forestry, or farm forestry, in which you expect another crop."

Paul Roberts recalls that the first trucking of lumber out of the Sitgreaves Forest was done by John Zahala from the Standard mill.

"He had two Coleman trucks," Roberts said.   "These trucks had hard tires.   John started hauling lumber with trucks, and he went to Winslow with it—went down through Holbrook to Winslow.   The Goodyear Tire Co. talked John into equipping the trucks with pneumatic tires.   Under the deal, they were supposed to keep him furnished with pneumatic tires if John would use them on his trucks.   I had a letter from John when I was digging up some information a few years ago.   He said he didn't know who got tired first, he or the Goodyear Company, but they had so many blowouts that finally they quit the pneumatic tires and went back to hard tires.

"Jimmy Douglas, the late Jimmy Douglas, who was father of Douglas the ambassador to the Court of St. James in the Roosevelt administration, and one of the promoters of the mines at Jerome, had quite a few interests in the country . . . some, I believe, in lumbering.   He was out to see John one time and saw John hauling lumber with trucks, and he said it was the craziest idea he had ever heard of, hauling lumber out with trucks."

Arthur J. "Crawford" Riggs, of Santa Fe, was working on the Sitgreaves in 1928, helping to scale logs and marking timber for the McNary mill logging operation, and he recalls that even with three men working they had a difficult time keeping ahead of the loggers.

"I'll never forget what Jim Monighan told us, that if we scaled as many as 300 logs a day, we could consider that a real day's work," Riggs said.   "After the company moved on the Forest and really began to cut timber, if we scaled less than 500 logs a day we thought we were falling down on the job.   We had to do it, we had to—to keep up.

"There are some things about that old timber sale that I'll never forget.   We used to have to ride—in wintertime we weren't able to use a car to get out to the sale—so we'd ride this train. Of course the Forest Service had no other way at that time for us to get out on the job except by pickup.   So we'd ride the train. Many times we left McNary at 6 o'clock in the morning, when it was real dark and 15 to 20⁰ below zero, and try to find a warm place on that train to ride, especially a safe place. You'd ride on one of the cars and you'd freeze to death, even though you might feel a little safer. If the train jumped the track you might be able to jump, but you finally gave that up and thought, 'Well, I'll just take my chances up in the cab with the engineer, I won't freeze to death at least.'

"It was quite an experience. We had lots of snow, seemed like, during the two winters I was there. The second winter I was promoted, I guess, to check-scaler, and did mostly check-scaling and cruising, and some survey work. Bill Beveridge and I stayed out in a camp, oh, about 20 or 25 miles north of McNary. We got snowed in during the winter and couldn't get out for about two months. We couldn't move our cars from this ranch house where we were staying. The railroad track was about a mile from the ranch house, so we were stuck. If we wanted to go to town, we'd have to catch the train. But we had a lot of fun and we cruised a lot of timber, all on snowshoes."

The railroad logging operations continued through the winter. The logging company skidded their logs onto landings along the spur railroad track that connected with the main line to McNary.

"They did their skidding with these old cats—the Caterpillar 90, I believe they called it," Riggs explained. "They were real good machines for that time. What would irritate the scalers considerably was that you'd get on a spur where they skidded in a lot of logs, and scale those all up and figure, 'Well, I've got it made now. I won't have to worry about getting behind on logs.' Then here would come a woods foreman and say, 'How about comin' over on this other spur and scalin' some logs? We've got a whole trainload of cars over there we'd like for you to scale.' Well, we did that for quite a while. We humored them and we'd get over there and work ourselves to death to keep ahead of the loader, loading out these cars.

"Then, finally we got wise to ourselves and we told them they'd load where we had the logs scaled, instead of having us chase all over the woods.

"I remember one incident. I had scaled a landing of logs one afternoon before going in for the night. Six or eight hundred logs were along this landing, a good trainload of logs anyway. Next morning I stopped at a place along the main line where they had skidded in a lot of logs and started scaling there. In about 30 minutes, here comes the woods foreman riding the log train. He ran over and said, 'I want you to come over to this other landing and scale some logs.' I said, 'You have a landing of logs back on this other spur.'

"He said, 'Well, I want to clear out this one over here.' I said, 'Well, you'll just have to wait until I get these scaled, and then I'll go scale those.'

"He made some remark about seeing my boss and reporting me to the Forest Supervisor. My marking hatchet was sticking in a log pretty close by, and I nonchalantly walked over and jerked this axe out of the log and stepped toward him. I had no intention of using it. So he spoke up—he got a little bit excited—'Now, wait a minute . . . wait a minute, Mr. Riggs. We can take care of that all right. Don't worry about it. We'll get along all right.'

"So I wasn't bothered then after that, about scaling any logs. And he didn't report me to the Supervisor. But, that's the way it went."

Jim Monighan spent several months in McNary in the winter and spring of 1927-28, and he discussed experiences similar to Riggs' concerning the railroad logging operation.

"The logging at McNary on the old KD Lumber Co. sale was strictly a skidding proposition when they first came on the Forest," he said. "They used chokers around the logs, skidding them directly into the landing where they were unhooked. The loader lifted them and put them on the cars, and they were taken into McNary every night. This type of logging in the early days, before we made many plans, really chewed up a lot of the soil, and made deep gouges from the logs being towed directly on the ground. In a good many places, it did make a good seedbed and in many areas where we had done this kind of logging, we got excellent reproduction in good years when we had good seed crops.

"One interesting thing about this old sale was the marking along the county road that went from McNary to Vernon. When we first started marking timber around Lake Mountain and along this road, we left a strip—I believe it was 200 feet wide on either side of the road—where there was no marking whatsoever. We left it in its natural state. Shortly afterwards, maybe within a year or so, the policy was that you could take out decadent trees and lightning-struck trees and trees that you really thought were going to die within a short period. Then after that you could mark about 30%. The policy changed again and you could mark 50%, and shortly afterwards, the policy changed again and you couldn't mark anything. As I remember, when the sale closed out, or just before it closed out, you could do the same type of marking along the highway, on this county road, as you did on other areas surrounding it.

"After the winter, spring, and summer at Los Burros we were finally moved into cabins that the Forest had built on Indian Service land in McNary, or just outside the town limits.   We moved into the cabins there.   Marge and I had two cabins that were about 8, 10 feet apart.   We had a bedroom in one, and a kitchen, office and everything else in the other.   The john was an outside john.   Water was piped in from the town of McNary and we did not have flush toilets.

"We spent the winter of '27 and the spring of '28 in McNary, at which time, in the spring of '28, I was offered the timber sale job on the Grand Canyon unit, which is now the Tusayan Division of the Kaibab, as timber sale man.   We reported in the spring of '28 to Williams.   We lived in Williams for several months while George Kimball, Arthur Gibson, John Schroeder, and a few more of the boys on the Tusayan that could drive a nail, built us a house.   As I recall, it was 20 by 20, and divided into four rooms which were about 10 feet square, which didn't give us too much space.   The headquarters logging camp for the Saginaw was on the Santa Fe Railroad, halfway between Oneida and Grand Canyon.   Our water was hauled into the camp in big tank cars from Williams and put on a siding.   We had two 8- or 10-gallon galvanized buckets and we had to walk 400 yards or so, and turn the water on in the tank and get a few buckets of water.   It took a long time to get down there with a few buckets of water to fill the tub that we put on the old wood stove to heat water, so you could have your Saturday night bath.

"During the early days of the Grand Canyon sale, we were not furnished with a car by the Forest Service, nor did we have a speeder to run on the Saginaw Railroad tracks.   The logging train would leave the headquarters camp with the empty cars between 4:30 and 5:00 o'clock.   We had to get on a car and go up to the logging camp and then walk out to where we were marking trees or supervising the brush, or skinning the logs, or doing the other jobs that were necessary around a big logging operation.   Then we came back in with the loaded cars at night.   We'd get home anywhere from 6 to 8:30, if the cars stayed on the track.   And if they didn't, it might be midnight, or the next morning, before we got home.   We did this for months.   I recall that there were a couple of the assistant scalers' wives came up to our house one day and just chewed into Marge and gave her the devil for me taking their husbands away from them for so long every day in the week and not getting them home 'til way after dark, and taking them to work before the sun ever thought of coming up.   Marge listened to it as long as they wanted to expound, and finally she says, 'Well, doesn't Jim go with them?   He's not at home, so he goes with them too.'

"A short time after this incident we did get an old Model T roadster that had belonged to the Supervisor's Office in Williams. When they got a new sedan, or a new pickup, I believe it was, we got the old Model T roadster. We didn't have to leave home until about 6:30 or 7 to get up into the woods in the Model T. But on the days when it was muddy or snowy, you'd still have to ride the train. A little later, we got a motor scooter to run on the railroad track to take us back and forth to the woods. These scooters were very, very treacherous. The railroad tracks had these high joints. They're not smooth. The curves aren't good. If you're not careful, if you got up too much speed, the scooter would be just as apt to leave the track and throw you off and skin you up. Several times, in riding the scooter, we'd be thrown off and get skinned up, but then get right back on again because that's the only way you had to get around.

"The logging operation there was two-fold. First, they skidded entirely with horses and high wheels. This went on for a year and a half, then they went to skidding on the ground with cats, and after a while they went to arches, steel arches with a track on either side, instead of wheels. They'd lift up the front end of the logs about 6 feet off the ground and take 'em into the landing where they were dropped and loaded onto the cars and taken to the Santa Fe Railroad and then into Williams. On their outlying areas that they considered too scattered to log, they had a contract they gave to an old fellow by the name of Pat McCoy and his brothers, Jesse and Zinny. They were quite an outfit. They were hard workers. They used 8-wheeled wagons pulled by horses. They'd just skid them up into a wagonload in the woods and they'd cross haul; load by crosshauls, and then take them to the landing. They were paid so much a thousand. They did all the work on these outlying areas, the cutting and the swamping and the brush disposal work, and getting the logs to the landing. The McCoys were good contractors and they knew their business, and they knew what the Forest Service regulations were. Though there were times when we might have a few arguments with Pat, why, they were just honest arguments, things that he believed in."

Monighan remained on the Grand Canyon unit until the latter part of 1933 when he was assigned to the Williams office. In early 1934 he was promoted to Assistant Supervisor, then later served as Supervisor on the Sitgreaves and Cibola National Forests prior to retirement in 1963.

Norman Johnson, of Flagstaff, spent 27 years on the Coconino National Forest in timber work and likes to recall that it was often said that "the Coconino trains most of the timber-sale boys in the

Region." While not true nowadays, for awhile it was just about the situation.

"We got two to four new men just about every season," Johnson explained. "Sure there were exceptions during the War years, but there were a lot of boys comin' through the timber camps on this Forest. Of course there have been a lot of others who've had a hand in the training of these men."

Johnson said that he had a few failures, but wouldn't call them failures. "I would say this," he went on, "they just didn't fit. This brings to mind something that will let you know that your bosses sometimes realize more than you think they do about what's goin' on. If you get four new men a year, you'll get one out of the four who's above average, two average, and one below average. So, naturally with myself as the trainer of these men, when they ask for my recommendation when it was time for them to move on, naturally, I'm gonna recommend the man who has made life easier for me, who is generally the better man of the group. So he goes first, and then the average fellow, and that leaves the lower-than-average. When this happens for a few years, what do you wind up with? It actually happened that way here on the Forest. The Supervisor came out and talked to me and said, 'I realize what's happening, but don't know what to do about it.' There was a build-up of a force of men that were below average. They were all good fellows, nice to have here in camp. Their greatest failings were that they couldn't do things with their hands. I think of one who was raised on the streets of New York. He couldn't even open a gate. What help was he to me? Oh well, he could do the leg work—if I told him which tree to mark, why, he'd go ahead and mark it. He did save me some leg work, but he just didn't fit. So I'd say we didn't have failures; we just had fellows that didn't fit."

Gordon Bade, of Williams, who retired from the Forest Service in 1958 to become a practicing consultant in forestry, believes that a better job of technical forestry was accomplished on project sales in past years than today.

"We had a trained timber crew that did nothing but handle timber," Bade explained. "They got a better job done, and I think more efficiently than today when it's under the District Rangers who seldom see the sale. The job of forestry is assigned to temporary, green people, untrained people."

Bade went on to say that project sales were handled by "practical foresters like myself, Lafe Kartchmer, Carl Johnson, Homer German, John Churches, Paul McCormack, and of course, Norman Johnson."

Bade speaks as a timber man and in presenting his ideas on timber management thinks "we should encourage more technical foresters to follow the timber management profession."

"Of course," he said, "in this Region, it's all range. I've had young fellows working, junior foresters, who said, 'Well hell, we want to get into range management so we can get somewhere.' That's wrong in my opinion. Our major resource is timber. As a matter of fact, special use fees are about to catch up or pass grazing fees. Put it on an economic basis."

Like Monighan, Gordon Bade had problems with transportation in the woods. "There was the time when Ed Groesbeck and I were scaling right-of-way logs on the Sitgreaves out of McNary," Bade recalled. "We had a little railroad speeder. The railroad tracks they built in those days weren't fit to walk on, let alone run a locomotive over, or a speeder. We would scale a bunch, then start the speeder up and go up for the next batch. We were going up this steep grade and we didn't make it. The speeder just didn't have enough power to do it. So we rolled back down and I says to Ed, "Shall I cock her back?" He said, "Yeah, cock her back; give her hell." So I cocked her back, and going up this big hill, up this steep grade, we came to a cut and the expansion had pushed the rails down. The steel crew had done what you never should do, they had joints opposite instead of staggered, and it just made an angle bend in the track. I saw it, and I said, 'Hold it, Ed, we're going to jump the track!' I knew we couldn't get around that sharp turn and, sure enough, we left it. I turned a somersault over the top of the thing and I come up, kind of stunned, and when I came to, there was Ed in agony. He had broken his leg.

"I had a job getting the speeder back on the track, and Ed back on the speeder, and tying his leg up with my belt, my shoestrings, and lunch box strap and getting him on the running board of the speeder and taking him down the country. Then we had the problem of running into a log train, moving empties out backwards. Kind of scary. We got down to the foot of the hill and we found a sedan there that I knew was with the survey crew—a company crew running out railroad spurs. We located them and they took Ed to the hospital by car. He was laid up quite a while with that.

"We had quite some experiences on those railroad speeders. Got some scarred heads to show for it. Once we pitched Bob Salton off head over heels. The gauge would vary so that the wheels would drop in—so would the locomotives. I've seen five locomotives on the ground at one time. That was no way to log.

"Another time we had a locomotive off. We were plowing snow. We had a home-made snow plow. Speed was the criteria, you know—you had to get up speed to push the snow. I felt the ground kind of rough under me, and I looked at the engineer and said, 'What happened?' He said, 'We're off.'

"We had run out into the woods about 50 yards. The ground was so hard that the drivers didn't sink. We just jacked the damned thing up, built a track under it, and ran it back on again. That took a couple of days."

Edward Groesbeck, of Albuquerque, was assigned to timber sales on the Coconino Forest in 1937. His experiences were typical of timber staff men.

"We were cutting quite a bit of timber when I went there," Groesbeck said. "The A.L. & T. was cutting. The old Southwest had the Rock Top and the Sawmill Springs units under contract, but they closed down at the first of the Depression. In 1927, I believe was about the last time they cut there and they were closed down for about 10 years. They didn't open again until about 1937. They opened up and started cutting again out there at Sawmill Springs. The old Flimflam Railroad was still in place there and they worked out a joint agreement with the A.L. & T. to where they used one railroad instead of maintaining two railroads running parallel right down through the same darned country. The old Flimflam track they pulled that out and junked it while I was there, and actually it was the old Southwest Railroad that they operated. Then they extended the railroad from there on up into the Rock Top unit and down as far as Allen Lake, and that's where this thing still is.

In November and December of that year, Groesbeck recalled that he marked out two million feet of timber in the Big Springs District out of Williams.

"I was running back and forth to Williams trying to keep track of that stuff," Groesbeck said. "There was no place to live. The old Jacobs Lake Ranger Station was there, but there was no water. The well had caved in, gone dry or something. The only place to stay was Jacobs Lake Lodge. They closed down the first of November, but they had old Devereau Bowman up there, kind of watching things. I'd stay there with old Devereau. The darned guy didn't like to get up in the morning until about noon, and then he didn't like to have supper 'til about 10 o'clock at night. I'd get a big hunk of bread, and in the morning that was all I had for breakfast. No coffee or nothing. I'd go out and mark timber 'til noon and then come in and get my breakfast and dinner combined with old Devereau. Then I'd come in at night and the darned guy—come supper time he liked a drink of wine. We'd have to drink about four bottles of wine, and by that time it'd be 10 o'clock, and we'd have a good supper. He'd really cook up a good supper. But breakfast was a bad deal; I didn't get any breakfast at all. By gosh, you know, when you're wading that darn snow out there all morning a fellow needs a little food to keep soul and body from getting too far apart. They were sure long mornings, I tell you.

"Along early in the year sometime the Whitings had that sale and they decided to put a mill up there. When I went there the timber was going down to Glenn Johnson's mill there at Kanab. They built that mill there at Orderville.

"Then we made another sale to the south that we called the East Fork unit, and then we worked out a cruise on the old Fracas unit in Fracas Canyon, in that area, and also the Big Saddle. We made a sale over on the Little Mountain. That was sold and they started in cutting pretty earnest, and they finally built the mill down there at Fredonia and got pretty well set. The big sale unit was just ready to go about the time I left the Kaibab.

"I left there and went to the Apache. But I had the cruise made and got the sale ready to go. They finally put it up the next year. That's the one they had all the fancy bidding on. Sold at $44.10 a thousand, which was one devil of a price. When you stop to think that the whole Kaibab timber had been offered for sale somewhere around 1910 or '12 for a dollar a thousand, and then in that short time—that sale was made at $44.10 a thousand. Nobody had ever paid a price like that for timber in Region 3. You know, they thought that was kind of a screwy thing, but you know that E. I. Whiting was a pretty sharp fellow. His contract covered an estimated 168 million feet, as I remember it, of which 15 million feet had to be cut at the bid price, and with re-appraisals at 3-year intervals. Well, I think the timber was advertised at around $7 a thousand, or something like that. That old boy was pretty sharp, you know, he was bidding for position and he wanted that sale. It required that he build a mill down there at Fredonia, and cut 20 million feet of timber per year. Anybody looking at that 15 million feet at $$44.10 a thousand, why, it was quite a jag of money, all right. But the old boy was smart enough to know that when time for reappraisal came along, why, the price wasn't gonna be that. It'd be back down. He was actually thinking, I'm sure, 'We're willing to buy timber at the price of the Forest Service appraisal plus so much a thousand over the total amount.' He was paying a premium on that 15 million. Now you take that money and distribute it over the whole 168 million, you know it'd only made $2 or $3 or so above the Forest Service appraised value.   But of course he had to have a few bucks salted down to pay that first jibe.   They had it, but you know, that was a pretty stiff poker game those rascals were playing when they went in on that stuff.

"The Whitings and Southwestern got to battling, you know, when Buck Elmore was vice-president in charge of operations there at McNary.   He was kind of a rough-shod old boy.   They got to squabbling with the Whitings over there on the Apache on some of those sales.   A sale would come up for the Whitings, why, old Buck would get over there and he'd run 'em up.   He'd run 'em up to about $35 a thousand on one of those units.

"Another sale on the Sitgreaves, down around Pinedale, he jumped in an' run 'em up there pretty high.   At Cox Canyon unit, on the Gila, he ran that up to $16 a thousand.   Mr. Whiting was getting kind of irritable about it.   Bucky failed to remember, by gosh, that they were gonna have units of their own coming up some day.   One of these units did come up on the Sitgreaves, I guess it was on the Heber District.   Bucky woke up with a heck of a start one day and remembered that he had a unit coming up, and he thought he'd better go over and patch fences with Mr. Whiting or he's really gonna make 'em pay for this timber.   So he called up Art Whiting, E. I.'s brother, and told him he realized they'd put over some pretty sharp deals but he'd kind of like to bury the hatchet.

"Well, sir, you know, it was a funny thing.   Whitings had had a deal with the Southwest that they would cut a couple of million feet off of the old P83 Forks unit, a deal that was made years and years ago.   Bucky Elmore was about to cancel that deal out and kick them off of there.   They needed the timber themselves, and they were about to terminate that thing.   But someway or other, along about that time they had a change of heart, and Whitings kind of increased their cut there.   They got four million feet a year instead of two off of that Rock Top unit.   They run that Alpine mill and part of the Eager mill for quite a long time off of that extra timber they got from the Rock Top unit, off of the Southwest lumber mill sale.   When the Southwest sale came up apparently the Whitings didn't bid on it at all.   But it was kind of interesting that they happened to get all this extra timber off of the P83 Forks unit just about that time."

CHAPTER XII
No Lady Rangers—But Lots of Paper Work

There have been no lady Rangers in the Forest Service. But many a Ranger's wife filled in for her husband to handle routine matters when he was on patrol and to help with his accumulation of paper work.

The earliest Supervisors had Ranger-clerks, who were paid the munificent sum of $60 a month, but these were men who, presumably, could also be sent out in the field.

The lady who broke the sex barrier in the Forest offices was probably Frances M. Elliott, way back in 1903, when the Forests were still under the General Land Office. Frank R. Stewart, Supervisor of the Prescott Forest Reserve, buried under an avalanche of paper work that day in March, 1903, decided to take a bold step. He would hire a girl as clerk and stenographer to help him catch up with the more than 140 mining claims on hand to be processed, and the reports on 15 to 20 timber sales, awaiting action.

Stewart sat down at his desk and wrote a letter to the Commissioner of the General Land Office asking for the appointment of Miss Elliott as clerk-stenographer at $25.00 a month.

". . . I should by all means have at least six Rangers but with five good men on the range and a clerk in the office I can keep up with the work, and I would prefer the appointment of a clerk at $25.00 a month to that of an additional Ranger at $60 a month," Stewart wrote, and went on to discuss the very great amount of record keeping.

He ended his letter by saying he had "no application blank for clerks but I enclose one of our regular forms of application for a position in the Forest Reserve Service."

Some years later a girl clerk at the Alamo-Lincoln National Forest office took the Ranger examination and passed it, according to O. Fred Arthur, former supervisor of the Cibola.

In 1917, Miss Anita Kellogg went to work for the Forest Service when Charles Jennings was Supervisor. In 1920, she took the Ranger examination and the Civil Service Commission notified her on January 24, 1921 that she had passed the examination. Supervisor Andrews of the Santa Fe National Forest offered her a job, but the Regional Office (then called the District Office) would not approve the appointment because she was "an unattached female." A few months later she transferred to the Coronado, and the next year while serving as chief clerk she was made a special deputy fiscal agent to pay off the firefighters on the Coronado and on a Class C fire on the Mogollon Mountains in the Gila Forest. Fred Winn, Supervisor of the Gila, objected to the assignment because she was still "an unattached female."

That summer she received a letter of commendation from District Forester Frank Pooler* for work on the fire as an "unattached female"—and also a promotion in pay from $1200 to $1400. She married the next year and, no longer unattached, she resigned from the Forest Service in 1924. A few years ago Anita Kellogg Blanchfield, former lady Ranger and "unattached female," was reported living in Mountain View, California.**

As the paper work increased in the Regional Office and in the Supervisors' offices throughout Region 3, the number of young ladies employed kept pace with the growth of the Forest Service. In the field, the Rangers still handled their own diaries, "bed sheet" reports, application forms, correspondence, etc.

When Edward G. Miller was assigned to the Datil National Forest in 1914, he went down to Magdalena to look over the setup. Bert Goddard was the Supervisor. The office staff consisted of Bass Wales and the girl who later became Mrs. Goddard. Years later when Sam Servis was a Ranger on the Datil and was reminiscing with Cole Railston at his ranch, Railston told him that when Bert Goddard died, Mrs. Goddard could just as well have taken over and would have made a good Supervisor.

In the early years of the Forest Service, the Supervisor's Office for the Tonto National Forest was located in one of the Reclamation Service buildings at Roosevelt Dam. A. O. Waha once said that "Supervisor W. J. Reed was the sickest man I had ever seen working. He was suffering intensely from an acute form of asthma." Reed was also fortunate in that he had an efficient wife. Waha said: "His wife, who had an appointment as clerk in his office, was a wonderful help."

---

*Frank C. W. Pooler had a distinguished career in the Forest Service. He went to work at $60 a month when the Forests were still under the General Land Office. He became Regional Forester in 1920 and served in that office until his retirement in 1945. During his years with the Forest Service he achieved a national reputation as a pioneer in the field of conservation. He died in 1960 at the age of 78.

**Mrs. Blanchfield died in 1972.

Reed and his wife moved to sea level the following year, and he was succeeded by Roscoe Willson. The clerical staff increased to two girl clerks, and Willson remembers the Forest Service built a house for them. But when Willson first went to Nogales in 1907 as Supervisor of the "Sneeze-Cough" group, he was alone for awhile.

Willson once recalled that a temporary Ranger who preceded him had rented a building for an office "and he had correspondence and what records there were scattered all around on the floor." Willson got permission to hire a part-time clerk—a man.

Later the Forest Service established what Fred Miller called the "statutory rule." "That meant," he explained, "that there were so many Forest Supervisors, so many Assistant Forest Supervisors, so many Rangers, etc. Along about 1923 on this Forest (the Carson) there was a Supervisor, an Assistant Supervisor, a technical assistant, and two girls—that was the staff."

Ray Kallus, of Alamogordo, who spent his years in the Forest Service in administrative work, recalls that even in the 1930's "everybody had lousy offices." He and Wayla Ellis went to a Tonto National Forest Ranger District one time to make an audit and began to work over the cardboard file boxes. "Ellis pulled open the bottom drawer of one of those file cases, and there was the nicest rat's nest you ever saw in your life."

Kallus went to the Coconino National Forest in 1938 and was there during the war years. "We had a lot of things during the war," Kallus said, "I know that Ethel, who is now Ethel Sutton—she married Gordon Sutton—and I constituted the clerical force most of the time."

The early Rangers did not pay strict attention to following all the rules regarding paperwork and reports, and this had serious consequences for one Ranger, as Kallus recalled.

"In 1934 I was sent to the Sitgreaves, as an assistant to Nicholson," Kallus said. "Nicholson had been a Ranger on the Mormon Lake District. One of the tragedies of the Forest Service is that while he and somebody else were trying to install a telephone pole—they had a jim-pole rigged up and were trying to get this big pole down in the hole—all at once the pole slipped and hit Nicholson in the side and knocked a kidney loose. He was physically unable after that to continue the work of a Ranger, so they made him principal clerk of the Sitgreaves. He later died from that injury. But like so many early Forest men, he didn't pay much attention to following the rules. He completely ignored the compensation law and failed to make a report of this accident. After he died, his widow was completely unable to get anything from that accident. I made up my mind at that time that I would never let an injury be neglected where a man and his family might suffer because of my not reporting it."

Kallus said there were other such cases. There was, for instance, the time when a Ranger on the Flagstaff District was out on Lake Mary and lightning struck him. His widow received no compensation.

In contrast, Kallus said that while he was on the Coconino, a man named Skoulson became ill with pneumonia and died. The fiscal agent in Albuquerque was asked if an injury report should be made. The answer was no, but "we went ahead and made the report anyway. Lloyd Dahl went out and spent three days in the field. He interviewed ranchers and CCC foremen and enrollees and everybody he could contact. He came in with a complete resume in statements of what happened and how this man got pneumonia. (We sent it on to the fiscal agent and he sent it on to the Compensation Commission, and the Commission made the allowance and Mrs. Skoulson received $120 a month compensation."

When Kallus went to the Sitgreaves as assistant clerk it was the year that cost accounting was instituted by the Forest Service.

"None of the administrative assistants, or whatever they were called, knew anything about cost keeping," Kallus said. "There I was, a new man in the Forest Service, and I didn't know anything about it either! About the time one of the reports was due, Nicholson took off on an extended vacation and he says, 'Ray, I want you to make out this report.' I got on it and nearly went nuts trying to figure out cost accounting. I studied and studied it, and I couldn't get it. I'd read the books over and over and over. Finally, after a month of just the hardest kind of studying, the thing kind of opened up, unfolded and was clear to me. So I made out the reports on the Sitgreaves.

"I had to work about 24 hours a day to learn the doggone thing. They were having trouble at different places. On the Tusayan and the Kaibab, they consolidated that year, and Hugh Putnam was up there—Hugh had just come down from Utah—and he had his hands full without trying to learn how to make a cost account report. He had two of them to make, one for the Tusayan and one for the Kaibab. So Albert Morris (Regional Fiscal Agent) called the Sitgreaves and told them to send me up there to make those reports. Walter Mann was Supervisor on the Kaibab. So I made the reports. By that time Leo Anderson, the administrative assistant on the Tonto, was having trouble; he was having more than he could do with all the new CCC camps, and the ERA and different programs.   He hadn't even looked at the book.

So Albert Morris called the Kaibab and said, 'Send Kallus down to make this report.'   And so I made out the Tonto report. There were troubles on other Forests, so they sent me in to the Regional Office to make out the Regional report, and while in there I had to re-make several of the other Forests' reports.   It wasn't that I was smarter than anybody else, it just happened that I had to concentrate on that one subject.

"This cost-keeping was quite a problem.   Nobody knew it, and nobody wanted to learn it.   The thing theoretically was fine, and would have been OK except the New Deal brought in such terrific conditions as to nullify the good work of the Forest Service, in that you would depreciate roads and all investments against operating accounts."

The cost accounting procedures were later dropped.

Kallus recalled the concise report that Ranger Harold Linn sent to Coconino Supervisor Edward Miller regarding trail building. Miller had given Linn an allotment of $200 to build a trail on the Beaver Creek District.   Several months went by and nothing had been done, and no money spent.   Supervisor Miller sent a stiff letter to Linn asking why he didn't go ahead and spend that money and build the trail.

Linn wrote his report on the bottom of the letter: "It snowed all around, and I couldn't help it."

Kallus was telling about a time around 1937 when the Forest Service people were involved in a number of accidents in the Phoenix area.   They involved paper work and legal work.   One of them was the death of an old postman in Phoenix, who was hit by a transient camp truck while riding a bicycle.

"It was in the red light district of town," Kallus recounted. "The Regional Office was getting real tired of all these people getting killed in Forest Service accidents.   They sent Judge French down.   French says to this truck driver, 'What were you doing in that part of town?   You had no business in that part of town where the man was killed.   What were you doing there?'

"Well, his story was the doggondest thing you ever heard of. We had been giving credit cards for drivers of government cars. We kept no records of these cards.   This fellow had a credit card.   He went down there and got 10 gallons of gasoline and got a rebate of one cent a gallon.   That enabled him to get a glass of beer.   That was the reason he was in that part of town, and that is how this old man happened to be killed.

"After that we started being pretty careful with the credit

cards.   As you look how careful the Forest Service is now in the matter of credit, the inattention that all of us gave to credit then must have been criminal."

Kallus said the payment of gasoline bills was about the biggest job the Supervisor's Office had.   It took a clerk a whole day to make out a voucher for one Forest, checking tickets pro-rating appropriations, showing account numbers.   Kallus made up a mimeographed form and supplied the gasoline company with the invoice form.   "That was the first invoice that any oil company ever gave the Forest Service."

As Kallus commented, today for such a suggestion he probably "would have got a $10 award under the present awards program."

Walter L. Graves, Chief of Operations of Region 3 who retired in 1972, started with the Forest Service in the CCC camp days, went up through the ranks, and got into administrative management in the 1950's.   During a stint in Washington, Graves headed the workload measurement program.

Discussing this program, Graves said that Earl Loveridge, who got his start in the Forest Service on the Carson Forest, was the "father" of workload measurements.

"Earl Loveridge did a tremendous amount of work," Graves said, "some of which was very good—and some was proven to be not so good.   Some of the theories and practices he initiated are still in operation.   Probably one of the worst fiascos I can recall in my career in the Forest Service was what was known as the old 26A, which was put into operation while I was at Pecos.   This was a large atlas-sized form on which the Ranger and his assistant were required to first plan all of their work for the month, down to 15-minute intervals and, secondly, to account for everything they did, down to 15-minute intervals.   As can well be imagined, this became so cumbersome that in a very few months it was dropped completely.   But as I recall, it took me about two days every month to make this out for the Ranger and myself at the beginning of the month, and about a day and a half at the end of the month, to record all of our accomplishments.   Our diaries had to be in such detail that it took an exceptional amount of time merely to keep the diary, because we did have to account for our time down to 15-minute intervals.

"After this was dropped, several different methods were tried.   One of the major ones was the old Region 3 Green book which was, in effect, an annual plan of work, in which all of the jobs that are ordinarily done on a Ranger District were listed in a book, with space at the side for planning the amount of time that the Ranger was going to put in on each job.   Now this was then segregated by months of the year and was used by the Ranger as a tool for planning his monthly work.   It worked reasonably well, but was still quite cumbersome.

"During the time that I was in Washington, although this was not in my branch, the uniform work planning system was started, and has been in operation since, and appears to be one of the best systems that we have come up with as far as work planning is concerned.   The workload measurement is tied in with work planning certainly.   I think that the method of workload measurement that we used until just recently was not too sound, primarily because no one in the field was able to take the workload as published in the manual and re-compute the workload on a Ranger District and arrive at anywhere near the answer that was listed in the tabulation in the manual for that particular District.   This was primarily due to some factors that were introduced at the Washington level that the field knew nothing about.   This was one of the major complaints of people in the field.   I think the present system is good.   We have all the information that is necessary to re-compute the workload any time we wish, and update it and keep it current to any extent that we feel necessary."

The daily diary that was so important a part of the paper work operation of the Rangers in the past has been eliminated, but Graves believes that present methods of reporting are more satisfactory.

"The diary itself was largely a repetition of monthly work plans," Graves said, "and frequently was inaccurate and in many instances was rather meaningless.   I think the present periodic or monthly work plan, with provision for recording accomplishments of jobs that were done, is all that is necessary.   And it certainly reduces the amount of time necessary to maintain a diary.   I for one am happy to see the Forest Service finally eliminate diaries."

Just to keep up with the great volume of rules, regulations, laws, interpretations is no mean task in itself for men in the field and in the offices.   When the Forest Service was headed by Gifford Pinchot in the early days of its existence, he developed a Use Book in 1906 that consisted of less than 100 pages of rules, regulations, and instructions to Rangers.   By 1908, the Use Book had grown to a volume of 341 pages.   From this bulky single Use Book, the collection of laws, regulations, and rules has grown to a whole bookshelf of 28 volumes!   And in addition, there are 78 handbooks of interpretations and instructions on every conceivable subject or problem that might confront a Ranger.

CHAPTER XIII

From Horses to Horseless Carriages

In the early days of the Forest Service horses were the only means of transportation in the Forest and each Ranger usually owned two or three horses. Even though he received only $75 or $90 a month, the Ranger was expected to buy and maintain his own horses and equipment. In fact, the first Use Book in 1906 noted that "Each Supervisor (and Ranger) is required to keep at his own expense, one or more horses, to be used under saddle or to vehicle, for his transportation in the Reserve."

The Datil National Forest also owned a team of horses which were stabled at Magdalena. Blueberry, a large roan, was an excellent saddle horse. Strawberry, also a roan, was a powerful bucker when the mood was on him. When the two horses were first acquired by the Datil office they were so wild it took three or four men to hitch them up to the light buggy inside the stable before the doors were opened. When the doors were opened, the horses made a wild dash for the open air, with the light buggy sailing over the ground. The team developed a bad habit of balking in the morning when they were supposed to be ready for a trip, which resulted in rather low mileage for the day.

Typical mileages for horseback or buggy trips were, from Magdalena: to Rosedale, 35 miles, eight hours; to Durfee Wells, 21 miles, five hours; to Tularosa Ranger Station, 85 miles, $2\frac{1}{2}$ days; to Hood Ranger Station, 115 miles, $3\frac{1}{2}$ days.

When Morton M. Cheney, as a tenderfoot young lawyer out of the East, joined the Forest Service in 1913, one of his earliest assignments was to attend the 1913 fall meeting of Rangers at Willow Creek in the Datil Forest. One of his most graphic memories of that Ranger meeting was the arrival of the Rangers from the Apache National Forest.

"One of the prettiest things I ever saw was when we were already in camp," Cheney said. "The Apache Rangers came in, the entire Apache Forest, including the cook. They made the two-day ride from Springerville to Willow Creek. As you drop into Willow Creek, you drop off the first ridge and the switchback down into the flat—and that group of Forest Officers, in uniform, with John D. Guthrie on a big black switchbacking down into camp, it was a beautiful sight."

Fred Miller used to enjoy talking about riding horseback to Los Pinos to go fishing. "I had one interesting experience there," he related. "I was there by myself and there was a little one-room overnight cabin. The front door step was about that high, and the back of the cabin was right up into the slope of the hill. I had a great big horse. He weighed about 1200 pounds, a big stout animal. I went down to get some water from the spring, and when I got back, here was my horse inside the cabin! I couldn't get him out because the door wasn't high enough—only about five feet high, and when the horse stood up, his head was higher than the door. I just couldn't get him out, and I didn't know what the devil to do. Then I remembered he was an oat hound, so I put some oats in a box, and when he put his head down to eat, I finally got him out. But it took me half an hour to get that horse out of there."

Edward Ancona, another tenderfoot forester out of the east in 1913, was assigned to the Coconino. "I remember getting on a horse that first day in Flagstaff," Ancona recalled. "I had rented a horse, and the Ranger had his horse, of course, and he said, 'We're going out to a point east of here—we have some sheep to look over.' I came out of the livery stable, and I didn't know how to steer the darned beast. So I sat on top with a pair of reins and used two of them. Well, he didn't know where he wanted to go, and neither was I quite sure where I wanted to go. We ended up crossing the street. The horse went up on the sidewalk and mounted part-way up the stairs of the Opera House before I got him turned around and back into the street. In the meantime, the Ranger had jogged off down the street in a typical jog-trot. I think he was pretty disgusted. I trailed him all the way out, some 12 or 14 miles, and 12 or 14 miles back, and I was 'skunned' from here to there! That was my first horseback ride. I learned though after that, because all of my work was on horses. You just had to adapt yourself to it, or you were sunk."

Later on (in 1916) Ancona was assigned to Taos. There he said, "we had to have driving teams, a team of horses that could both ride, pack and drive. I had two teams toward the end of the job because we went enormous distances there. We'd drive clear from Taos out to Dulce and the Jicarilla country. We'd drive to Tres Piedras and all that country, clear over to Canjilon. That was big country and the roads were very primitive, lot of them in deep sand. So you had to have horses that could drive, pack or ride, because we'd go as far as we could driving, then we'd leave this mountain wagon and put on our saddle and pack outfit and go on."

Roads in the Forests of the Southwest were almost non-existent in pre-World War I days.   Outside the Forests they were nothing to brag about.   New Mexico was building state roads with convict labor in those days, and in 1917 boasted that the Camino Real "is an improved road from end to end"—Santa Fe to El Paso—and that a 5-year plan was being developed for an elaborate system of state highways, aggregating 3,540 miles.

Arizona had the advantage of a number of military roads that crossed the state, but mostly the roads were "natural roads" that could be traveled only in dry weather.   In the northern part of Arizona this offered some hazards.

Early in the century, the Bureau of Reclamation had undertaken construction of Roosevelt Dam.   To make transportation of materials to the damsite possible, the government constructed 60 miles of road from Mesa to Roosevelt.

Describing a trip he made to the dam while it was under construction in June, 1908, A. O. Waha called the road "certainly the best in the Southwest at that time."

"Many freighters with their 8 to 16 horse or mule teams were on the road," Waha related in reminiscences some years ago. "My trip was made in a Concord stage (leather springs) which was drawn by four horses.   Horses were changed four times during the trip so twenty horses were required for the trip which was made in a day.   For the first 18 miles the road traversed the level desert country where the giant cacti grow; then through foothills country for about 30 miles and then into the mountain country.   The road has splendid grades and a good surface.   Fish Creek hill was the real scenic spot along the road.   Here the road was made by blasting some solid rock walls.   Approaching the highest turn on this hill, the stage driver hit up his horses taking it on a high gallop. While there were passengers inside of the stage, I sat on the high seat alongside the driver.   It was surely a real thrill when we were rounding this high point on the curve and I could look down over the sheer cliff which was about 500 feet high."

In May, 1909, a few months after John D. Guthrie had been appointed Supervisor of the Apache National Forest, he was directed to locate a feasible route for a road over the Blue Range and White Mountains of eastern Arizona.   At Clifton, Guthrie was joined by District Engineer Jones of the Regional Office in Albuquerque, and by David Rudd, an Apache Forest Ranger.

Seventeen years later, Guthrie told the story of that trip in a paper presented at the dedication of the Coronado Trail Road. Here is an excerpt from that unusual story:

Forest Service truck stuck in mire along Grand Canyon trail, Kaibab National Forest, 1920.

Customary locomotion up Luna Hill, Alpine (Ariz.) Reserve (N.M.) road, June 1920.

Jones knew nothing of the country, having come into Clifton by train; my knowledge was limited to what I had been able to see from the bottom of the Canyon of the Blue, which wasn't much to worry about. Only David Rudd was familiar with the region through which we were to go. He had accidentally shot himself through the side about a year previously and not having recovered, it was decided not to take a pack outfit on this trip, but to stop at what ranches or cow camps there might be encountered; we encountered none!

From all possible sources of information about the country and from what maps were then available (and these were few and poor), the most likely route seemed to be to follow the old Mitchell Road out of Metcalf and then keep on the divide between Blue River and Eagle Creek, to the top of the Blue Range, to go around the head of Black River and the Campbell Blue, and on into Springerville. How to get to the top of the Blue Range, that was to be a problem.

That became the route later, but when we started we didn't know just where we'd land, nor where we'd stop for the nights. David could not tell for he did not know whether we'd go up Eagle Creek, up the Blue, or up the divide.

Anyway, we started out, three men, three horses, three saddles, and one canteen and three small lunches. The first night out from Metcalf I well recall. It was somewhere on the southside of Grey's Peak. There was a spring with watercress in it; there were pine trees and pine needles, and only Arizona's blue sky overhead for a cover.

No bedding, no chuck, except the dried remains of a lunch we had had put up at Metcalf. We sure slept out. Somehow we put in the night. I wonder if the new road goes by that spot?* The Spanish captains of Coronado's caravan may have camped in that spot on their way from Mexico to Zuni in May 1540. Who knows?

The captains may have known as little about the country as we did, but they did have 600 pack animals and provisions. Our caravan of 1909, 369 years later, certainly was traveling lighter. Their record speaks of big pines, watercress and fish in the streams, and wild game. That first camp of ours was Spartan in its simplicity. We just stopped, threw off our saddles, hobbled the horses, built a fire (merely for social purposes), and somehow the night wore way.

The next morning Dave Rudd did something I never saw done before. He had an old-style army canteen, the kind with

---

*It does.

Road between Alpine, Arizona and Luna, New Mexico, May 1924.

Coronado Trail, Apache National Forest, is one of the most scenic in Arizona

the laced canvas cover.   Dave had some ground coffee along, but there was no pot, no cups, no cooking outfit.   There wasn't even an old tin can left by some former camper.

Coronado must have left a clean camp and a dead fire.   May all his followers over this trail do likewise.   Dave's Ranger ingenuity came to the front.   He ripped off the cover of the canteen, filled it with water, set it upright between two rocks, and built a small fire around it.   When boiling well, he lifted it from the fire, poured in a lot of coffee—and, after steeping and cooling, we took turns at the breakfast coffee urn.   The coffee was strong—*muy fuerte*, as the local saying is, but it was our life-saver.   That was our breakfast and coffee never tasted more wonderful.   Perhaps Coronado's men quenched their thirst in a heavy Spanish wine, but it could not have tasted better than our canteen coffee that May morning in 1909.

I don't think the engineer cared for the camp nor the coffee particularly, especially since he was wearing on this trip a stiff white collar.

We were simply looking over the country to see if a road were feasible, on not too heavy a grade, and at not too prohibitive a cost, from the copper towns of the south to the cool, green forests to the north with the fish, water cress, pine trees, and wildlife of Coronado's day.

We followed as best we could the divide between the Blue and Eagle drainages, through Pine Flat, circling Grey's Peak and Rose Peak, and struck the rim of the Blue Range, climbing it over a trail that went nowhere but up.

That was the third day out from Clifton.   Dave supplied the knowledge of the country that could not be seen; the engineer (in a collar now not quite so white) took many "sights" with his level and made many notes, and we climbed to Hannagan Meadow and rested there the third night.   The snowdrifts were plentiful and deep.

The engineer still wore his stiff collar, now past all semblance of its former self.   There was neither fence nor cabin at Hannagan Meadow.   Two deer came out in the Meadow early next morning to feed.   A grouse whirred away from the spruce tree under which we slept.   There was white frost on the aspen poles around the spring when I went down for a drink.   Across our trail down to Black River that morning stalked a flock of wild turkey.

That day we rode into Springerville from Hannagan Meadow, a right nice little ride, via the Slaughter Ranch, Big Lake, Pat Knoll, and Water Canyon, with big appetites and tired horses, and one dark-brown, still a collar, on the neck of the engineer.

The conclusion at that time—and that was in 1909—was that such a road could be built, with a fairly good grade, but that it would be expensive. Somewhere in the Government files are Engineer Jones's report and maps covering that reconnaissance for a road from Clifton in Greenlee County to Springerville in Apache County. The next year (1910), another government engineer (Howard B. Waha) made another reconnaissance, but his route ran up Eagle Creek, through the Indian Reservation, and around the west end of the Blue Range.

This is now 1926. It has taken 17 years to build that road. Governments move slowly and cautiously. That looking over the country for a road in May, 1909, was the very beginning of the Clifton-Springerville Road. Coronado went over it, but he was looking for gold and treasure, not roads.

His historian, Castenada, did set down what are destined to become treasures of the region, perhaps as valuable as the mythical gold Coronado sought—the tall pines, the fish, the watercress, the wild flowers, and the wild game.

Now people will again come up over this route from the south, as Coronado and his captains came, seeking something. I wonder if the Spaniard put out his campfires, if he left camps clean. With 600 pack animals and 1,000 men he must have had many camp fires gleaming in the pines along the route from the "Red House" to Zuni. Being a soldier, I suspect he had order in his camps; I suspect he left his campfires safe; he must have left some fish, some game, some watercress, and the oak, pine and spruce trees, for they are still to be found along his old trail.

By 1917, the Forest Service was ready to start the actual survey of the Clifton-Springerville road, and Fred H. Miller was assigned to the task. World War I interrupted, and Miller along with many other Rangers and Forest officers, enlisted.

From its earliest years, the Forest Service had made allotments for roads and trails, but for the most part these were small ($42,000 for New Mexico in 1916)—and as with the Coronado Trail, accomplishments in road building were slow in realization.

After the war, the Forest Service again resumed plans for road building or truck trails as they were called. Ed Miller (not to be confused with Fred Miller) recalled that he arrived in Flagstaff from assignment in Prescott in 1919—"at about the beginning of the rainy season."

"Ray Marsh was Forest Supervisor," Miller said. "He had succeeded John D. Guthrie. He wanted to show me a part of the south end of the Forest, but was afraid we couldn't make it by car and he didn't have time to start out with a pack outfit, so we hired a man who was running a country taxi business there at Flagstaff. We started for Winslow and bogged down on the way, got there after dark. There were no built roads. The only graded road on the Coconino at that time was a strip that Howard Waha had built between Flagstaff and Williams. It was, as I recall, about 14 feet wide; part of it was made of cinders. There was another little strip of road from Long Valley east across Blue Ridge. It has been constructed but not surfaced.

"Anyhow, when you started out on a trip in a rainy season you never knew how many miles you would make. Ray and the driver and I stayed all night in Winslow and started for the Bly Ranger Station, southwest of Winslow about 20 miles. We bogged down at about the half-way point, worked three or four hours in getting out of the mud. We cut greasewood and branches from junipers and found a few stray rocks. We got to the Bly Ranger Station and Fred Croxen, who was there at the time, said it was impossible to get on toward Long Valley so Ray Marsh called up Bill Brown and had him come over on horseback and we chatted there for an hour or two. Made it back into Winslow that night, and made it back to Flagstaff without bogging any more.

"Jim Mullen was out in 1923, made a roads inspection trip. The clouds looked like a heavy rain was coming on so we left the Long Valley Ranger Station somewhere around 3 o'clock that afternoon. We bogged down—had on chains of course—bogged down about the east end of Blue Ridge. One chain was broken almost beyond repair. We got down pretty close to the east boundary of the Forest. We had figured on going on into Winslow, even though darkness came on and our lights shorted. It was pouring down rain. Jim and I pulled out at the side of the road, built a fire, cooked our supper, bedded down in the old Dodge truck. We were thankful that we had a truckbed long enough to accommodate our beds. Along in the middle of the night we heard a big car pass us, slopping through the mud. We got up in the morning and the rain had stopped. We cooked our breakfast and leisurely packed up and headed for Winslow. In a big flat pretty close to where Ray Marsh and the taxi driver and I had bogged down in 1919, we found a big Cadillac with Boyce Thompson and his driver in a rented car bogged down hopelessly. Thompson was the man who established the Boyce Thompson Arboretum at Superior, Arizona. He said, 'Have you boys any spare gas?' We said, 'Yes,' and he said, 'Thank God for the Forest Rangers!' We put a 5-gallon can of gas in the old Cad, but there wasn't enough manpower available to move it an inch. Mr. Thompson asked us if we would have the owner of the White

Garage in Winslow send a car out with plenty of planks and plenty of gas. They told us in Winslow that they would go right out, which they did. Jim and I found that we couldn't make the road north of the Santa Fe Railroad back to Flagstaff without danger of bogging, so we took a route south of the tracks, in places as much as three or four miles south. We came to the first big *arroyo* west of Winslow, probably four or five miles out, and it was in flood stage. It was still raining—rather raining again. We watched a lot of those people try to go across. Several of them bogged down. Jim and I finally decided instead of hitting the water hard, we would creep through, which we did, with the old Dodge. It was impossible to do anything for the people who were bogged down. It was a case of more help than we could give so we made it back into Flagstaff that night."

Discussing the building of the truck trails on the Coconino, Miller said that one of the all-time foremen was John McMinnimum. His wife was cook. "We wanted to build a fire trail across East Clear Creek Canyon," Miller related. "We worked Mac down there two winters with a bunch of burros and five or six men. They camped down on the water most of the time at Clear Creek. Mac was one foreman in a thousand. He had learned blacksmithing when he was a boy. He had an eye like an eagle. You could rough out a line with an Abney level, and he'd do the rest. I don't suppose any foreman ever built more road in two winters than Old Mac did, with less supervision, because he didn't need it. The Ranger would go down occasionally to see what supplies were needed. But Old Mac would work all winter, maybe lay off one or two days. He built trails, truck trails and fences for us until the CCC boys came along. Then he went on as road foreman for the CCC. We always figured that people like the McMinnimums made America. There were many fine people in the rural areas in those days—in the Zuni mountains, on the Datil, on the Prescott, and the Coconino."

Ask any Ranger about problems of the early twenties, and the reply will be transportation. When he went to the Sitgreaves Forest in July, 1922, Paul Roberts found that there were no good roads, away from the main roads, on the Forest.

"The program of truck trails was starting," Roberts said. "We cleaned out the old Rim Road, the Apache-Camp Verde military road along the Rim, as far as the Coconino Forest. The Coconino cleared it out from there on. Of course, all the canyons headed up close to the Rim, so the road headed the canyons. Once we got that cleared out we built truck trails. There wasn't much building. We cut truck trails and cleaned them out down between the canyons so we could get in to fires with men and equipment a good deal faster than we could in the old days with pack horses.

"One of our early experiments—somebody got the idea that we might put a truck equipped with tools, fire-fighting equipment, between Wildcat Canyon and Chevelon Canyon. So we rented a truck took it up around the Rim and down between the canyons, and placed it where we could get to it as quick as we could get over there on saddle horses.

"The first fire we had was a lightning strike, and it was right near the truck. It burned the whole outfit up before we could try out how effective our experiment was. It took us about a year to get approval to pay the fellow for the truck.

"Then the next flurry—we decided to build a road, a crossing on Wildcat Canyon. Aldo Leopold was Chief of Operation, and I was just a young Supervisor and inexperienced. Leonard Lessel (Assistant Supervisor) had more experience than I had, so I took him into the conference. When we asked for an allotment to build a road across Wildcat, Aldo was so dumfounded he said, 'Well, that is a crazy idea.' Since I was a young Supervisor and inexperienced, I wouldn't be reprimanded for such an idea, but it was totally impossible.

"But the next year, Evan Kelly, who was an engineer and a road builder, came along on an inspection, and he said, 'Paul, why don't you build a road across Wildcat Canyon—and across Chevelon, too, so you can get across there?' We built the road across Wildcat Canyon while I was there, and soon after I left they built a crossing on Chevelon Canyon.

"I remember particularly about a road up to the lookout on Lake Mountain. I checked up with Lessel and he said we had plenty of money to finish that road. So I went ahead and built the road, and when I got through I found out that I was $800 short. So I wrote in—Jim Mullin was handling allotments then—so I wrote in to Jim and I said, 'We're $800 short; we need to increase our allotment.' And Jim wrote back a little note and said, 'You can overdraw on the checkbook, but you can't overdraw at the bank.'

"I had a well-experienced clerk there and he said, 'The Government always pays its bills; let's just wait and see what they do.' So we never wrote in to the Regional Office about that any more. We just sat there, and in about a couple of months, along came an increase of allotment in the amount of $800.

"There were no paved roads in Arizona, except a few miles out of Phoenix at that time. As I remember, along in '30 or '31 they built a mile of experimental oiled road between Holbrook and Gallup. That was the first oiled road that we had. Of course, as I have said, transportation was slow. Right after the War, while I was still in Albuquerque, the office asked me to take a Ford sedan, which was a transfer from the War Department, out to the Tusayan from Albuquerque. Tusayan was having some fire difficulties and they wanted to speed up their transportation.

"I thought that would be a good trip for my wife to go along, so we left Albuquerque that morning about 10 o'clock and got to Thoreau that night, late that night. But before we got into Thoreau, we'd gone through an *arroyo* and twisted the hose connection off the radiator and had to walk in about a mile. They were having an oil boom at Thoreau at that time and the oil men were having a poker game in the hotel and one of them said as soon as he'd lost his stack he'd go out and pull me in. He won a little money before he lost it, but he finally lost what he had, and we went out to get the car and bring it in. We made the necessary repairs that night and started out at sun-up the next morning and by driving real fast and hard we got into Holbrook that night about 9 o'clock. We left there early the next morning and got into Williams after dark that night. That was three days from Albuquerque in a Model T Ford. After that we took a vacation and went up to Grand Canyon. That gives you some idea of the speed of transportation in those times.

"Then, in the fall of 1929, or '30, the first emergency money that we got was still in the Hoover administration. They asked us how soon we could start crews to work if we had the money. I told them we could start the next morning. I believe we got an allotment of about $3,000. Right at that time, or about that time, we had started the road crossing, at what we called the Mormon Crossing, on the Chevelon District, down near the old Marquette Ranger Station. All the drilling for use of powder was done by hand. Well, we got a jackhammer. It was the first one on the Forest. Bill Baldwin had laid out the road so we'd have the easiest going with the ordinary methods of construction, and I'd approved the location. About two or three weeks later I went back out there to see how they were getting along. In the meantime, Bill had gotten the jackhammer and he'd completely changed the location of the road. He was going around a rock ledge which really was a better location. They were really usin' that jackhammer to blow out that road and get around there. They thought that was really something. Those tractors and that jackhammer were the first pieces of real equipment that went out on the Sitgreaves."

Today there are Wildernesses and Primitive Areas in the Forests where vehicles are prohibited, but otherwise Rangers can cover their patrols with pick-ups and 4-wheel drive vehicles. But the old-time Ranger still loves his horse as the way to get around the country. As Ranger Henry Woodrow of the McKenna Park District once said, "I expect to keep riding them as long as I am able to—up until I am a hundred years old anyway."

Stanley Wilson, a technically trained forester, graduate of the Yale Forestry School, spent his entire career in Ranger and Supervisor positions, and he summed up the feelings of a lot of old time Rangers about working their Districts on horseback:

"As a retiree who knows nothing about the facts, I just want to make an observation or two. In my day, of course, we rode horseback. We were encouraged to make trips where we had nothing in particular to do except to see the country. I never made a trip of that sort but what I came up with something I ought to know. I remember the trip I made on the Catalinas. I just went into an area to see the country. I found goats in trespass. I didn't know there were any goats in the Catalinas. I found a fence that had been built. Basically we were doing this to get acquainted with our District. We did know the nooks and corners, but as I say, we almost always found some good reason for being in that place that we couldn't think of. Now, of course, there are roads everywhere. We have roads to our lookout; we have roads everywhere . . . but I can't help thinking that men don't know their Districts as well, traveling in a car."

Wilson said that when he moved to Phoenix as a retiree, he ran into Hugh Cassidy at Springerville.

"Stan," Cassidy said, "when you move out here and get settled, come on up and take a week's trip with me."

"Well," Wilson said, "I'd love to, Hugh. I haven't forked a horse in 15 years."

"Who said anything about a horse?" Hugh asked. "We're going in a car."

"Go to the devil," Wilson said. "I don't want to ride with you."

And he added, he never went.

CHAPTER XIV
CCC Days

Edward G. Miller was Supervisor of the Coconino National Forest in 1933 when the telegram arrived at his Flagstaff office advising him that some 500 to 600 CCC enrollees would be assigned to the Flagstaff area. Miller was advised to be prepared to take care of them.

Similar telegrams were being received by other Supervisors as the Federal government's emergency program to combat the Depression got underway. With about one-fourth of the population of the United States between 15 and 24 unemployed, and as many employed only part-time, the government was taking dramatic action to cope with the problem.

Chief of the Forest Service Robert Y. Stuart had estimated that 25,000 men would be put to work in the National Forests. Within a month he had been asked to increase the number to 250,000 as plans went ahead to enroll young men in the Civilian Conservation Corps. At its peak the number of camps increased to 1,500 and an enrollment of half a million.

In the Regional Office in Albuquerque, Hugh Calkins was Chief of the Operations Division and Stanley Wilson was assistant.

"I was rather amazed at how wonderfully Hugh Calkins found camp sites and places and work for all of the camps," Wilson recalled. "My own part of it was handling personnel."

The establishment of the CCC camps put a great drain on available supervisory forest personnel and new technical foresters had to be obtained and obtained quickly. Prior to that time when technical foresters were needed, it was customary to send word to the forestry schools for the names of people and resumes of their qualifications.

"We'd peruse the lists and look wise and pick the people we wanted," Wilson recounted. "Of course it didn't do us any real good."

Because he was not happy with the system, Wilson—shortly before the start of the CCC program made arrangements with 10 forestry schools for selection of candidates for employment.

"I don't want your histories of these men," Wilson told them.

"They mean nothing to me.   What I want to do is to be able to call upon you for so many men to be either camp superintendents or camp foremen—and here are the qualifications.   I don't want their qualifications, because I want you to be willing to stand behind them.

"So when the CCC program broke, I sent for 80 men from the 10 forestry schools.   Then there was a delay in the program, and for a day or two we didn't know whether we were going ahead or not.   I was afraid to take the men, yet on the other hand if I cancelled the order for them I would be out of luck.   So we sat tight, and fortunately the order came to go ahead.   We got 80 men, and the heads of the forest schools did such a good job that actually we had no lemons in those 80 men.   I think we had unquestionably the best group of technical foresters any Region got."

The various Forests were setting up camps to handle the influx of enrollees.

Edward Miller reported from Flagstaff that with Major P. L. Thomas from the regular Army, his lieutenant and a sergeant, "we looked over several possible camp sites and agreed to put one camp north of the city reservoir, out from Flagstaff where water could be obtained from the city power plant; one camp at Double Springs on the west side of Mormon Lake; one camp at Woods Springs on the Munds Park District."

"By the time the enrollees showed up," Miller said, "our boys had installed water mains, storage tanks, had made some clearings and were ready for the CCC camps to be established.

"We had some of the technical foremen, forestry graduates, start on timber-stand improvement work as soon as possible.   We started some fencing work, some erosion control, like building little check-dams in some of the *arroyos*.   Looking back, it seems to me that those spring developments were mighty important from the viewpoint of forest grazing permittees.

"We also started in on some recreation improvements.   Recreation was just coming into its own on the Coconino.   Oak Creek was a favorite spot, also Mormon Lake, and Lake Mary."

The level of Lake Mary was low in 1933, and a lot of water was being lost from holes and fractures along an old fault line in the limestone bottom of the lake.   It was decided to try to plug the holes.   The State Game Department provided truck loads of cans to save the fish before the repair program got under way.   CCC boys seined for days getting out bass, crappie, and ring perch, which were then transported to other waters.   Then crews of CCC boys with trucks and other equipment began the task of repairing the leaks in the lake bottom.

"I remember one crack that must have been 300 feet long and several feet wide."Miller said.   "One of the big holes that had been filled with brush and clay in 1905 and '06 had opened up. We decided we would put in layers of limestone rock, carefully laid, then layers of clay.   We found a sizeable clay bank, from which dump trucks were loaded by hand.   Weeks were spent on this work.   The clay was compacted as it was put in.

"By the time the camp was to move to winter quarters, the boys had filled all holes and all cracks that were visible in Lake Mary.   That was one job where the CCC boys really accomplished something that meant a lot to a lot of people.   Lake Mary is a favorite camp ground, a favorite fishing lake for a lot of people from Phoenix and other points in the desert as well as local people.

"Other recreation work included fireplaces, tables, water lines.   One water line in Oak Creek was extended from the Upper Spring in Oak Creek Canyon down to Pine Flats campground. Other springs farther down were also developed.

"Incidentally, it is interesting to think back and realize the change in thinking.   The most desirable places, like Pine Flats and Oak Creek Canyon, were laid out by Aldo Leopold and his helpers as summer home sites back in 1917, '18, or thereabouts. Fortunately, most of those summer home sites were never rented. But now I understand that people come from California, and other distant States, for a few days' camping in that beautiful canyon.

"Sedona was winter quarters for one CCC camp; another was placed on the upper part of the Beaver Creek Ranger Station site, and another on the upper end of the Clear Creek Ranger Station site.   Those camps were located so that considerable recreation and range improvement work could be accomplished.   Thousands of little check-dams were put in, camp sets were constructed up in Navajo Creek Canyon, stream bottoms were fenced, checkdams put in.

"Unfortunately, we had no guides for them and the engineer who gave advice had to go by rule of thumb.   I just do not know how many of those checkdams were destined to last until the present time.   We fenced some of the stream bottoms as we figured that by reseeding those stream bottoms and keeping cattle out, Old Mother Nature would revegetate and that possibly more permanent good would result than would be accomplished there by the construction of checkdams.

"A person would have to admit that a lot of those kids that came out as CCC workers were pretty poor help for a few months. Very few of them knew how to use tools.   We didn't get too

The Civilian Conservation Corps, organized during the "Depression" days of the 1930's, accomplished many worthwhile projects on the Southwestern National Forests.

much use of them in firefighting. Even though the actual work accomplished amounted in real permanent values to only about a dollar and a half a day, those boys certainly received permanent benefits from their experiences at the CCC Camps. The foremen reported that they developed some fine Caterpillar tractor drivers, some good road-grader operators. Unfortunately, too much of the first equipment that was available was of poor quality; some of it was almost useless. But it served the purpose in a training program. I have no doubt that a lot of the CCC boys who learned to operate equipment filled important places overseas in the Second World War.

"I can say that CCC camps alone did not and cannot meet the needs of some Forest-dependent communities. The local boys in communities like Camp Verde, Winslow, and Flagstaff, Northern New Mexico, need the work on roads, trails, firefighting. It seems to me that our local people cooled off a little after the CCC boys came in, because they felt that they and their boys would not be used on the various jobs that required temporary labor during the summer months. However, I think that the provision that allowed Forest officers to enroll some local enrollees, who were qualified to guide the boys from the big cities, had a tendency to cool off some of the local farmers who thought that we were doing them an injustice by bringing in outside boys to do the work that they had participated in over the years. Actually, when we found that so many CCC boys were afraid to use tools, we used local men when it was possible to get them."

With the availability of CCC boys to do the work, recreation sites got increased attention.

"We began to develop recreation areas all over the Region," Zane Smith, a Ranger on the Prescott and Cibola Forests during the late 30's and early 40's said. "There were over 400 recreation sites developed in about a ten or eleven year period. Some of those were quite small admittedly, just a toilet and maybe a dug garbage pit with a cover over it, one table and a fireplace. They went all the way from that sort of a set-up to a 50-or-60-family unit, comprised of table, fireplace, and essential facilities.

"Recreation use began to pick up along through the '30's, with the various alphabetical programs that were helping the country get its feet back on the ground and pull out of the depression. There was a five-and-a-half-day week, there were roads being built making it a little bit easier for people to get around and into the forests. Recreation began to command quite a spot of importance in Forest Service work."

One of the interesting little projects accomplished by the CCC was the construction of the Catwalk bridge in Whitewater

Canyon near Glenwood. They made use of hangers and material that had held up a pipeline through the canyon during the early mining days.

Sam Servis was a Ranger in the Magdalena District during the later 1930's, and he recalled an old report in Socorro, written in longhand regarding the mining operation in Whitewater Canyon.

"They piped water some three miles down Whitewater Canyon to the Competence Mill site," Servis said. "To pipe this water, they laid an 18-inch pipeline. To maintain it, the miners got to walking the pipeline. They are the ones who called it the catwalk because of walking the pipeline. It was just suspended there in the canyon. They climbed up it and walked on up it.

"The water was piped down, generated electricity and ran the machinery at the mill. At one time they had so many people around there, they called it the town of Graham. The town flourished and they shipped out many thousands of dollars worth of ore. The first office of the old Gila River Forest Reserve was located there before it was moved to Silver City."

The mine and water line had ceased operation in 1914, but the stream was popular with hikers and fishermen and the bridge built by the CCC as a successor to the pipeline was also called the Catwalk, as it is today.

The CCC bridge rotted out in recent years and was replaced by a steel bridge, which had been moved from the Sitgreaves Forest.

Servis recalled that the Regions engineers who had first started out to design a new bridge for the meandering catwalk location finally gave up in disgust and despair "and threw all their papers and pencils out the window and told Bob Leonard (improvement foreman on the Gila) to go get his torch and a couple of helpers and put the bridge in. It was a good winter job and so old Bob and his helpers went up and put that bridge in—with just a torch and his own ability to make it fit. It was an extremely fine job. For a good many years that steel bridge will be there and handle lots and lots of people."

Walter Graves, who became Regional Chief of Operations in 1961, was one of the 1933 forestry graduates who had come to New Mexico for work in the CCC program.

"As a matter of fact," Graves said, "I was only one of two in my graduating class that were still at Iowa State for graduation to receive our diplomas. The rest of the class had already gone to CCC camps all over the country.

"I arrived in Santa Fe about the middle of June 1933, and at the same time a forester from Oregon arrived to be in the same camp. The Supervisor, Frank Andrews, was so busy getting CCC camps established that he was not available for the first two weeks that we were in Sante Fe. Each morning we would go to the office and receive word that the Supervisor was still out, and that we would not be assigned to a camp until he returned. So for two weeks this other man and I spent our days reporting to the office and finding out that the Supervisor would not be back, and then just waiting until such time as he did show up. After two weeks, Mr. Andrews finally came back into town and called the two of us in and told us that we would each be assigned to different camps. He assigned each of us to a camp by flipping a coin. The camp I was assigned to was the one at Hyde Park, about 10 or 15 miles out of Santa Fe. This was a tent camp and was composed mostly of boys from Southern Texas. We spent all that summer at the Hyde Park camp doing mostly erosion control work in the Hyde Park area, with a small side camp in Santa Fe Canyon doing some erosion control work there, as well as timber-stand improvement work."

In the fall a permanent camp with wooden barracks and all necessary facilities was built at the edge of Santa Fe. (During World War II this became a Japanese Detention Camp and later the site was sold and became the Casa Solano subdivision.)

Graves had assignments other than CCC camps for several years then in March '39 became a full-fledged District Ranger with headquarters in Coyote on the Carson National Forest.

"While at Coyote, we had a CCC camp just below the Ranger Station that was there until World War II was declared.

"The Ranger's house at Coyote was rather primitive. When we moved there, there was no electricity. We used gasoline lanterns and later Aladdin's lamps for light, and a kerosene operated refrigerator for refrigeration. There was no plaster on the interior walls of the house, just mud, but the year after arrival I was able to get the CCC crews to replaster the house.

"One of our major problems at Coyote was the distance we had to travel to do our shopping. There was one small store in Coyote. The selection was quite limited and about all we could get were canned goods and a few staples. We made a trip every two weeks to Santa Fe for all of our supplies. During the summer, of course, with fire season, I was not able to go with my wife when she went on her two-weeks shopping tour, so she had to go by herself. It was quite a sight to see her come home to the Ranger Station with two youngsters in the car, two weeks supply of groceries, 200 pounds of chicken feed, 10 gallons of kerosene for the refrigerator, and five or ten gallons of white gas for the lanterns. The car was so loaded it would hardly clear the wheels."

Commenting on the CCC operations, Graves said that "the Army had the responsibility of organizing the camp and handling all of the logistics, and the complete operation of the camp itself. The involved agencies, land management agencies, were assigned the boys in the morning, took them out on the job and were responsible for them until they returned to camp in the evening, at which time the Army took them over and of course was responsible for them until the following morning. The regular Army was the nucleus of the camp operations, with a number of reserve officers assigned, particularly in the later stages of the program. At the time the program was dropped, it was operated almost entirely by Reserve officers. Of course the program was stopped when World War II started. Had it not been for that, we undoubtedly would still have a CCC program, would have had it all through these years.

"We built many miles or roads, lots of range fences, range improvements of all kinds, erosion control, and while this Region did not concentrate on the construction of administrative improvements such as Ranger stations, a number of Regions did, and of course these buildings are still in use today.

"We had men in our camps out of Santa Fe who had doctors' degrees, and a number of men who were high school and college graduates. But they were not able to find work at all, and this program was aimed at providing work for those people who just could not get a job. Some of them came hungry—very hungry—men who had been out of work, with families to support, been out of work for months and months."

Norman Johnson, of Flagstaff, was a construction foreman on the Coronado Forest, and one of his CCC assignments was to build a combination guard and fire cabin at Cima Park.

"It was a complete installation, telephone lines, water system, a large cabin. In the building specifications, it called for two fireplaces to be built back to back. Every fireplace I had had anything to do with in those days either smoked or provided inadequate heat. You'd have to stand up to the fire, and if you were facing it, you're warm on that side and you're cold on the opposite side. I had no idea how to build a fireplace back to back and the plans didn't detail it enough to know. So I wrote the Government Printing Office and sure enough, they sent me the details that I needed to get the job done and it worked very satisfactorily—a double fireplace with one chimney.

"Another thing about the building—we had to cut the logs, skid them with a mule. As a matter of fact we had to pack everything in from Rustler Park, at the end of the road, to Cima Park. So everything had to come in by pack animals.

"The plans called for windows lying horizontally, like log cabins were in those days. Now, I'm rather a tall person, and the windows were either too low when I was standing up to see through or too high to see through if I was sitting down.   I came up with the idea I wanted a window I could see out of.   I took it upon myself to stand the windows up and down so I could see out.

"Fred Winn, (Supervisor of the Coronado and by then an old timer) came up on an inspection trip, accompanied by Mrs. Winn.

"I doubt very much whether Mr. Winn noticed this change. But certainly Mrs. Winn did—and I really heard about it! It was a log cabin that wasn't a log cabin."

Johnson stayed with the CCC program through the rest of its existence until it folded in 1942, working mainly with campground construction.   Several summers were spent operating what might be termed side camps, which were camps away from the mother camp.

"I recall that it was rather an imposing task to be camp commander, educational advisor, the 'doctor,' the project superintendent, all in the camp, plus running the crew during the day," Johnson said.

"I can remember having side camps on top of the Huachuca Mountains and we would be there for weeks on end, because a person would have to walk off the top of the mountain and it wasn't worth walking off the mountain to go to the main camp. We furnished our own recreation in the form of hikes, horseshoe games.   There wasn't any place level enough for a baseball diamond, but we'd have an area where we could play catch, so we were rather a complete camp."

As the CCC program was getting started, Ranger Zane Smith, who had just been transferred to Alamogordo, drove up to Albuquerque on a personal business matter one week-end, and visited Landis Arnold, who had just been put in charge of recreational programs for the Southwestern Region.

"Pink, who had shown a great deal of personal interest in this sort of thing, had scrounged around and managed to build a few old tables out of scrap lumber, and give some attention to the recreationists from Albuquerque, out in the Sandias.   This caused him to be selected to head up this work.   He was a real good administrator, but surveying and mapping was something beyond him; he was never able to grasp it.   About the time I came to Albuquerque on this little private business trip, Pink was looking for somebody who could fit into his organization and head up the mapping side of it.   I just happened to come into view and he knew me, knew that I could do that sort of work, so I was imme-

diately tapped for that.   I remember we had moved into an apartment in Alamogordo that was a second choice.   We were told if
we would occupy this temporarily, one of the better apartments
would be available soon and we could have it.   Well, the weekend
that I came to Albuquerque my wife got the new apartment and
moved into it.   When things firmed up on my move to Albuquerque I had to move her out of it.   We did a lot of moving in a short
space of time.

That was quite a move, to be attached to the Regional Office,
for a youngster getting started.   My working area suddenly became
all of the National Forests in the States of New Mexico and
Arizona.   I was probably feeling pretty cocky over what I considered to be my good fortune.   I took off with a lot of confidence
and no knowledge of recreation development, but I was still under
Pink Arnold's guidance, making plans for picnic and campground
developments throughout the Region.   With the rapid increase in
the CCC program and the number of camps, which I believe got
to number up around 40 during the 30's, we were pretty busy
making plans and developing camp and picnic grounds for all the
National Forests.   In fact, some of the improvements are quite
serviceable."

CHAPTER XV
Ranger Humor

Oscar McClure, a Ranger on the Coconino and Prescott for more than 30 years, was telling of some of his experiences and he mentioned that "we fellows were always playing tricks on each other."

"There was a kind of funny one that has to do with Bob Monroe," he said. "One time we were down on Secret Mountain —went down to survey a fire and make an inspection. Coming back, our trail went down into Secret Canyon. There are water brakes every so far apart on the horseback trail. On one of these there was a small oak log that had about a two-inch hollow in the middle of it. The yellow jackets had built a nest in there.

"Well, now, if two fellows rode along there and they stayed right close together, they could get by all right. But if they were a little ways apart, the yellow jackets would be disturbed, and the fellow behind usually got nipped.

"There was another fellow with me and Bob that day and this other fellow was in a little bad humor with Bob, so he cut around and went someplace else before we got to this log. I trotted up— and Bob hit 'em just right!

"He was riding a big horse that weighed 1300, 1400 pounds, and he had one of those little old McClellan saddles. That horse squealed and took off. And Bob did too. He managed to stay with him until he got him under control.

"I never did tell him who did that. Bob would have killed him."

Perl Charles thinks that the funniest things that ever happened to him were back in the mid-20's when he was in the Jemez country.

"There was a fellow named Bert Pfingsten, who had the Ranger District next to mine when I was at Espanola. Pfingsten had the Bland District. This Bert Pfingsten was a very interesting man. Bert and I were always figuring projects where we could get together. One time we had to post the game refuge line around the Bandelier National Monument. We had to put a strip of black paint, then a strip of yellow paint. I took a packhorse and

Bert took two pack mules and we were to bring supplies and stay there a week. Bert had the paint on his white mule—and the mule got scared and bucked the pack off and spilled black paint on one end and yellow paint on the other. He scattered groceries all over the hillside. When we went back to pick up the potatoes, we found everything but the baking powder. We had enough bread for two or three days and when we ran out, we had to make biscuits without baking powder—flapjacks—and they weren't very good.

"Another time we caught a little cub bear—Bert and I. There was a permittee named Pedro Garcia with us. We were trying to teach him to salt out where the feed was. We were working on this permittee when we found the bear.

"We were riding along, and we saw this little bear climbing a tree. Bert said, 'Let's stop and get him.' I told him I hadn't lost any bear. Well, Bert wanted him.

"Bert says, 'I'll go up and get him; you stay down here and keep the old bear away.' In those days everybody carried a gun, I don't know why, but we did. Bert got about half-way up the tree. I had a little .32 automatic and fired it a couple of times. Bert yelled, 'What's the matter?' I said, 'I think the old bear's coming.' He said, 'Don't let her come up here!' I waited a minute or two and I fired this gun a couple of times again and said, 'I don't think I can stop her.' He said, 'Well, I think I can jump out into this little white fir tree over here.' Then I burst out laughing, and he knew I was kidding. So he went to the top of the tree, and this little bear went just as far as he could. Bert had a little pigging line and he tried to slip it over the bear's head, and the bear would knock it off.

"So Bert climbed up just a little bit higher and grabbed the bear by the hind leg and called 'I got him!' I was standing out where I could see him, and about the time he yelled, 'I've got him!' the bear got him. He just reached down and caught Bert on the wrist. Bert yanked—gave quite a pull when the bear bit him, and pulled the bear out of the tree. Here he came, right down through the branches on this white fir. He hit the ground, and the first time it looked like he bounced about six feet high and the second time about half as high, and away he went. But he was a little groggy. I had a little rope, so I flipped it over his head and pulled him up.

"The bear turned around and looked at me. He was just about so high and he said, 'GRRRR' and here he came! I thought I could sidestep him, you know, and yank him around again. I started to sidestep him and I don't know what happened.

I had my boots, spurs, chaps, everything on.   I probably tripped over a spur or something.   I fell down and as I started to fall I thought, 'Well, I may as well get this over with,' and I just made a header for that bear.   I'm telling you, I wrestled that darned bear all over that little flat there.   Talk about the cat and the bird.   We really tore that place up!   This Bert Pfingsten was up in the tree watching, he was having the time of his life.   I'll never forget when I finally got that little bear choked down.   I took a deep breath and up and here was this fellow, Pedro Garcia, and he was laughing.   He had his shirt collar open, and tears were running down his face and were runnin' down his neck.   He said, 'You're crazy.' Bert came on down and we put the bear in a sack and he said, 'Who's gonna carry him?'   I said, 'I just don't need that bear, that's all there is to it.'   He said, 'Maybe I can carry him on Old Buck.'   He couldn't get Old Buck near him.   I was holdin' the bear.

"Finally Bert got back about 30 yards and yelled, 'I'll run by you and when I do, throw me the bear.'   He got up all the speed he could on that old horse and when he came by I heaved him the bear, and he caught him.   That horse got his head down and really took off.   Bert rode him—all the way—and took that little bear home.

"He had it down at the Bland Ranger Station, chained to a tree.   They fed him in a little bowl, and that little bear, after a week or ten days, you'd go out there in the morning and he'd bring his bowl to you and wanted you to put some food in.   They finally gave him to Albuquerque zoo."

The old-time Rangers all have horse stories to tell.   Ranger Bob Ground liked to tell one about G. L. (Lee) Wang, who served for 15 years as a Ranger and additional years as a Supervisor. Back in 1928 when Harry Naylor was Ranger on the Tres Piedras District he arranged for a round-up of wild horses on the District.

"Naylor had bought a horse and it had a bad leg," Bob Ground reminisced.   "The horse had gotten away, and in the round-up we rounded up this horse of Naylor's.   Harry said, 'Put it up for sale just like the rest of 'em.'

"They put this horse up for sale, and Lee Wang was up there and he began to bid on it.   Harry told him, 'Lee, you don't want that horse.   It's only got three legs.'   'I want a tradin' horse,' Lee told him—so he bid it on up.   I don't remember what he paid but it was something around $20.   Anyway, he got the horse.

"He took it home, and he tried to trade it off down around Vallecitos, to some of those natives around there, but he didn't have any luck.   They seemed to know more about the horse than Lee did!

"Then they had another round-up over on Canjilon District. Jim Newton was Ranger over there.   Lee went around tryin' to trade this horse, and he couldn't find anybody to trade with except some people named Trujillo.   They had a bunch of horses, so he finally talked up a trade, and got in trade a cayuse, a wild little bronco.   Lee traded his three-legged horse for this little wild cayuse.   When they got ready to leave, why they packed this little horse up.   Jim Newton put the pack on, and he put it on to stay. Lee Wang started out ridin' his old, long-legged Sam horse, goin' off across the flats.   I think Jim Newton was out there kinda shooin' the horse behind, 'cause the horse wouldn't lead.   Finally, Lee got out of sight and Jim Newton came back.   Some of the fellows sittin' on the corral fence there tellin' stories looked up and saw this little horse goin' across the flats with the pack on him—old Lee Wang behind it on his old Sam horse, just givin' it heck, tryin' to catch him!   Of course, he didn't get him.   After while he came back to the corral there.   Of course the fellows couldn't keep from laughin' 'cause they saw the whole show.   Lee told 'em what happened, said he'd give $5 reward for the horse, or the outfit.   Things drifted along for a day or two, so he raised the ante, said he'd give $10.   Still nothin' happened.   Finally, he raised the ante again and told 'em they could have the horse, just bring his bed back.   About that time, Manual Trujillo went out and shot the horse and got the bed and brought the bed in to Lee and collected his reward.   The rumor was—I don't know whether there was any truth in it or not—they said he shot a hole through his bed.   That was the end of Lee Wang's horse-tradin'!"

As far back as 1908, the Forest Service had sought to discourage the use of intoxicating liquors.   One of the earliest orders issued by Chief Forester Pinchot was Service Order No. 12, noting that "the excessive use of intoxicants by members of the Forest Service is a bar to their efficiency and will be dealt with as such."

The order even discouraged "moderate drinking" at official gatherings, although it noted that "it is not competent for the Forest Service to require total abstinence."

A. O. Waha noted that Service Order No. 12 probably caused more discussion among field men than other more important orders, but said the order was "pretty generally followed."

Jim Monighan remembered one time when it was not "generally followed."

Monighan was scaling logs on the Sitgreaves National Forest, and working out of the old Los Burros Station.

"After a hard day's scaling in the mud and rain, we came into the old Los Burros Station," Monighan said.   "Everett Hamilton was chief cook at that time, and he was making a cake. He had it in the oven. Duncan Lang and I came in together. It had been raining off and on all day and we were cold and wet—and hungry. We sat around for a little while and finally the weather got the best of us. I guess we had cabin fever, because we were chewing each other out and hard to get along with. For some reason, it just happened that I had a little bit of apricot brandy in my suitcase. Not knowing whether Dunc or Everett ever took a drink, I went in and got the bottle and set it up on the table and said, 'I don't care who knows that I take a drink. I'm gonna have a little drink.' So I took a little swig and Hamilton got up and said, 'I don't care who knows I take a drink,' so he took a little swig, and then Dunc Lang got up and said, 'I don't give a damn who knows I take a drink,' —so he had one, too. And after a while, you know, that cabin warmed up, and I don't know to this day whether we had a good supper or not!"

The oldtimers remember a lookout who had been hired for the Baker Butte lookout in the Long Valley District during World War II when men were hard to get. This one hadn't read—or certainly had not paid any attention to Service Order No. 12.

One time the lookout went into Payson, drunk, and was going to shoot up the town. After his arrest, it was discovered that his distillery was in the attic of the lookout tower!

Among oldtimers, Ralph Hussey, an early-day Ranger on the Gila and later Supervisor on the Coconino, was both a teller and subject of stories. Ray Kallus was telling about Hussey's entrance into the Forest Service.

Fred Winn, the Supervisor, told Hussey: "Ralph, there's a fire out there. Go, put it out."

Huss told Kallus, "Ray, I got ready and dashed 65 miles to the fire on a mule."

Later in his career, Hussey was on the Lincoln Forest making a land classification study with Sim Strickland, and they were just about to finish the assignment when a big snow came on and they were snowed in. Their food was about to run out, so as Kallus recalls the story, Huss said, "We'll just take our guns and go out and get a deer." They went out to get a deer. Huss went over one hill and Sim went the other direction. Sim saw a rabbit and he thought, "Well, maybe I won't see a deer," so he shot the rabbit. And he never saw a deer. Huss heard the shot and thought, "Well, maybe he didn't hit that deer." He saw a rabbit about that time, so he shot a rabbit. Sim heard the shot. Each of them thought, "Well, we're gonna have venison tonight, and until we get out of this snow."

They got back to the cabin about the same time, Kallus related, and each one was carrying a rabbit.

"Fred Arthur, Supervisor of this Forest, had a kind heart," Kallus said, "he wasn't gonna leave these land classifiers out in this snow-covered mountain where you couldn't get through. He would get through to them. He sent a fellow out—it could've been Reuben Boone—sent him out on a horse with a bag of flour, a little bacon and some other stuff, such as could be carried on the saddle of his horse, to give to these fellows to help them out. That grub was needed. They made whoever it was sit down and eat rabbit with them that night."

Kallus said that "Bill Brown was another character. Bill didn't believe in cooking anything but meat. He was the Ranger on the Long Valley District, and an oldtime Ranger. I don't know how long he was at Long Valley—for many years before I came to the Coconino, though, and that was in 1938. I remember that Hussey and he were always arguing. Bill Brown was telling about an incident that happened when he and Hussey were out on a trip. Hussey says, 'I just can't figure where it was that you are trying to tell me.' And Bill Brown says, 'Why you remember; I was eating an apple and I had the core, and I threw it at a squirrel.' Hussey says, 'Damn you, Bill Brown, you can confuse me more than any other man alive!'

"Old Bill Brown had a really hazardous fire district. You couldn't ever get him to lay off a lookout. The excuse always was, 'It rained where you say, but it hasn't rained at Bly.' That got to be a byword, 'Call Old Bill and find out if it rained down at Bly.'

"We had a fire meeting one time, and Bill finally told how bad it did rain. Huss was cussing him out because it never rained at Bly. Bill says, 'It does rain down there. Right now it is raining so hard the trees are sinking into the ground.' Well, there was a humorist who did a lot of writing who lives down in that part of the country, and he got hold of this story, that Bill Brown had said the trees were sinking out of sight. So he wrote it up, but he said that the fence posts were sinking out of sight. That story got all over Arizona.

"One time during the hunting season, Bill Brown didn't want a bunch of hunters in a certain area. There was one place along the entrance road where, if a certain tree fell down it would keep hunters from driving into that area. They couldn't get through without getting out and moving that tree. In some way or another, that tree did fall down!

"There was some evidence that it had been blasted by dynamite, but of course, we would never have thought that Bill Brown could have done it!"

Some of the incidents that Rangers remember as humorous now were not so humorous when they happened—at least not to some of the victims of practical jokes or unusual accidents.

Gordon Bade recalled an unusual incident when he was scaling logs on the Coconino. "I watched a couple of log cutters cut down this fair-sized yellow pine, and when it hit the ground it burst open," Bade said. "It was hollow, and alive with bats! Bats fluttered on the ground and crawled around. One of the log cutters went to another tree and started cutting, and all of a sudden I noticed him peeling off his overalls. . . . shook them out. One of the bats had crawled up his pants leg. We yelled—wow! We thought that was great. About that time one of them got up my pants leg—and I had to shake my own. They've got sharp claws. There were scores of them. The daylight blinded them, and they were stunned, I suppose, from the fall, and they were trying to get back where it was dark—and pants legs were the nearest spot."

Perl Charles was telling about a trip he made in the field with Ranger Ed Tucker of the Mt. Taylor District of the Cibola Forest and remembered they got caught on top of Mt. Taylor as it was getting dark and starting to snow.

"I didn't think we had a chance in the world of getting back to our camp before dark, and neither did he," Charles said. "And we knew if we wandered around in that country after dark, we'd have trouble. He said, 'Well, can you do without your coffee tonight?' And I said, 'Sure, why?' He said, 'Well, we can go up and stay all night at La Mosca cabin on top of the lookout.' We went on up and the wind was blowing forty miles an hour, stacking a little snow up on the side of the trees. We found some boxes and got a little wood and built a fire. We had some emergency rations from World War I, and we dragged them out. I had eaten them before, so that didn't worry me too much. Finally, I said, 'Where's the water. I need a drink of water,' 'Water?' he asked. 'Didn't I tell you that you couldn't have any coffee?' 'Yes,' I said, 'you told me I couldn't have any coffee, but you didn't say I couldn't have a drink of water.'

"Oh, that fellow was having fun. He sure enjoyed it more than I did."

Perl Charles had a similar experience earlier with his Supervisor, Frank Andrews, when he was a Ranger on the Espanola District. But that time it was Frank Andrews who went without his coffee.

"I never knew a man in the Forest Service—or anyplace else —that I had a higher regard for than I had for Frank Andrews,"

Charles said. "That was one of the best men I ever knew in my life—and one of the crankiest. He came over there one time to the south side of the Baca Location and wanted to put an emergency lookout on Rabbit Mountain. We had a bunch of World War I telephone wire, but I didn't have a packhorse. He said, 'Well, get a packhorse and pack it up there.' I met him, but I'd had trouble with the packhorse and was a little late. So he wasn't in a very good humor. He said, 'Aw, I'll go on. I'll meet you on top of the mountain.' He started off, and then he came back and said, 'Can you put this on the pack, too?' I said, 'Certainly, what is it?' He said, 'That's my lunch.'

"I thought he was making a mistake, but he was the boss. Who was I to question him? That was my first year on the District. Instead of getting up there at noon as he thought I would, I got there about dark. He said, 'I don't feel very good, I've got a headache. Do you have enough outfit with you that I can stay all night?' I said I thought so. So we hobbled our horses, and I built a fire and was stirring around to fix us a bite. Finally, he said, 'Where's your coffee?' I said, 'Mr. Andrews, I don't drink it and when I'm by myself I don't carry it.' He said, 'Well, I'll be God damned!'

"He never said another word. He turned around and went out and got that old bay horse, saddled him up and went down the canyon in the dark. Didn't say good-bye or anything.

"I thought my Forest Service career was ended right there. In later years I could kid him about it. He said, 'Oh, it wasn't the coffee altogether. That was pretty much of a hen-skin outfit you had there anyway. I didn't like the looks of it.' "

Fred Miller was a Ranger on the Zuni District soon after World War I and one time was riding from McGaffey to El Morro. "I remember I came down a very steep slope that was covered with woodland type, and here was a Navajo girl—or woman—riding a burro," Miller related. "She was wearing a voluminous skirt, and she was wearing a beautiful concho belt. She had on an old brown jacket and a voluminous skirt with this beautiful belt. I wanted to buy the belt.

"There I was, sitting on my horse, a great big horse—trying to make her understand. I couldn't speak Mexican or Navajo, and she couldn't speak English. Using a kind of sign language, I started pointing to the belt. Finally she started to laugh, and after a while she got down from her donkey, sat down under a tree and started to pull her dress off. I was still on my horse. I started shaking my head and yelling, 'No, no, no!'

"Then she got real mad and started picking up rocks and

throwing them at me. You can bet that I decided about then it was time to hightail it out of there!"

Back in 1911, Assistant District Forester J. K. Campbell was the victim of one of the practical jokes that Rangers sometimes staged—but it had no serious consequences. The story is told in an old report of the Datil National Forest.

Campbell had gone to Magdalena to make a grazing inspection on the western part of the District. He and Supervisor Goddard drove the District Office's well known team of horses —Blueberry and Strawberry—to the Tularosa Ranger Station. As has been noted before, Blueberry was a gentle horse under saddle, but Strawberry was a powerful bucker when the mood was on him.

When Campbell and Goddard got to the Tularosa station, they saddled up the team for their inspection ride. The Ranger at Tularosa station was Bill Bunton. He had known Campbell well in Albuquerque, so he took him aside and warned him that Supervisor Goddard was quite a practical joker.

"If Bert tries to get you to ride a certain horse, you insist you want to ride the other one," Ranger Bunton warned.

When Goddard suggested to Campbell that he ride "Blue" because it was a gentle horse, Campbell said no, he'd ride the other one.

Goddard reluctantly consented but warned that Strawberry was a rough actor.

Campbell, probably smiling to himself that he had outmaneuvered the Supervisor, mounted the powerful Strawberry. Thinking all was well, he sank his spurs into the horse—and away they went. Strawberry put his head down and began to buck. He did his best to throw his rider. Campbell, taken by surprise, was almost thrown—but his skill as a horseman saved him, and he was not unseated.

He later learned the real joker was Bunton—not Supervisor Goddard.

When Model T Fords began to get popular before World War I, some of the Rangers decided to try them out—and probably decided they would never replace the horse.

Back in 1916, Don S. Sullivan, a Ranger on the Coronado Forest bought a Model T, and he recounted his early adventures with it in a report to Supervisor Don P. Johnston:*

"I have purchased a Ford this week, and the designs I left on the road, while not copyrighted, have drawn considerable atten-

*The story of Ranger Sullivan's trials and tribulations was told in the Ari-zona Star, December 3, 1916.

tion.   When I first started it up, it was a success—until I tried to stop it, and as I did not know the combination, I failed on this point.

"After circling the yard twice, I concluded I needed about four more gates and as the only gate was closed, I compromised between the gateposts and took the gate on the northwest corner of the radiator.

"The conquest seemed to stimulate Lizzie and I was carried on an independent excursion over the mesquite thickets.   I soon caught sight of an authority on Fords and tried to draw his attention by following his lead.   By a flank movement he boarded and shut off the gas.

"By a liberal supply of paint and by moving the accordion bellows design out of the starboard fender, Lizzie and I have been able to recognize each other and expect to become fast friends."

CHAPTER XVI
Grasslands

Walter J. (Jim) Caserta was sitting at his desk in his cubby-hole in the office of the Soil Conservation Service in Amarillo one day in 1954 when three men walked in and introduced themselves —McCutchen, Davis, and a roly-poly Irishman name of Monighan, long-time Supervisor of the Cibola National Forest.

McCutchen stuck out his hand and said, "Caserta, welcome to the Forest Service!"

"Believe me," Caserta said in reminiscing about this meeting, "I had had about 20 years in Federal service, and that was the first time that anybody had welcomed me anywhere, let alone to the Forest Service. I thanked him. I guess he could see the amazement. He said, 'There's nothing in the world to worry about. We just came over to tell you that you are still holding your present position, and your responsibilities are the same, except you are going to be paid by the Forest Service."

The Land Utilization Project lands in New Mexico, Western Oklahoma, and the Panhandle of Texas had been transferred from the Soil Conservation Service to the Forest Service. The administration of these lands was placed with the Cibola National Forest temporarily.

The LU project had started back in the dust bowl days when the Federal government was buying up farms and ranches that were blowing away and attempting to stabilize the land and return it to grass when possible.

"We finally leveled enough land in Dallam County (Texas) to start a planting," Caserta said of the early activity. "We couldn't buy grass seed. Nobody harvested grass seed in those days. The only kind we could find was some fool had harvested Amaranthus—pigweed—and we had enough pigweed to sow probably three or four sections of land. Now this sounds perfectly ridiculous, but in those days of panic you did anything you could.

"You couldn't plant ryegrass—the wind would come along and blow it out. Amaranthus seed had some sort of ability to stick to the soil, as they say. We had a good firm seedbed up there, since Joe had wallowed around on the thing for quite a while, while the wind was taking the loose stuff off and it left a hardpan. Well, we got this stuff in the ground and, one of those unusual occurrences, it rained, and we got a good stand of pigweed, and that was the basis of a nurse crop. Later on we started to harvesting our own grass seed and made some plantings that proved quite successful as the years went on. Of course, I'm going over a period of development of maybe three or four or five years, and very quickly, but that was the start of the thing."

Early projects included recreation areas also, and Caserta recalls that he and Clancy Waneka went to the settlement of Hope, New Mexico, with a thousand dollars to spend for a recreational area:

"After spending the night with an old character by the name of White over in Hope, and getting up early the next morning and getting a pail of water out of the irrigation ditch, after moving the manure off the water surface, we got a pail of water and washed our face and hands. We didn't dare drink it. The only other available liquid there was bourbon whiskey or beer.

"We had a very fine breakfast with Mr. White. This was in July but we had deer meat. He called it 'summer beef.' Where he got it, I don't know, except that it was a delightful breakfast, grits and 'summer beef.' Well, Clancy and I decided it was about time to do something for those people. They couldn't afford to drink whiskey all the time, and there wasn't enough beer in the country, no ice to keep it cold, and hot beer is a very unpleasant beverage. We looked around and asked about water. Old Man White said, 'Yeah, there's a well around here; it's about 12 miles off. The thing's over a thousand feet deep.' Right away Clancy's eyes lit up. So did mine. We had a thousand dollars, and we were thinking very seriously of the possibility of the people at Hope gathering around a well and being able to talk, or sit down, and get a pitcherful of nice cool water—an unusual drink. I don't recommend it, but it is an unusual drink. So we decided that we would make a try for a water well. We talked to some local drillers and found out that water was available at about 800 or 900 feet, and there was a possibility that it would cost about a dollar a foot. That left us with enough money for possibly a windmill or a hand-pump, although I don't know who would've pumped a 1,000-foot-deep well by hand. But we were thinking that way. We were a couple of young squirts and just full of ideas. The only thing I think was successful about Hope was the water well. It did come in at about five gallons a minute. We were successful in convincing the Washington Office that this was a good expenditure of recreational funds. We got approval and put it in finally, and put in a couple of picnic tables which you could build for about $10 apiece in those days. In other words, we set Hope up.

"When we got back we found out that the magic wand of Congress had waved, and we had 10 million dollars to build dams with. Ten million dollars—that's a lot of money. So we started the dam projects, and incidentally in that deal such places as Tule Lake, Buffalo Lake, Lake Marvin, which the Forest Service still has; McClellan Lake, another Forest Service endeavor; Wolf Creek Lake, one over near Clovis which never did jell, but we had the money and did plan it. There's another one up by Dalhart, Rio Blanco Lake, and we had plans for about seven or eight more scattered around the Panhandle of Texas. The people we used in construction were largely from WPA. We had as many as 5,000 WPA men on our own payroll, BAE payroll, at one time working on these recreational projects, identified usually as lake projects.

"Now while this was going on, Norm Buck had other duties, too, that he was following up, the stabilization of wild lands. Have you ever been in a dust storm?" Then you know what wild lands are. The land takes off. Today it may have a cover of soil, silt, sandy land, from four to six feet deep. Tomorrow, after a good storm, it may not have any. It may be right down to where you can see the old plow furrows, where the plow point had cut in and left a little groove in the hardpan below. Well, this I saw. One of the places I saw that was Manhattan, Kansas. Clancy and I used to travel a lot together and that was one of our favorite places to visit. An old boy, George Atwood, was the Project Manager there. He had lost one of his hands, I imagine during World War I; he was an ex-soldier and quite a pleasant sort of fellow and an interesting man to meet. They had a dry summer when we went through Manhattan, Kansas, and alongside the river there was a cemetery. We bought cemeteries; we bought cities and towns. La Bajada is one of them, right out here close at hand in case you want a reference on that. Another one was up here near Mora, in the Indian lands south of Mora. But this one at Manhattan was unusual since the cemetery had a wrought-iron fence and swinging entrance gates, the posts of which were cast-iron and they had little round black balls on top of them. Well, the first time I visited the place, all I saw was about a foot of post and a black ball on top of the ground. Later on I went up to see what George was doing; he was always proud of the fact that on one side of the river he had Democrats, and on the other side he had Republicans, and the cemetery was on the Republican side and they had to wait until they had a dust storm to bury the Republicans and preserving those guys was really something.   I think it was two years before I made another visit with George. We drove through the gates of that cemetery.   It had been uncovered.   Those posts were fully six feet high; that much soil had moved in two years.

"That was the type of project that started the Land Utilization program that led toward completion of the developmental stages of the lands and placing them into management stages for utilization by the general public.   Six lakes were completed in 1939 and the early 1940's, and opened to the public for recreation use.

Buffalo Lake was dedicated in July, 1941, and Caserta recalls that Dr. H. H. Bennett, Chief of the Soil Conservation Service came out from Washington for the dedication, which attracted 50,000 people.

"He liked to sail," Caserta said.   "So that night after a little mosquito bite preventative and things like that, I had the honor of taking him for a sail in Howard Finnell's sailboat.   Doc Bennett was dressed in a silk hat and tails.   Caserta had on his very best— a tuxedo, which was all I could afford.   We got quite a kick out of it.   Doc wanted to stand up and walk from one end of the boat to the other, and I knew good and well if he did, he'd fall overboard, because it was all I could do to sit down and stay in the boat.   We finally made it back to shore and went back to the group again.   Doc never forgot that because on a future broadcast, some several months later, he mentioned the 50,000 people who came out to Buffalo Lake to watch him go sailing.   Actually, it was to dedicate the Lake, but Doc remembered the sailing I think more than the dedication."

World War II brought new problems and Caserta recalls that the LU program was able to furnish lands for bombing ranges and air fields and also "the longest runway in the world then was constructed at Dalhart out of caliche mined on the Rita Blanca Lake Project, right inside the city limits of Dalhart."

"Out of this mining operation on the LU Project," Caserta said, "we sold caliche to the Army's contractor for three cents a cubic yard—millions of yards."

During the war, development projects stopped.   Caserta explained that "you couldn't hire people to do development; you couldn't hire people to harvest."

There were hundreds of German prisoners of war in the Dalhart area, and thousands of Italian prisoners in the Buffalo Lake area, but government agencies could not use prisoners.   The prisoners could be used by the farmers, however.

Caserta recalls that there were some good wheat crops and that the pick and shovel drainage work by prisoners resulted in one of the finest wheat crops ever seen in that country.

After the war, Caserta said, "the stockmen wanted all this good grassland back into private ownership."

"We were just living from day to day, so to speak," he said. "We didn't know when some cowboy was going to ride up and say, 'This is mine, by an Act of Congress'—and it almost occurred several times.

"The cattlemen were quite anxious to get this land back, and they were told by their own counties, 'You can't have it. We're going to oppose you.'

"And that's the reason the LU Program has continued. We made a reputation, locally, of good land managers. Our policy of use of only the available grazing made sense to them. Our grazing was based on land, not on the number of head. Ours was an established preference for so many acres, and that was adjusted annually to what forage there was available. It's still a good premise to handle grazing. There's no use putting 1,000 cattle on a hundred sections if you can't raise 500 on it. It doesn't make sense. If it was capable of supporting 500, we ran 500. If it was 10, we ran 10. And they had no choice.

"Oil was found on much of the land, and of course the counties benefitted from the 25 percent in lieu of taxes. Our 25 percent was solely restricted to school and road funds.

"Our policy of use of only the available grazing made sense to them. Our fees, compared to National Forest fees, were exorbitant.

"When I left, we were getting a dollar and a half per animal unit a month for grazing. And of this, 25 percent went to the county. So they wanted us to be good land managers."

Hoyt Harvel went to work for the Soil Conservation Service in 1950 and spent 11 years on LU projects developing—or "attempting to develop" as he put it, the area that had been purchased by the government during dust bowl days.

One area had once been part of the land traded by the State of Texas to the XIT Ranch syndicate in return for building the capitol at Austin. Some of the land was sold off and sub-divided into smaller ranches and farms, and the sale of the land was promoted by real estate operators in the East.

"The cultivation started back there in about 1927 and 1928," Hoyt Harvel said, "and they did pretty good with their farming the first year and made a good crop. In 1929 they made a good crop and got a pretty fair price for the commodity produced. And

The dust storms of the 1930's forced this farmer to abandon his farm.   He lost 1200 acres of wheat.

Today, the National Grasslands, the former dust bowl lands, are again productive.

then the drouth hit, and at the same time the depression came on. The cash they got for their crops was very small. Production was very low. Along in the early 30's many of those people said, 'To hell with it!' and got up and left.

"When I say 'got up and left' that's exactly what I mean. There were several of those old farm homes that had dinner sitting on the table. When I went there you could still find old homes that had dishes and plates on the table and dried pinto beans that had been cooked and left sitting on the table. Syrup pitcher with the syrup long since turned to sugar still on the table. They'd moved out, went back to Missouri, Pennsylvania, or wherever they might have come from—and turned the farm back to whoever was holding the mortgage on the land. In many cases it was the Federal Land Bank, and in other cases it was life insurance companies."

Harvel said that he enjoys a "feeling of pride" to go back and see some of the old areas that were fields of sand ripples and see a good stand of side oats gramma, blue grass or switch grass "and cattle grazing all over the place."

"To go back now and see some of those places that I personally had a hand in developing, seeding and putting a fence around, putting windmills on it, and then writing a permit to so and so to put cattle on there, it does give you a feeling of accomplishment," he said.

Harvel said that in 1956 "we almost had another dust bowl." "I firmly believe," he went on, "that if we hadn't had so much of that country back in grass to break up strip cropping, we'd have had another dust bowl then. We had less rain that year than we did any time in the dust bowl years. And we had the wind. The only thing lacking in a dust bowl was bare ground, bare soil. That was what we had in the 30's—no stubble, nothing to hold it. It was dry and the wind always blows. So the three elements for a dust bowl were there in the 30's, whereas we had only two in '56— that was the wind and the drouth, lack of moisture. We did have something on the soil, something on the ground to hold it down."

The Grasslands came under the administration of the Southwestern Region of the Forest Service in 1953. They were managed as a part of the Cibola National Forest until 1960, when they became the Panhandle National Grasslands. Supervisor's headquarters were at Amarillo, Texas.

The Grasslands covered approximately 300,000 acres of rehabilitated lands that were once "dust bowls." From 1958 to 1970, there were five individual areas in the Panhandle National Grasslands: the Kiowa in eastern New Mexico; Rita Blanca, which lies across the border of Oklahoma and Texas; Black Kettle in Western Oklahoma, and the Cross Timbers and Caddo in North Texas.   In 1970 the administration of the Cross Timbers and Caddo was assumed by the Southern Region and the other Districts again became part of the Cibola National Forest.

The Grasslands are predominantly suited to grassland agriculture.   They are being managed and developed by the Forest Service on a multiple use basis to provide not only feed for thousands of cattle and wildlife but also to offer a variety of forms of recreation, such as picnicking, camping, swimming, boating, water skiing, fishing, and hunting.

A Ranger is in charge of managing each of the Grasslands for maximum utilization of resources in the public interest.   Rangers are stationed in Clayton, New Mexico; Cheyenne, Oklahoma; and Texline, Texas.

Forage is one of the most valuable crops produced on the Grasslands, and today more than 13,000 head of cattle owned by more than 360 local ranchers graze the Grasslands under paid permit.

Outdoor recreation is the fastest growing use on the Grasslands.   The big attractions are Lake McClellan, Lake Marvin, and Dead Indian Lake.   Camp and picnic grounds have been developed at these lakes and at other recreation areas.   Range and watershed improvements have enhanced wildlife habitat and the Grassland Districts are growing in popularity among hunters in search of big game—antelope, deer, Barbary sheep, turkey—as well as small game.

Thus the prairie land dust bowl has come back into production in a big way.

Southwestern National Forests

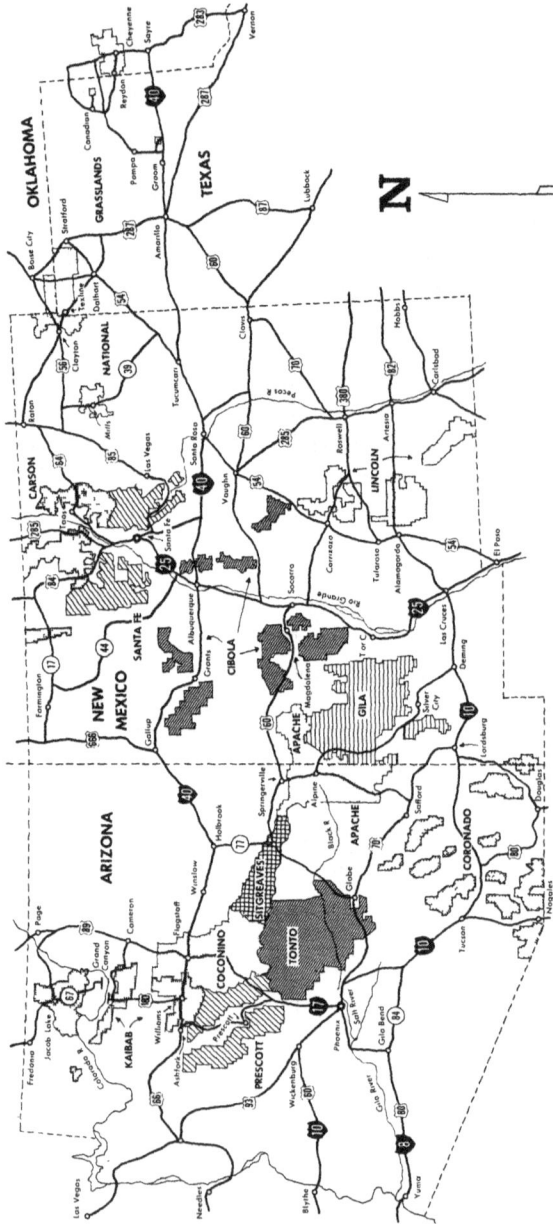

CHAPTER XVII
The National Forests of Arizona

Apache National Forest

John D. Guthrie had been Supervisor of the Apache Forest for only a short time back in 1909 when he and A. O. Waha made an inspection trip of the Forest. They were in Hog Canyon south of Fort Apache when night caught up with them, and they came upon the camp of a young cowboy. They had no equipment for overnight camping, so they asked the cowboy if they could stay with him.

"I didn't have anything but a tent," Benton Rogers, the cowboy, recalled nearly 60 years later. "I told them O.K., that I could stand it if they could. I had a blanket on back of the saddle. I told 'em I'd give 'a part of my bed, and we'd make it all right.' "

They stayed over night and shared breakfast with the cowboy. Before they left, Guthrie asked the cowboy how he liked his work. He told them he didn't like his present job too well.

"What do you think of the Forest Service?" Guthrie asked him.

"Never heard of it," the cowboy replied.

Guthrie explained and told him to write a letter applying for a position in the Forest Service and to be in Springerville a month later.

Benton Rogers did go to Springerville and he got a job as fire guard on the White Mountain Indian Reservation. That was the beginning of more than 30 years with the Forest Service, most of it as a Ranger on the Apache National Forest.

Back in those days most of Benton Rogers' work besides fighting fires was grazing permits. As the demand for lumber from a growing population expanded, the Apache National Forest began to supply that need.

Today, the pine, spruce and fir forests of the Apache are capable of providing an annual cut of 69,000,000 board feet of lumber on a sustained yield basis. The Apache also supplies pulpwood to the Southwest Forest Industries' paper mill at Snowflake. Seventy thousand cords per year are under contract for the next dozen years.

Timber is only one of the important resources of the Apache. This Forest encompasses some of the highest water-producing land in the state of Arizona—and the Forest is managed to produce the maximum possible amounts of usable water. A research project has been underway on Burro Mountain where different cutting practices are tried to determine their effect on water yield and on reestablishment of trees. Watershed erosion projects were also undertaken.

The Apache National Forest is host annually to more than 15,000 hunters and as many as 250,000 fishermen. Improved highways have made the Forest easily accessible and 10 times as many visitors are entering the Forest today as did 15 years ago. (The total for 1971 was more than 659,000 visitor days.) By 1973, it is estimated that the total of recreation visits will reach nearly a million, and the Apache crews are hard put to keep up with demands for recreation facilities.

The original industry—grazing—is still important, and more than 26,000 cattle and horses and 7,300 sheep graze under paid permit on the forest.

Part of the Apache National Forest extends into New Mexico, covering 616,160 acres in Catron County, to make the total acreage of the Apache 1,807,925 acres.

Coconino National Forest

One of the sharpest memories Fred Croxen has of his early years in the Forest Service was that 64-inch snow during the winter of 1915-16 at Flagstaff. It snowed for three days then cleared for a week and got down to 25 degrees below zero.

Today on the Coconino, snow is an important resource. Though they may not appreciate 25 degrees below zero, the winter sports people and the ranchers certainly appreciate those heavy snows that fall on the Coconino. The nationally-famous Arizona Snow Bowl attracts thousands of skiers and the facilities are heavily used throughout the winter.

Like the Apache, the Coconino provides an important annual harvest of timber on its nearly 2,000,000 arcres. Logging and mill operations have been a key factor in the economy of Flagstaff since before the turn of the century. Allowable timber cutting on a sustained yield basis is nearly 60,000,000 board feet. Actual timber cut has sometimes exceeded that figure and—depending upon demand—often fallen as low as 30,000,000 board feet. More than 10,000 sheep and 19,000 cattle and horses graze on the Forest under permit. The sale of logs and pulpwood and fees from grazing and special use bring in more than $300,000 a year—one fourth of which is returned to Coconino, Yavapai and Gila Counties.   And those special uses are varied and numerous—about a thousand special use permits in all, including such a myriad of uses as public schools, transmission lines, radio and television transmitters, observatories, rifle ranges, cemeteries, water developments, roads and highways, city parks.

Since 1957, the Forest Service has been operating the Beaver Creek pilot test watershed project, covering more than a quarter-million acres in the Coconino Forest.   The project is developing information on how to and how much it costs to effectively manage a watershed.   The project includes juniper removal, grass seeding, pine thinning and pruning, water measuring, and the relationship of watershed management to livestock grazing, wildlife management and to timber production.

Recreation knows no season on the Coconino, and nearly a million visitors each year enjoy camping, riding, hunting and fishing, skiing, and hiking.

Hiking is a popular recreation on the Coconino today, but Paul Roberts, reminiscing about his early days on the Coconino, recalled a time when hiking was just pure misery.

In 1912 he was with a horseback reconnaissance party, and one of the members of the party was Jim Sizer, an oldtime cowboy and wagon boss, who later became a Supervisor of the Apache National Forest (1922-25).

"I remember our first camp was out at Dead Man's tanks," Roberts related.   "Coming back, we were so heavily loaded that Sizer and I were walking.   I don't think Sizer had ever walked that far in his life.   We got to the top.   It was a fairly warm day, and old Jim sat down and leaned against a tree.   He had on a pair of heavy boots.   He looked down at his boots, and he groaned, 'By God, I'm about caught up on this walkin'.'   And he sure was."

Coronado National Forest

The Coronado National Forest is made up of a number of the old Forest Reserves, including the "sneeze-cough group": the Baboquivari, the Huachuca, the Tumacacori.   The other consolidations were the Dragoon National Forest and the Santa Rita and Santa Catalina Forest Reserves.

As a result of all these inclusions under one name, the Coronado is a group of "islands" in the desert of southeastern Arizona and about 70,000 acres extending over into Hidalgo County, New Mexico.   Lumped together they make a very sizeable 1,800,000-acre Forest.

When Gilbert Sykes started on the Catalina District as a fire lookout in 1919, the only access to the Catalinas was by the old Sabino Trail.

"Everything was packed up on a string of burros by the Maggie Pack Train," Sykes said. "All the supplies, all the furniture, everything up the mountains by pack train. There were some cabins up there then, not many. Groceries, everything went up by pack train. They charged 2½ cents a pound for packing things up.

"There really weren't any recreational facilities, no improved campground. Three or four years later they started a little layout just above Soldier Camp . . . called it a campground. They finally piped water down from Bear Wallow and that was the first recreational area laid out in the mountains."

Today with improved roads and a variety of recreational facilities available in the Santa Catalina Mountains, the Forest provides a popular playground for Tucson and visitors to southern Arizona. Other recreation developments have been undertaken in the Chiricahua Mountains, Madera Canyon in the Santa Rita Mountains, and various developments in the Graham Mountains. At the entrance to Sabino Canyon, fifteen miles from downtown Tucson, a new visitor center was built in 1963 to provide information for the more than one million annual visitors to the Coronado Forest. A self-guided nature trail showing plants in a desert watercourse was dedicated in Sabino Canyon. Explanatory signs and turnouts on the Hitchcock Highway which leads to Mt. Lemmon interpret the Forest terrain and geological formations.

Though outdoor recreation is the Coronado's fastest growing business, it is concerned with watershed rehabilitation, development of improved hunting and fishing, development of forage resources. Timber harvesting is confined to salvage of overmature, dead and dying trees since timber-growing sites on the Coronado are limited and in demand for recreation sites.

Where once there were only horseback or game trails, today there are more than 1400 miles of road system in the Coronado National Forest and about a thousand miles of trails. And where once Gilbert Sykes helped to build a single telephone line and where he used a heliograph to signal other Rangers, there are now 50 permits for radio and television electronic sites, and a hundred and forty miles of telephone and telegraph lines.

Prescott National Forest

J. R. Williams, whose syndicated cartoon "Out Our Way" was so popular in other years, operated the K4 Ranch on Walnut Creek during the 1930's. Jesse Fears, Ranger in charge of the Walnut Creek District, was a good friend of the cartoonist, and they often visited together.   Williams used the Prescott National Forest as the locale for many of his cartoons, featuring cowboys and Forest Rangers.

The Prescott National Forest is rich in history, for it surrounds the town of Prescott, which was the first Territorial Capital of Arizona.   Within and adjacent to the Forest are locations of old army outposts.   There are shafts and tunnels all over the Forest, dating from the years of the mining booms that started when gold was discovered on Lynx Creek in 1863.   Where once there were busy mining communities, today only a prospector or two remains.

The settlement of Prescott began during the Civil War when gold was discovered, and the need for sluice boxes was met by the miners who whipsawed logs into lumber.   In 1865 a portable sawmill was set up just south of the present city of Prescott to use logs from the Forest.   The Forest continued to supply wood in many forms for the mining industry throughout the territorial days of Arizona.   The Prescott National Forest is still supplying the wood needs of mining and a variety of other industries, including utility poles and railroad ties.   Two sawmills operate yearlong.

Because of the growing importance of recreation in the Forest, the Rangers are pretty choosey about where logs can be cut, even to selecting individual trees for cutting so as to preserve scenic values and to protect recreation sites.   More than 600,000 visitor days in the Prescott Forest are tallied each year, and it is estimated that in the 70's this will be a million visits.   The Prescott is particularly popular with residents of the Salt River Valley seeking relief from the heat during the summer in the cool million-and-a-quarter acres of Forest.

This part of Arizona has always been an important ranching area, and today the Prescott has grazing allotments supporting 15,400 cattle and horses.   Sheep driveways cross the Forest from winter to high summer ranges, and 28,000 sheep use the driveways.

The Prescott National Forest has had some bad fires—some of which were started by people and could have been prevented! In 1955, the Johnson fire burned 19,000 acres near Crown King, and the next year the Mingus Mountain fire burned 14,000 acres. The Battle fire in 1972 burned over 28,000 acres south of Prescott.   The Prescott has air tankers, based at Prescott Airport, which are used to cool down a fire or prevent it from spreading.   The tankers use a mixture of fire retarding chemicals and water to drop on fire areas.

Watershed management is an important part of Prescott Forest work since the Forest has few "live" or yearlong streams.

Watersheds that have eroded are being rehabilitated and two small areas are under continuing study as part of watershed management research.

Kaibab National Forest

The deer herd of the North Kaibab Division of the Kaibab National Forest has been famous since before the turn of the century. This was one of the favorite hunting areas of Teddy Roosevelt, and it is the favorite hunting ground of nearly six thousand hunters annually—more than half of whom get their deer.

In years gone by the deer herd had so multiplied that it was necessary to reduce the deer population by thousands upon thousands, for the herd had reached the point where many thousands were dying off from lack of forage. Today, as with the other forest resources, the deer herd is controlled scientifically to maintain a balance between numbers and the forage supply.

Timber harvesting is big business on the North Kaibab. Large scale operations began in 1942 and increased to 42 million board feet allowable cut.

Kaibab is an Indian word for "lying-down mountain." Indians believed that the high plateau north of the Grand Canyon was a mountain lying on its side.

The Kaibab National Forest is split into four sections. One surrounds the town of Williams, the second along the south side of Grand Canyon, and the third division, the North Kaibab, and the fourth a small isolated Forest area north of the Colorado River, west of the North Kaibab Division.

Recreation visits to the Kaibab have been increasing rapidly in the past few years and it has been estimated that the present 900,000 visitor days will reach a million by 1972 when there will be a total of 8 campgrounds.

The famous deer herd of the North Kaibab has overshadowed the deer herds south of the Grand Canyon, but there is also good hunting on the South Kaibab and the number of hunters has doubled in the past 10 years.

Arthur J. "Crawford" Riggs, of Santa Fe, spent five years as a Ranger on the North Kaibab beginning in 1937, and he recalls that when he first went there range conditions were just starting to come back after the big die-off and reduction of the deer herd. "You could still see the old deer line in the brush and trees, about four to six feet high," Riggs said. "I was there five years and when I left you could hardly see the deer line, which shows how fast, how quickly, the country can recuperate, when you reduce your grazing animals."

Scientific management of the available forage for wildlife and domestic animals has been a continuing process. During the eight-year period from 1954 to 1962, range technicians analyzed over 1,000,000 acres of Kaibab range land, and a management plan for more efficient use of 900,000 acres was developed with stockmen. This includes a rest-rotation stagger system so that forage is not subjected to grazing on all allotments during the growing season. Twelve thousand cattle and horses and 10,000 sheep are grazed on 58 allotments. The Forest Service works with the Arizona Game and Fish Department as well as with grazing permittees in order to keep deer breeding herds and cattle numbers in balance with the existing forage conditions.

Special use permits on the Forest include more than 100 public service facilities such as an airport, cemetery, reservoir, school, waterline, playground, resort and privately operated ski area near Williams.

Sitgreaves National Forest

Timber is big business on the Sitgreaves National Forest. The allowable annual cut of logs on a sustained yield basis is 56.2 million board feet.

The establishment of a pulpmill at Snowflake, on the edge of the Forest, was an important stimulant to the economy of Arizona and intensive forest management. The demand for pulpwood makes it economically feasible to thin out the young, dense, overcrowded stands of trees. This practice makes it possible to furnish pulpwood for the mill and speeds up the growth of the remaining crop trees.

Five timber operators, employing hundreds of men, and production of a variety of forest products make timber the most important business in the Sitgreaves area.

This area of eastern Arizona is still ranching country, too, but today with only 4,100 cattle and less than 15,000 sheep on Forest permits, the business is considerably smaller than in those days of overgrazing before the turn of the century and before the establishment of the National Forests. The old-time Sitgreaves Supervisor Paul Roberts recalled that one outfit once unloaded "28,000 cattle in one fell swoop in the spring of 1885, and that was enough to overstock a lot of range before they got them distributed around."

Today the 800,000-acre Forest range is supervised on a scientific range management basis to provide for proper stocking and maximum sustained forage production.

Timber management, too, is on a more scientific basis than

in the past.   Watershed rehabilitation, tree planting, grass seeding, *arroyo* stabilization, and erosion control all enter into timber management.   This is a far cry from the days nearly 50 years ago when Supervisor Roberts had to depend on ex-cowboys to mark trees preliminary to a sale.   His files reveal complaints to the Regional Office that he did not have a single technical forester on the Sitgreaves.

"When I look back and think of the technical advancements over the years, why you know it's just a doggone wonder that we did as well as we did in those early years," Roberts reminisced. "We know so much more now than we did then, technically, there's no comparison.   I hear a lot of old timers say, 'Well, these young fellows—they don't do as good a job as we did,' and a lot of that kind of stuff.   As a matter of fact they're probably doing ten times better job than we ever did.   Because they've got much more basic information and are much better trained, technically, before they ever get out of the schools.   They can't help but do a much better job.   So I think they ought to be given credit for it."

In Paul Roberts' day, the Sitgreaves Supervisor and Rangers weren't much concerned with recreations visits, but today recreation is an important part of the job.   Annual visits have increased tremendously to nearly 300,000, and it is anticipated this figure will be about 450,000 by 1972.   Campgrounds and picnic sites, water systems, parking areas, sanitation facilities have been installed to take care of the growing demand.   Fishing and hunting are attractions, too, and Forest personnel works closely with the Arizona Game and Fish Department in improving wildlife habitat to provide another annual crop for harvest.

Tonto National Forest

Back in 1935 when F. Lee Kirby was in his first year as Supervisor of the Tonto National Forest, he received an application for a strange request.   N. B. F. "Uncle Mac" McCord, a retired railroader, asked for about an eighth of an acre within the Forest for his final resting place.

Uncle Mac had already picked out the place—a high, lonesome spot on a granite knoll on the slope of Screwtail Hill, 45 miles from Phoenix.   "I don't want no damned lawn mowers running over my grave," Uncle Mac had told friends.

Supervisor Kirby had been in the Forest Service as fire guard and Ranger for more than 20 years and had a lot of experience dealing with the rugged individuals who had helped Arizona to grow into a great State.   He honored the request.

Uncle Mac wrote to thank him, saying: "After I locate there, I will not violate any of the regulations that are enumerated in the Permit. Thank you, it won't be long now."

Today a modern highway passes 100 yards from the lonely grave, and there for all to see is the crude inscription chiseled on a giant boulder: MACK'S REST.

That's probably the strangest special use permit that has been issued in the Tonto Forest, where about 900 special permits are in effect. The others cover such things as more than 300 miles of power lines, nearly 400 miles of roads, 28 radio and electronic sites, many miles of telephone line, a number of apiaries, and even a seismological station.

Because of its location a short distance from Phoenix, the Tonto is a favorite recreation area for residents and visitors to the Valley of the Sun. Recreation visits have jumped from half a million in 1955 to more than two million annually, with an estimate of 3,750,000 by 1973. As a result, planners are working on a $4 million program of recreation development during the present decade. Camps, picnic grounds (for a million picnickers), boat launching ramps, swimming beaches, and other recreation sites have been built. Visitor information programs have been launched and vista sites established.

The Tonto does not have as much timber available as other forests, but timber cutting is the main industry of the town of Payson and total annual cut has been as high as $18\frac{1}{2}$ million board feed. Pulpwood harvesting has also been possible to help supply the needs of the pulpwood mill at Snowflake.

In watershed management, the Tonto has an important role. There are six reservoirs of the Salt and Verde River drainages: Saguaro, Canyon, Apache, Roosevelt, Horseshoe and Bartlett Lakes, and the goal is to manage the watersheds to provide the maximum possible silt-free water for these reservoirs. The reservoirs do triple duty in providing year-long irrigation, domestic water, and water recreation in the desert.

This is still ranch country, and the largest number of livestock on any Forest in the Southwest—more than 42,000 cattle and horses and 11,268 sheep and goats are grazed on the Tonto— the largest of the National Forests in Arizona, with 2,886,185 acres.

CHAPTER XVIII
The National Forests in New Mexico *
Carson National Forest

There was a time when the nearly million-and-a-half acres of the Carson National Forest provided one of the great sheep-raising areas of the West. Thousands upon thousands of sheep were moved into the Forest for summer range. Back in the days when Aldo Leopold was Supervisor of the Carson Forest before World War I, the first steps were taken to reduce the number of sheep because of the heavy overgrazing. During World War I, the allowables were increased, and one large permittee alone was running 23,000 sheep on the forest. Bob Ground recalls that there were 52,000 on the San Antonio District alone. The present allowable on the whole Carson is 43,000 sheep (and goats) and 9700 cattle (and horses). These 43,000 sheep and 9700 cattle are owned by more than 500 ranchers, the largest number of permittees of any Forest in the Southwest.

The Carson also supports a wide variety of wildlife, including deer, elk, antelope, bear, turkey, and grouse. The largest elk herd in New Mexico grazes on the Carson.

The Forest is managed to supply adequate forage for both the wildlife and domestic animals without overgrazing and damaging the watershed.

An example of what can happen to a watershed was the Taos Canyon area, which was heavily cutover for timber. The Forest Service acquired the land and in 1955 began a program of rehabilitation.

The late Fred Miller, of Taos, whose career in the Forest Service spanned more than 40 years, once said that the greatest accomplishment of the Forest Service on the Carson Forest was the stopping of erosion in the high grazing areas.

"Just look at Taos Canyon," he said. I can remember when that was just a goat range. In fact, nothing but *arroyos* starting.

---

*The Apache and Coronado National Forests extend into New Mexico but these are described in the previous chapter on National Forests in Arizona.

But go up there now.   I happened to go up and help one of the ranchers here with his cattle in that particular area, and by golly, in a good year grass is belly-deep to a horse.   I can remember when it was good for nothing but goat pasture, with erosion and nothing else."

The Carson has been a good area for logging through the years and has an allowable annual cut of 30,000,000 board feet. But the fastest growing business of the Carson is recreation. Spectacular scenery, cool summer climate, fabulous hunting and fishing, and deep snow for winter sports provide outstanding opportunities for recreation.   Today, summer resorts that used to close on Labor Day or right after the hunting season now stay open all year long to provide facilities for winter as well as summer visitors.   Snowmobiling is the new winter sport attracting thousands of winter sports fans to the Carson area, while skiing continues to grow in popularity beyond all estimates of a few years ago.

At the edge of the Carson National Forest northwest of Abiquiu on U. S. 84 is Beaver National Forest, the smallest National Forest in the world.   This Forest in miniature covers $1\frac{1}{4}$ acres at the famous Ghost Ranch Museum.   It is man-made, developed by the Charles Lathrop Pack Forestry Foundation with the aid of the Forest Service.

In 1970 the museum was transferred to the Forest Service by the Pack Foundation to ensure continuation of the facility as a source of public enjoyment and information on the flora, fauna, and geology of the area and proper multiple use management of forests and rangelands.

The tiny Forest within the museum, using half-scale models, demonstrates the use being made of the recreation, water, timber, forage, wildlife, and fish resources of the National Forests.   The figures inhabiting the Forest include cattle, sheep, deer, turkey, quail, duck, and people enjoying a family outing.   There also is a fire tower with a lookout on duty and two loggers are busy cutting down a tree.

Cibola National Forest

Reminiscing about his long years as Supervisor of the Cibola National Forest (1949-63), F. J. (Jim) Monighan decided that one of his biggest jobs (and perhaps the biggest headache) on the Cibola is "recreation on the Sandias and part of the Manzanos."

"There are hundreds of thousands of people that go to the Sandias every year for picnics and for overnight camping," he said. "Just to keep the areas maintained and cleaned up, and everyone happy, is quite a job for both the Supervisor's staff and the Rangers. It seems as if we were just maintaining and rebuilding recreation areas in the Sandias all the time."

Providing recreation facilities on the Sandias and other parts of the Cibola will be a continuing task for the Forest Service, for the number of recreation visits is increasing each year. The number jumped from 82,000 in 1943 to half a million in 1968.

But as big as recreation is, this is only a small part of the Forest Service's job on the Cibola. There's timber harvest and grassland and mountain pasture grazing, watershed rehabilitation, game and fish improvement work, and roads and trails construction.

The Cibola, like the Coronado, is a collection of scattered forest islands extending over a wide area of western and central New Mexico—more than a million and a half acres in ten separated sections of forest.

The Cibola National Forest is on both sides of the Rio Grande, and the headwaters of both the Rio Puerco and the Rio Salado are within the Forest—which makes watershed management an important activity. The Cibola undertook its first watershed project—the Bernalillo Watershed Project—on the northwest slopes of the Sandia Mountains in 1954. The pilot project was designed to protect the community of Bernalillo from floods which occurred every time a major storm struck the mountain slopes. The check dams, planting, and re-establishment of vegetative cover provided the protection that Bernalillo now enjoys.

As a result of this pilot project, watershed projects were undertaken in the San Mateo Mountains and several thousand acres of rangeland were successfully treated and stabilized for intensive grazing management. Additional projects are being undertaken as the forest management plan for the Cibola progresses.

The grasslands and mountain pastures of the Cibola have been grazed since the days of the Spanish *conquistadores*—and, unfortunately, many thousands of acres were overgrazed so that today there are still scars of early-day, unmanaged grazing.

Part of the Cibola's activity today seeks to heal and erase the old scars and restore the waist-high seas of grass that the historians have described. Present forage availability limits the number of cattle and horses to 17,000 and sheep and goats to 11,600.

Because of its central New Mexico location, the Cibola has an unusual variety of special use permits, including television transmitters atop Sandia Crest, telephone microwave stations, military, state, and commercial radio networks, power lines, and oil and gas pipelines, and a tramway.

The Gila National Forest

Zane Smith's introduction to the Forest Service in the 1920's was a three-day fire training session on Hillsboro Peak, and then helping to install some lightning protection on the old wooden lookout at Diamond Peak where he was to be stationed for the summer.

"We were having some dry lightning storms," Smith recalled. "There was no lightning even close; otherwise I would have left the tower and gone down into the cabin as we were instructed to do as a protective measure. All of a sudden a bolt of lightning struck the tower and burned big black strips down the legs where the copper wire was located, knocked the phone out and blinded me for about 30 minutes. It was tremendous white light and it just left me blinded. I couldn't see, and it just about scared me to death. I went down to the cabin, and I was still pretty scared. The lightning hit a big old fir tree right back of the cabin and knocked a huge slab off. This slab bounced over and hit the back of this log cabin. On the inside, we had an apple box tacked up there in which we kept our tin dishes, tin cups and so forth. All the tinware fell off on the floor, and the rattle and tremendous crash of thunder just about spooked me off the mountain. I almost quit the Forest Service and ended my career right there. Actually I wasn't hurt, and I'm sure my safety was due to the fact we had installed this lightning protection."

Smith did not quit the Forest Service that summer. He went on to a distinguished career. And the Forest Service went on to develop new and more effective methods of combating fire danger.

Lightning caused many of the fires on the Gila Forest in past years and still does today. Dangerous, explosive conditions can develop in the Forest during the dry season.

A series of disastrous fires burned 56,000 acres in 1951, 10,000 acres in 1953, and 11,000 acres in 1956.

To combat the high fire danger, the Gila now seasonally employs, in addition to its trained lookouts and ground attack crews, all the modern air attack methods available, including aerial observers; smokejumpers; helitack crews, who are trained firemen transported by helicopter; tanker aircraft carrying fire retardants; and aircraft equipped to drop fire-fighting equipment, food, and water by parachute to firefighters in remote wilderness and primitive areas. With this multipronged attack, fires on the Gila are now being kept to a minimum. And while lightning still causes fires, the record indicates that most disastrous fires on the Gila were those caused by careless or unthinking people.

The largest of the National Forests in New Mexico, the Gila

covers a total of 2,701,614 acres—an area twice the size of the State of Delaware.

Because it is not as close to large centers of population as other Forests in the Southwest, not as many recreation seekers were using the Gila resources in past years as visited in other Forests. That situation is beginning to change. Sightseers, especially, are attracted to the Gila for its great variety of attractions: the Gila Cliff Dwellings National Monument, now accessible by paved road; other Indian ruins, mountain streams and fishing lakes; a growing number of camp and picnic sites; wilderness areas; and scenic loop roads out from Silver City, headquarters of the Gila. Annual visitor days are estimated at nearly 600,000.

The Gila National Forest surrounds the Black Range and Gila Primitive Areas and Gila Wilderness. (These are discussed in another chapter). With so much game habitat, the Gila is a big attraction for hunters. More than 20,000 are tallied on the Gila and about one in five gets a deer. A few are lucky enough to get an elk or a bear.

The Gila has been ranching country for a hundred years and about 160 ranchers now run 29,394 cattle on the Forest under grazing permit. As with other Forests, the Gila is working under a range management plan to provide additional forage whenever possible. Stabilization of key watersheds is underway, and the Gila is also engaged in a one-year road and trail construction and reconstruction program.

Lincoln National Forest

The Lincoln National Forest is Smokey Bear country. This was the Forest where Smokey, the living image of the Forest Service Fire Prevention Poster Bear, was rescued—badly burned and clinging to a tree during the Capitan Gap fire of 1950.

Probably to many who see the fire prevention posters, Smokey is only a picture. But to the people of Capitan and the Lincoln Forest country, Smokey is real, for they remember the fire that burned 17,000 acres, and they can still see the scars in the Forest from the tragic carelessness of someone throwing a cigarette or match from a car window. They remember, too, that human carelessness provided the spark for the fire that devoured 25,000 acres in four hours in 1953.

At Capitan there is a museum dedicated to Smokey. The fire lookout tower which first spotted the Capitan Gap fire is Smokey Bear Lookout.

The Lincoln National Forest is a high fire danger area because of weather conditions resulting from hot, dry winds from the Pecos River Valley and Tularosa Basin, so there is a constant alert to "hit 'em fast and keep 'em small" when a fire is reported. The Lincoln Forest has the benefit of the Mescalero Red Hats from their neighboring reservation and the closeby military firefighting crews of Holloman Air Force Base and Fort Bliss, Texas.

The population growth of Alamogordo, El Paso, Texas and the Pecos Valley of eastern New Mexico has had a heavy impact on recreation use of the Lincoln.   Back in 1958, it was estimated that less than 300,000 persons visited the Forest that year.   The figure has jumped to more than a million.

Besides the construction of facilities to take care of this influx of both summer and winter visitors, the Lincoln is concerned with the usual problems of forest management: harvest of timber, improved forage for wildlife and domestic animals, watershed management and rehabilitation work, road and trail building.

The Lincoln is one of the best big game hunting areas in the state and is improving fish habitat, with the result it attracts nearly a hundred thousand hunters and fishermen each year.   The annual deer harvest averages 11,500 animals.   Two hundred and seven permittees graze 11,870 cattle and horses and 2254 sheep and goats on Lincoln allotments.

The Lincoln has some rather unusual special use permits in effect, including the Sierra Blanca Winter Sports area, operated by the Mescalero Apaches; the SAC Peak Solar Observatory, White Sands Missile Range, Alamo Lookout Radar Tracking Facility, 205 oil and gas leases, 217 miles of powerlines and a number of organization camps in the Forest.

The Santa Fe National Forest

The Santa Fe National Forest is "high country."   Here are located the 13,000-foot high peaks of the Truchas and the sister peaks that give birth to the headwaters of the Pecos, part of the Rio Grande, and the Red River.

When Frank Andrews was supervisor of the Santa Fe National Forest in 1942, it was his proud boast that "the Pecos area ranks high among the attractions supporting the tourist industry, which has been one of the leading industries of New Mexico."

The Pecos River Forest Reserve was one of the first set aside in the United States, and in 1942 Frank Andrews could write that "the Pecos Forest area has changed little with the passing of years, even though many changes have come about in Forest administration.   True, here and there is a fire lookout tower, or a Forest Service telephone line.   The old wagon road up Pecos Canyon has been improved by the Forest Service into a good motor highway.

The Forest Ranger of today has a sturdy pick-up truck for travel where roads are available. But he still needs a trailer behind the truck to carry his horse and equipment for riding on after the road ends. . . . The Pecos highway, in fact, still ends at Cowles. The trails that Stewart and other early Rangers blazed have been improved, but they mainly follow the same routes. There is still practically as much wilderness land here as in the early days."

Much of what Andrews wrote 30 years ago still holds true today—and the appeal of the Pecos high country, with its fishing, hunting, hiking the high trails, picnicking and camping are even stronger attractions.

The impact of population increase has changed directions for the Forest Service in the Santa Fe National Forest as it has with others. While there is still great activity in timber and grazing, there is big emphasis on recreation. Total recreation visits to the Santa Fe now approach a half-million a year, and this will probably go to a million in the 1970's. More miles of trails to open up more of the back country are being built each year.

Where once there was recreation activity only in summer and during the hunting season, now it extends into winter. The Santa Fe Ski Basin, for example, brings thousands of visitors to New Mexico from Thanksgiving until Easter.

The eight major campgrounds that existed in Frank Andrews' time were expanded to 16 by 1963, and the demand for more led to a program of planning at least two additional campgrounds each year.

The Santa Fe National Forest vies with the Lincoln in offering the best hunting conditions in the State. More than 50,000 hunters are in the Forest during the hunting seasons, and more than twice that many fishermen enjoy the sport on the lakes and streams of the Santa Fe.

While much is being done to improve recreation facilities, the revenue-producing activities of timber cutting and grazing are still big business. In the 1968-69 fiscal year, 47,768,000 board feet of lumber were sold, with a value of $660,018.15. The annual allowable cut on the Santa Fe is 41,000,000 board feet.

Grazing is still important, too, with 9,800 cattle and horses but fewer than a thousand sheep under permit on the Forest. Like the Carson, the Santa Fe has a high number of permittees grazing small numbers of livestock. In all there are 422 permittees. The Santa Fe is the only other Forest besides the Carson, which has more than 400 permittees.

CHAPTER XIX
Lost Mines and Buried Treasure

Perhaps the two most famous "lost mines" in the Southwest are the Adams Diggings in New Mexico and the Lost Dutchman mine in the Superstition Mountains of Arizona.

Men have been looking for the lost Adams Diggings since the 1870s. Some place in the vast area of the Gila or Apache National Forests—or perhaps even in the Cibola—is the vast wealth in gold nuggets that Adams found and then lost because he could not find his way back to the mine.

And in Arizona, the Lost Dutchman mine still defies searchers as it has for nearly 90 years. When Jacob Waltz died in 1881 in Phoenix, the secret of the location of his mine died with him.

In his roamings of the Gila Forest, Ranger Henry Woodrow did a lot of looking for the Adams Diggings in the more than 30 years that he was a Ranger on the McKenna District. Woodrow, in a paper he wrote after his retirement in 1942, said that a fellow named Horn Silver Bill (William P. Dorsey of Silver City) "came by the Gila and wanted me to go with him up into the mountains at the head of Mogollon Creek to look for the Adams Diggings. I spent some time looking for it myself and did not find it, so it can stay lost now, as far as I'm concerned."

Gilbert Sykes was for nearly 30 years a Ranger on the Coronado Forest—23 of those years on the Nogales District. This is an area where there are numerous mines and mining claims—"quite a few patented claims, and an awful bunch of unpatented claims," as Sykes put it.

When the uranium boom started in the Southwest "the mountains were alive with wide-eyed weekend prospectors," Sykes related, "and they would argue and squabble over their claims and want you to referee their battles."

"Then the Tumacacori Mission treasure down there was another thing we had lots of fun with," Sykes went on. "Right to this day there are two or three fellows out there hunting for the treasure. They have dug in numerous places. I had a regular treasure hunting clientele all the time. One old chap there in the main canyon, Pack Canyon, has been in there for about 14 or 15 years.   He's getting up in years, he's over seventy now.   I guess he has moved 250 or 300 tons of rock by himself since he's been there.   He's down in the bottom of one of these natural rock slides and he's decided the treasure is buried in under that.   He decided the rocks were put there by man.   Of course these natural rock slides are in numerous places all through the mountains there, and you see them in lots of other places.   If a rock is too big for him to load into his little ore car and wheel to the edge of the bank and dump over the hillside down into the canyon, he drills and shoots it. He shot several times when the ranchers would be riding down below.   All of a sudden a blast would go and a shower of rocks, and it took years to train him to yell 'fire' before he shoots.   Four or five of those rock slides I know treasure hunters have been digging in.   They file a mining claim and will get just enough color sometimes to hold their mining claim.   You know there is mineral pretty well all through the country there of one sort or another. They can get away with a mining claim when actually they are treasure hunting.

"After they get to know you they will break down and tell you.   'Well, I'm doing some mining there, yes, but I think we might find something else also.'   Of course I don't know that there ever was any Tumacacori treasure, but they have the old story down in the records at Tumacacori.   If you take the article and follow it out with a protractor and trace the lines out and bear west so many steps or yards or whatever they call for and then go east, you trace it out and you come back almost to the place you started from, following this yarn.

"Some of them have spent thousands and thousands of dollars there.   One old camp is up off the side canyon coming into Peck Canyon.   Mrs. Shipley operated there for several years.   She got thousands of dollars put up by two or three profs from the University here and a doctor or two and others, and she was excavating there.   She even had a machine gun set up at one time to guard this 'valuable treasure.'   Two of the fellows that were her bodyguards are still in Nogales; one is a contractor and the other got to be deputy sheriff in Nogales.   She sold a lot of stock in this venture.   There was all sorts of digging there.   In one place she had an inclined shaft.   One of the old ranchers there told me that one of the workers she had one time was a wetback from across the line. He was down in this precarious shaft digging for the treasure that was supposed to be down there and it caved in on him and killed him.   While no one knew particularly that he was a wetback from across the line, there was no better place to bury him, so he is still down in the shaft.   It caved in and that's that.   We called that

Camp Loco.   She hired a pack horse from this rancher, for several seasons. He ranted her a kind of an old sway-backed horse that wasn't much good for anything else.   She would tell prospective bait that he had got sway-backed from carrying out silver bars. Finally she got hold of some stationery of the Treasurer of the United States and faked some correspondence on that—I don't know just what—'your shipment of bullion had been received and the approximate valuation was so much and the exact valuation would be sent to her shortly.' She passed this around and they picked her up on that charge—doing things she shouldn't have done.   They sent her up but she came back after a while and went to operating again.   She finally moved over to the Coast and committed suicide.   That was the end of that.   She was quite a gal."

Zane Smith left a lot of "buried treasure" on the Verde District when he was transferred out of there in 1940.   Telling about a local stockman and lion hunter, Nick Perkins, Smith said that he had made a lot of interesting trips with Perkins, who liked to prowl around old Indian ruins.

"This Sycamore Wilderness country was full of old Indian ruins," Smith related.   "We'd usually stop and have our sandwiches in the middle of the day somewhere where we could prowl around the old ruins and pick some arrowheads and that sort of thing.   I found a number of old *metates* in that country that I never quite got out.   I always wanted to bring one out, but they were too heavy to carry, and I never seemed to find one when I had a pack animal with me.   I would cache them around a tree or a rock butte or something, hoping one day I'd pick up one.   So I guess the 10 or 12 *metates* that I cached away maybe are still back there."

Nick had a few treasures cached away, too, according to Smith, as he discovered on trips with him.   He recalled one trip and a particularly hard day back into the mountains.

"It was away into night when we got the horses taken care of," Smith said.   "There was a sort of overhanging cliff that Nick camped under occasionally, particularly if it was bad weather.   He always had a little firewood gathered up there and sometimes had a sack of salt or something hung up.   In the summertime, he might even keep a few cans of vegetables or canned meats so he wouldn't have to pack so much food in.   Anyway, we'd had a real rough day and way into the night, and the next morning it was frosty. Nick crawled out of bed before I got fully awake, and built a fire. Then I heard him rustling around in one of the kyacks and could hear plates and tin cups rattling, and pretty soon I heard Nick at my bedside.   I threw back my tarp, and here was Nick with a tin cup and a bottle of Old Yellowstone that he cached away, over in

the rocks.   He thought that would be a good way to wake me up
and get me out of bed.

"I'll never forget old Nick and his bottles of Yellowstone that
he cached away at almost all of his more favored camp spots—
all the way back through the Sycamore Wilderness there.   He
never drank much that I ever saw, but he would have a little short
nip of a morning to wake up."

Sam Servis has a story about buried treasure, too, but this
time it's a buried church bell:

"In the early days there was a young couple at Deming who
decided to spend their honeymoon fishing on the West Fork off the
Gila.   They came up to the West Fork and the fishing wasn't too
good so they took the zigzag trail that dropped off to the meadows,
and fished the Middle Fork for a while.   Coming back up the trail,
a rain storm struck them and they got turned around and lost.   In
wandering around there, they came upon some rocks and *adobe*
ruins that might resemble a church.   This fellow went over there
and dug under what would have been the place for the altar, and
I'll be darned if he didn't find two bells, both mounted in silver.
Two sizes, a small one and a large one.   Well, they started packing
them, but the large one got too heavy, so they buried it beside the
zigzag trail.   Apparently it was buried between the top of the hill
and Big Bear Canyon, or even in Big Bear.   Anyway, they carried
the little bell out, and it was on display in a bank in Deming for
many, many years.   The bank burned down and the silver melted
off, so it isn't in good condition today, that is, there isn't too much
silver on it.

"That woman who was the bride is now in her eighties, and
you know as you grow older you don't remember too well.   She
can't remember exactly the description of the area where that bell
is buried.   They had always meant to go back and get it but they
never got around to it.   There is a silver mounted bell buried
somewhere between the zigzag and the trail, dropping off to the
meadows, and there's also a ruin up there that I would like to find,
because there may be more.   That's all they took time to do, was
just to scratch around and they found it just under the surface, so
maybe there's more."

Servis recalls that there were a couple of easterners who did
find Eldorado:

"They were looking for a place to start mining and came to
Magdalena.   A bartender just stepped outside the door and
pointed toward a little hill outside Magdalena.   He said, 'Well,
boys, you just go out there and dig.   There's lots of ore in that hill.'

"So the boys immediately bought some supplies and went out

—it's a couple miles from town—and went to digging like fools. Of course, the people sat around and laughed at them. Be darned if they didn't strike silver and take $80,000 worth of dough out of there. Oh, my Lord, those people never told anybody else where to go and mine!"

The greatest treasure in the Forest is the Forests themselves! The annual income from the National Forests of the Southwest exceeds several million dollars a year.* This money comes from many sources, but chiefly from timber and grazing fees. Carson National Forest has revenue from producing oil wells and potential for more. There has been active leasing also on two other Forests, the Sitgreaves and Coconino; and the underground wealth in minerals has probably only been sampled. There is no way to estimate the tremendous value of the treasure that the Forests hold for the future.

---

*Twenty-five percent of this money is returned to the counties in which the National Forests are located. Ten percent is returned to the Forests for roads and trails within the Forests.

CHAPTER XX
Ah Wilderness!

Wilderness has magic in the very sound of the word, though it may mean many things to many people. It may be the poet's enjoyment of the quiet beauty, the artist's fascination with the colors of autumn, the hunter's excitement of stalking the trophies of the Forest, or the sightseer's delight over spectacular vistas. Whatever the magnet, there is strong empathy between man and wilderness.

As urban populations continue to swallow-up the greenery of the countryside, the importance of the existence of areas of unspoiled forests untouched by the inroads of modern civilization becomes all too apparent.

The pioneers of the Forest Service in the Southwest were men of vision. The technical forester had been trained to think in terms of years and decades, not merely days and weeks. They early saw the advantages of setting aside areas of the forest that would remain for all time in their primitive state, where no roads would be built, no trees cut, no mechanized equipment permitted. Such areas would be control plots in the forest for watershed protection for research and study and a tremendous recreation resource for those seeking solitude and refreshment of the soul away from the clangor and trappings of modern civilization.

Ward Shepard, who in 1914-15 had been a Ranger on the Gila National Forest when his District was part of the then-named Datil National Forest and who later served in the Regional Office was one of the first along with Aldo Leopold, the famous conservationist, to argue for setting aside wildernesses. They convinced John D. Jones, Chief of Lands of the Regional Office in the early 1920's, that an area in the Gila Forest should be set aside as a Wilderness.

"As Chief of Lands," Jones recalled, "I wrote the first plan— you might say the first limitations of what we would do. Ray Marsh signed it with me as Chief of Forest Management. It was about a paragraph and a half long. We made it fairly simple because we didn't know just how far we could go, so we left it so it could be amended later on. It was the first thing that was ever written in this Region, officially, on Wilderness areas.   Leopold was always arguing for it, but Shepard was just as much in it as he was."

The first area of Wilderness in the Gila National Forest, the first in the Nation, was officially set aside by the Region in 1924. From that beginning evolved a National Forest Wilderness System comprising over 14 million acres in 73 National Forests.

In the Southwest—Region 3—there are now 1,669,535 acres within 16 wildernesses and Primitive Areas on 10 National Forests. Sixty percent of the Wilderness acreage is in New Mexico, the balance in Arizona.

Besides the Wildernesses, there were also Primitive Areas set aside by the Secretary of Agriculture in special recognition of their unique qualities and for further study for possible inclusion in the National Wilderness Preservation System.*

Recognizing the need and desirability of perpetuating Wildernesses, the Congress in 1964 adopted the Wilderness Act, setting up the National Wilderness Preservation System.

The Wilderness Act spells out the design of the Wilderness "in contrast to those areas where man and his own works dominate the landscape is hereby recognized as an area where the earth and its community of life are untrammeled by man, where man himself is a visitor who does not remain."

It is further defined to mean "an area of undeveloped Federal land retaining its primeval character and influence, without permanent improvements or human habitation, which is protected and managed so as to preserve its natural condition and which (1) generally apears to have been affected primarily by the forces of nature, with the imprint of man's work substantially unnoticeable; (2) has outstanding opportunities for solitude or a primitive and unconfined type of recreation; (3) has at least 5,000 acres of land or is of sufficient size to make practicable its preservation and use in an unimpaired condition; and (4) may also contain ecological, geological, or other features of scientific, educational, scenic or historical value."

The Southwestern Region Wildernesses that have been formally designated under the Wilderness Act are the Chiricahua, Galiuro, Mazatzal, Mount Baldy, Pine Mountain, Sycamore Canyon, Sierra Ancha and Superstition in Arizona, and the Gila, Pecos, San Pedro Parks, Wheeler Peak and White Mountain Wildernesses in New Mexico.

More than a quarter million visitors to the Wildernesses indi-

---

*These are discussed in a later chapter.

Gila Wilderness, Gila National Forest, was established by the Forest Service in 1924.

The colorful Sycamore Canyon Wilderness on the Prescott, Coconino, and Kaibab National Forests is sometimes called the "Little Grand Canyon."

Riders in the high country of the Pecos Wilderness, Santa Fe and Carson National Forests.

cate their popularity in the Southwest.   But such popularity also poses problems.

A report by the Region 3 Office notes that a Wilderness "can properly accommodate only so much recreation use without damage."   It goes on: "Uses and values vary among parts of an individual wilderness.   There are wide differences in vegetative types and wildlife.   Patterns of use, local customs, traditional attitudes of users and interested nonusers also differ.   Consequently, acceptable uses and management practices necessary on one National Forest Wilderness are not always necessary on another.

"Wilderness values cannot be measured by the number of people who actually visit an area.   Wilderness is a resource which can be destroyed.   It has a capacity.   It need not be used to realize its benefits."

The Pecos Wilderness, which was the second one to be established in New Mexico, has gained great popularity in recent years.

In the past several years the Forest Service has had an intensive program to survey trail construction, rehabilitation and maintenance needs in the Pecos Wilderness.   This has resulted in an improved trail system for safer, more enjoyable hiking, pack tripping and trail riding.

A. J. Riggs was a Ranger on several Districts in the Gila Forest, and when the Wilderness District assignment opened up in 1949, he asked to be transferred there.

"I think I enjoyed the Wilderness District as much as any, even though I did have some bad fires there," Riggs said.   "It was wonderful country to be in during the summer time—wonderful country to hunt in, and fish if you were a fisherman."

Long-time career man Zane Smith credits Henry Woodrow with the fine system of trails that existed in the Gila Wilderness country.

"He was quite a colorful character—one of the most colorful old-time Rangers the Southwest ever had," Smith said.

"He had the adjoining District to the Mimbres, on which I was located, and my lookout served a lot of his country.   At least, it overlapped with lookouts that were on his District, and some of his country was blind except to my particular lookout.   Henry had lots of fires.   He was a pretty rugged, self-sufficient individual and he didn't call for help.   He took his little trail crews and he put 'em out.   They used to call up Henry because the lookouts would be reporting in that smokes were boiling up.   They'd ask Henry if he needed any help.   We'd have to make a special damage report on any fire that exceeded 10 acres.   It was kind of a joke around the Gila that Henry Woodrow never had fire over nine acres in extent.

"I remember how effective Henry could be sometimes in handling situations. It was contrary to the usual practice, but for some reason or other, it was a stepson of Henry's that was employed on one of his lookouts up there. I guess it was at a time when help was pretty hard to get. They were probably pressed to get someone who knew the country. This fellow, named Bob, was certainly an excellent woodsman, knew that country well, and was employed by Henry on Granite Peak. The lookout tower was about a mile from the cabin. Bob rode up to the lookout each morning and stayed until sundown, then rode back to his cabin. Henry became a little suspicious that Bob wasn't handling his job according to instructions. One morning when he gave the test call, which was a particular ring on the old grounded telephone line that connected all the lookouts and all the stations in the Mogollon Mountains, why he checked off each lookout very carefully. When he got all through, Bob checked in properly for Granite Peak lookout. Henry said, 'Bob, are you up in the tower?' Bob said, 'Sure.' Henry said, 'That's funny, I am too.'"

Henry Woodrow's reports were as laconic and to the point as his speech. "During the year 1909 about all I could do in the way of trail work was to blaze a trail up to Mogollon Baldy and down Mogollon Creek," he wrote, "cut out a log here and there in box canyons where I had to get through."

His report for each year showed new trails built or old ones undergoing maintenance work, as for example in 1915: "I hired a crew of men and started trail work at head of Little Creek—followed down Big Turkey Creek to a point one mile above Bear Moore Cave, then turned out across ridge to Miller Springs and over Granny Mountain to Gila River, two miles above Sapillo Creek, then down to Sapillo and out across ridges to the Davidson sawmill."

Woodrow remained on his Wilderness District until 1942 and his reports show trail work each year, even the last year when he reported that "We went into White Creek and got a trail crew started on some of the trails to get them opened up for the fire season."

Today the work that Henry Woodrow did is a major part of the Gila Wilderness trail system and something of a monument to a pioneer Ranger.

The Pecos Wilderness, which used to attract a few hundred people annually, recorded 58,600 visitor days of use in 1971—hikers, campers and trail riders. Perhaps the most famous who went in was Greer Garson, the motion picture star, who hiked to Hamilton Mesa.

A new Forest Service employee in the Wildernesses is the "wilderness contact," whose job is just what the title implies. Craig Nordyke, formerly of the Pecos, is typical. He rides the trails all summer long, stops to visit with hikers and campers, accompanies trail rider groups, answers questions, gives nature talks, and generally keeps track of what is going on in the Wilderness, and keeps in touch by radio with Ranger headquarters.

CHAPTER XXI
Recreation

The figures aren't in yet, but it would be a good bet that the total estimate of visitors to the National Forests in the Southwest during the next 10 years will be up above twenty million. The figure couldn't be far off because the total of the 1971 season was 11,677,900 visitor days.

This is quite a contrast to the years when visitors were counted in thousands instead of millions.

Recreation is the fastest growing business of the Forest Service. It is also a much more recent activity. In the early years of the Forest Service, fire protection, grazing and timber sales were the principal work loads.

M. M. Cheney, for many years in the Legal and Lands Divisions of the Region 3 office, remembers when the first *national* appropriation for recreation was made. It was $15,000. Today many times that much might be spent on a single campground. The cost of maintenance and clean-up alone for the Southwestern Region recreation areas runs into hundreds of thousands of dollars.

John D. Jones was Chief of Lands in the 1920's, and he has recalled that he helped lay out most of the early recreation areas in the Southwest.

"Mr. Burrel and I laid out the areas on top of the Catalinas and out in the Santa Ritas, and some of them down on Oak Creek, and all of these up here on the Sandias and the Pecos," Jones recounted. "I made the first recreation plan for the Region, an outline for working out the basis of laying out lots. I didn't agree with laying out lots like city lots, in squares. My idea was to stake out the location that you wanted to put the house in and then—the expression I used was, 'wrap the lot around it,' so they'd have a reasonable amount of privacy from the adjoining area. And that was the system we used. We didn't follow the regular rectangular lots. I didn't think they were practical. And we encouraged people to chop as few trees as possible. The habit of most people was to trim as high as your eye, then when you sat down there was no privacy. You could just see through the whole area. So we always tried to encourage people to leave the shrubbery and just clear what was needed around the place itself.

"There was very little known about recreation layouts in those days. I used to correspond with Dr. Francis of Syracuse University, who wrote a few items on it real early. Outside of that, he was about the only person working on it besides myself. I made a trip to Montana; I made a trip to Los Angeles and covered that famous area in the mountains north of Los Angeles, which everybody was bragging on, and when I saw them, they weren't as good as some of ours here. I didn't see that they had done anything new whatever, and the same thing was true in Utah. Then I made a trip with Mr. Knight in 1924, up in Colorado, over the Squirrel Creek area, that everybody was bragging about. It was real nice but no different from what we had here."

Jones was transferred from the Lands Division to the newly designated Information and Education Section, and he was succeeded by Mr. Cheney, who had been his assistant. Cheney had no assistant, so he asked Landis (Pink) Arnold to come into the Regional Office to take charge of recreation.

"At that time, the recreation problem was entirely different from what it is today," Cheney said. "Albuquerque at that time was under 40,000. Today it is 300,000."

That was about the time the CCC work was getting started, and Zane Smith recalls that for the first time "we had a definite program of constructing recreation facilities for camping and picnicking in the National Forests."

"Pink, who had shown a great deal of interest in this sort of thing, had scrounged around and managed to build out in the Sandias a few old tables out of scrap lumber and give some attention to the recreationists from Albuquerque," Smith related. "This caused him to be selected to head up this work."

With the increase in recreation site construction under the CCC Arnold needed an assistant, and he chose Zane Smith who remained in the Regional Office until 1937 when he was given his first Ranger district on the Prescott National Forest in Arizona.

Ed Miller came into the Regional Office as Chief of Recreation and Lands. Miller had been supervisor of the Coconino Forest when the CCC program started and he had used the Corps to build recreation facilities.

"Recreation was just coming into its own on the Coconino," Miller said. "Oak Creek was a favorite spot, also Mormon Lake and Lake Mary. Recreation work included fireplaces, tables, water lines. One water line in Oak Creek was extended from the Upper Spring in Oak Creek Canyon down to Pine Flats Camp-

The National Forests have always attracted campers. This family enjoyed the Santa Catalina Mountains (Coronado National Forest) in 1900.

A family enjoys camping at Santa Barbara Campground, Carson National Forest.

ground. Other springs farther down were also developed. Incidentally, it is interesting to look back and realize the change in thinking. The most desirable places, like Pine Flats and Oak Creek Canyon were laid out by Aldo Leopold and his helpers as summer home sites back in 1917-18 or thereabouts. Fortunately, most of those summer home sites were never leased. But now people come from California and other distant states for a few days camping in that beautiful canyon."

Trail rides into the National Forests were becoming popular in those days, too, and the American Forestry Association selected the Gila for one of its sponsored trail rides in 1935, and for two rides in 1936. And interestingly enough, that 1935 ride attracted only three men—but 22 women. They followed the trails that Henry Woodrow had built in the Wilderness, and one of the highlights of the trip was a ride up that first trail that Woodrow blazed in 1909 to the top of Mogollon Baldy Peak for a view from the fire lookout tower.*

Writing in the November, 1943, issue of New Mexico Magazine, Landis Arnold could brag that the Forest Service now had 120 campgrounds in New Mexico's seven National Forests and that 500,000 persons visited the seven Forests in a normal year.

Today the recreation people talk in terms of millions of visitors, not hundreds of thousands.

While there had been some recreational development during the CCC camp days, little was done after World War II until 1957 when a start was made with the advent of "Operation Outdoors."

This program really only got under way in 1958 and 1959. By the 1962 fiscal year funds for recreation construction were up to $591,000 in the Region, while operation and maintenance funds were only $353,000. In contrast, 1969 fiscal year construction dollars were $382,000, while operation and maintenance funds had increased to $1,342,000. The high year for construction was in 1964 when $940,000 became available for this purpose.

Since the end of World War II, the State Game and Fish Departments of Arizona and New Mexico have greatly expanded their lake development program with the aid of Federal funds. New lakes constructed in this program along with other impoundments built in the past by either state or Federal agencies are becoming increasingly popular with people of all ages. The construction of these lakes on National Forests made a large impact on the recreation construction program in the Region.

---

*The story of the 1935 Trail Ride is told in the August, 1936, issue of New Mexico Magazine, in an article, "Gila Trails" by W. W. James.

A report of the Outdoor Recreation Resources Review Commission has noted that water is a focal point for outdoor recreation, and in the report, one of the findings of the study was: "Most people seeking outdoor recreation want water—to sit by, to swim and fish in, to ski across, to dive under, and to run their boats over."   The construction of lakes in New Mexico and Arizona has greatly enhanced the recreation opportunities in the Southwestern Region.

The advent of the fee system, provided for by law in 1965, brought great changes in recreation administration in the Region. Prior to this time, recreation management activities were more or less directed towards cleaning the campgrounds and maintaining the facilities.   The fee system made it essential that the user be contacted and a fee collected.   This brought the recreation managers into closer contact with the needs and necessities of the people. It also brought about the tighter control of recreation use in the developed recreation sites.   The Region was quite successful in the implementation of the fee system, being number two in the Nation in collections in 1967.   In 1968, while only generating 6 percent of the reported use nation-wide, 11 percent of the total L&WCF fee collections were made in this Region.

In the last few years it became increasingly evident that there would be need for more law enforcement activities in the recreation field.   This became particularly true in those recreation sites that were adjacent to major population centers such as Tucson, Phoenix, and Albuquerque.   Training sessions were held in this activity, and law enforcement officers were employed in both New Mexico and Arizona on a zone basis.   In one case in Arizona, a particular problem area near Tucson, a law enforcement officer was employed on the Coronado National Forest for use in that particular area.

In a recent report on recreation, the Division of Recreation and Lands noted that the rate of increase in recreation use "depends on many factors, including economics and weather.   We expect the upward trend to continue."

Water and snow-oriented recreation use is increasing more rapidly than more conventional uses, such as camping and picnicking.

"Regardless of his particular pursuit, the user expects and demands more and better services and facilities than he did a decade ago," the report stated.   "Bathhouses, flush toilets, electrical power, and trailer sewage service stations are examples of new facilities that are now installed which were unheard of a few years ago.   We expect that such improvements may become the rule rather than the exception in many of the more heavily used sites.

"Depending upon the recreation experience level planned for a developed site, facilities and improvements may vary greatly. Most 'family units' of a developed campground normally contain these improvements: a parking spur, table, fireplace grill or other cooking facility, a level spot for pitching a tent, a garbage receptacle, and a pro rata share of water and toilet systems. The Southwestern Region has a total of 6,840 such family units in 382 developed camp and picnic grounds. This does not include improvements at observation sites, boating and swimming sites, recreation residences, winter sports sites, and visitor centers. All sites developed for public recreation use total 650, with a total capacity of people at one time of 75,967. These developed sites cover 6,896 acres.

"While it is generally true that the public may change preference for outdoor recreation experiences, these changes are quite gradual. Much work along this line is done by various state and local governments and universities as well as the Bureau of Outdoor Recreation, the National Park Service, and the Forest Service, in seeking guidance for economic development or exploitation of a given area or attraction. Bureaus of Business Research also delve into this subject.

"Users of the National Forests in the Southwest are generally from the metropolitan areas which lie adjacent or close to the National Forests. Climatic relief is sought by many people from Oklahoma, Kansas, Texas, and California, who drive farther to visit the cooler climate of the higher elevation in National Forests. Obviously, the most heavily used areas are those which are most easily accessible. The use pressure will shift and expand as the relatively remote areas are opened up and developed. Management plans are being written as rapidly as possible and specific management practices to meet current or expected impacts are implemented as fast as budgetary limitations will allow.

"As you would expect, the time spent by each recreation visitor varies with the activity in which he is engaged. As little as one hour might be spent by a group or an individual on a picnic in the National Forest near his home, while up to 12 hours might be spent by this same group or individual when it is necessary to travel long distances to the National Forest. All else being equal, however, we generally assume that the average length of stay for such activity is three to four hours. Camping length of stay is believed to be an average of two to three days for most sites. Wilderness recreationists usually stay six to seven days. Skiers spend about three hours per day actually skiing, with another estimated two hours spent in using associated improvements.   General enjoyment of scenery, recreational driving, fishing, hunting, nature study, etc., are all too abstract to attempt to define a length of visit.

"The Southwestern Region is not presently able to meet the demand for outdoor recreation at developed sites.   Our goal is to provide enough improvements to accommodate average weekday use.   We don't believe it is practical to develop sites for peak weekend and holiday demand.   Inventories of sites suitable for recreation development show that there is sufficient acreage of National Forest land available to meet expected needs through at least the year 2000.   We have not developed plans beyond that date yet.   Within the next two years we should complete an update of our long range plans.

"The control of use of recreation improvements and undeveloped portions of the National Forests is a tremendous job. Overuse of facilities, vandalism, lawlessness, and lack of respect for public property are examples of the problems.   Much time is consumed in this way, which could be much more profitably spent in actual management of the resources.

"The basic use to be made of a developed site by the public can usually be controlled by the physical layout of the site and the design of improvements installed.   The kind and amount of parking, the presence or absence of fire grates, whether or not tables are furnished, all influence and in a measure regulate demand and use on a given site.   The use of restrictions on fire is another way to regulate use in general undeveloped areas as well as in the sites developed for public use."

An interesting new trend in recreation in the National Forests is the growth of snowmobiling.   In the past couple of years, the village of Chama in northern New Mexico has been designated as "The Snowmobile Capital of the Southwest."   Each weekend, hundreds of snowmobile enthusiasts flock into Chama to follow the high country trails.   More than 300 miles of trails have been established by the Forest Service, Soil Conservation Service and the snowmobilers themselves.   One of the trips is a safari across the Carson National Forest from Chama to Tres Piedras.   The Cloudcroft Ranger District in the Lincoln Forest has marked two snowmobile trails; Santa Fe Forest has marked three trails in the Coyote District.   The Cibola Forest has marked several trails in the Sandia District and has some snowed-in roads in the Manzano Mountains and in the Gallinas Mountains that would be suitable for snowmobiling.

The Multiple Use Management Guide issued by the Regional Office for its Supervisors and Rangers notes that "winter sports are growing in popularity. Northern New Mexico National Forests contain most of the more desirable winter sports sites in the State. This area is the closest skiing available to western Texas. Northern Arizona provides winter sport activities within a three-hour drive from Phoenix on a high speed Interstate Highway. The nine winter sports sites in the Region have a capacity of 13,150 people at one time and their use constitutes 2.5 percent of the Region's total recreation use."

Discussing the recreation resource potential of the Forests of the Southwest, the Management Guide notes that "the Region is unique in that it has desert environment for enjoyment in winter, and cool mountains for summer use. Practically all of the 20.5 million acres of National Forest System lands in the Southwest have something of interest for the recreationist. Areas most valuable for recreation are generally those with some special attraction, such as a river, stream, or lake. Unusual vegetation, altitude, climate or scenery also draw visitors."

Noting the fact that Interstate Highways bring "an already mobile population closer to the National Forests," the Management Guide points out that new or improved Forest highways provide easy access to many Forest areas, and that as "use increases in the undeveloped areas, it will be necessary to provide minimum sanitary facilities and cleanup to protect public health and safety, prevent water pollution and enhance natural beauty."

Just to travel through the Forest is a form of recreation—whether it's by car, horseback or on foot. To come suddenly upon a flock of turkeys or to spy a deer by the side of the road becomes a recreation bonus. The landscape is a source of interest and the wildlife a special delight to the picnicker or weekend explorer.

The Rangers themselves never become so blasé about their jobs that they aren't sensitive to the beauty of the Forests or enjoy the same little delights that please the casual Forest visitor.

A good example of this is indicated in the story that Ed Miller related about a trip that he and Lefty Lewis, one-time State Game Warden of Arizona, made one fall into the South Pocket country of the Rogers Lake District of the Coconino nearly 40 years ago.

"The Ranger had wanted us to get Lefty down into that South Pocket country," Miller related. "He felt that the deer were too numerous down there, so Lefty Lewis and I went in—in a pickup as far as we could drive. As we approached the South Pocket Tank, which was the watering place for the D-K outfit, we thought we saw a movement inside the high wire fence that the D-K outfit had around the water tank. Lefty said, 'Ed, what's that? What are those things?' I said, 'They're cubs. Little bear cubs.' 'Well,'

Lefty said, 'we'd better be blamed careful or we'll have the old mother after us.' 'Well, we're not gonna cause any excitement,'

"We just took very, very slow paces down a little bit of wash, down to the gate. Those little cubs were standing straight up, watching us. Apparently they had never seen a man before. We walked slowly toward them. One crawled under the woven wire fence and stood by a yellow pine. The other one stood within about 10 feet before he moved from me. And then he started up a pine tree. I walked up so I could stroke his back. One cub was cinnamon, the other pure black. Lefty said, 'Ed, if I go back to Phoenix and tell people about this, they'll think I'm a damn liar.'

"That's the closest that either one of us ever got to a wild animal that wasn't sick. Where the mother was, we don't know. Her tracks were there at the water. It was a regular watering place. But since we didn't disturb the youngsters and make 'em set up a howl, the mother may have been unaware of what was happening. We both felt very sad that we had been foolish enough to have left the camera in the car. The sun was just exactly right for a picture of those cubs. I've seen bear in the woods, but I've never seen two babies along in September that were just as pretty as any cub you'll see in a zoo. Their fur fairly shone."

Discussing trends in Forest Service policies, Elliott Barker noted that the increase in population and demand for general outdoor recreation has changed the direction of the Service to a great extent.

"We used to think of the Forest Service as grazing and timber mainly, with recreation completely in the background," Barker said. "Now it's right out in the foregound. I think the increase in population is going to get worse. It's just a little hard for me to envision what inevitably lies ahead for the Forest Service. For instance, there are some who foresee the day in the not-too-far-distant future when you will have to regulate the number of visits that an individual can make to the National Forests or to a Wilderness in any one season. I can't quite picture that. Still, if we figure the increase, for instance, going back to about 1910 or '11, when I was at the Panchuela Ranger Station, we estimated that there were fewer than 300 people went into the back country— what is now the Pecos Wilderness—each year on recreation, that is, other than stockmen who went in on business. Less than 300. Well, that has increased steadily through the years, and when I went on as State Game Warden, I think we estimated—that was in 1931—we estimated it up to about 800. A few years ago it was between 15,000 and 20,000. How can anyone tell where we are going to come out? Our population is running away with itself."

A growing activity of the Forest Service in connection with recreation is the Visitor Information Service, which takes a variety of forms in the different National Forests and is designed to help the visitor interpret the Forest and understand its management. Visitor centers have been built in some Forests; nature talks are given at campgrounds; hikes are sponsored; nature trails established; attractive information displays are set up in Supervisor and Ranger headquarters.

On the Pecos Ranger District of the Santa Fe National Forest, there are nature talks and slide showings at three campgrounds every evening during the summer.   J. D. Woerheide, of the lands and recreation staff of the Pecos District reported that a collection of 3,000 color slides had been built up for use of the VIS staff.

Adjacent to the Gila Cliff Dwellings National Monument, 43 miles from Silver City, New Mexico, the Forest Service and the National Park Service cooperated to establish and operate the Gila Visitor Center that features the archeology and natural history of the area and management of the Gila National Forest.

One of the most popular visitor centers is undoubtedly that near Tucson, the Sabino Canyon Visitor Center, at the foot of the

Senator Clinton P. Anderson was an honored guest at the dedication of the Gila Visitor Center.   Anderson, former Secretary of Agriculture, was a personal friend of Aldo Leopold and the father of the National Wilderness Preservation System.

Santa Catalina Mountains, and its Catalina Desert Trail for the Handicapped.

In the planning stage is a visitor center to be built near Flagstaff that will house the Forest Service Museum, now housed at the Continental Divide Training Center.

Population projections indicate that by 1980, there will be 1,630,000 people in New Mexico and 2,050,000 in Arizona. Forest Service officials believe this increased population, coupled with the increased awareness of the public of the activities on National Forest lands, makes it imperative that the Forest Service continue on its established direction of comprehensive land management planning and activities.

CHAPTER XXII
Multiple Use

When the Forest Service was transferred from the General Land Office to the Department of Agriculture in 1905, Secretary Wilson issued a directive that the Forests were to be managed "for the greatest good for the greatest number in the long run." From that directive emerged the policy of multiple use management of the National Forests.

Congress recognized the soundness of the policy and in 1960 passed the Multiple Use-Sustained Yield Act, which establishes in law the policy of administering the National Forests for outdoor recreation, range, timber, watershed, and wildlife and fish purposes. The Act declared that the resources of the National Forests were to be used in combinations that best meet the needs of the American people. Prior to the passage of the bill, a Southwestern Regional Multiple Use Management Guide had been developed in 1959, and this guide was revised in 1967 to bring it in line with new Service-wide standards and requirements.

All resource and activity management plans, actions plans, and action programs are in accord with the overall coordinating requirements and management decisions contained in the approved District Ranger Multiple Use Plan. This plan can be revised annually with the Supervisor's approval, but the Regional Guide will remain in effect without major changes until 1973.

In his foreword to the Regional Guide, William D. Hurst, Regional Forester, noted that "Effective multiple use management requires close cooperation with permittees, adjacent landowners, conservation organizations, cooperating Federal and State agencies, and other interested groups and individuals. Much of the desirable and necessary coordination can only be effectively carried out through full understanding and support of all concerned. Big game, range, and timber activities are good illustrations of coordination that is being carried out through action programs of other agencies, groups and individuals.

"Multiple use planning, like most planning, is but a means to an end. The degree of planning success is measured by the end results obtained on the ground. I am confident that, through multiple use planning and coordination, land managers can more successfully fulfill their obligations to provide the maximum amount of quality products and services to meet the growing needs of the people in the Southwest and in the Nation."

In explaining the Multiple Use Management Guide, Regional Forester Hurst said that it "establishes nine management zones and explains how the resources, uses and activities within each zone will be coordinated to best meet public needs. Within zones, management direction and emphasis will vary, depending upon available resources and opportunities for public use and enjoyment. For example, in the Travel Influence Zone, which includes areas adjacent to principal roads, trails, railroads, tramways, and campgrounds, the objective is to maintain natural beauty of the forest environment. The management direction for this zone provides that cutting of timber, grazing of livestock, and development of wildlife habitat will be conducted in ways that will best maintain or enhance the natural environment."

Regional Forester Hurst said that a multiple use plan has been prepared for each Ranger District. "The plan, which incorporates a map and written section, has been developed within the framework of the Region's Multiple Use Management Guide. Management zones are shown on the map. Management decisions for each management zone are made by the Forest Ranger and recorded in the written section of the plan. Before a decision is reached careful consideration is given to all factors with the objective of coordinating present or planned uses within the zone to avoid or minimize conflicts. The plan will be revised to meet changing conditions."

The various zones established for planning are: Desert, Chaparral, Grassland, Woodland, Travel Influence, Intermediate, Water Influence, Crest, Special.

Desert Zone

Ranging from 1,400 feet to 3,500 feet in elevation, the Desert Zone is located in southern Arizona and New Mexico. It is an area of rugged scenic beauty featuring cactus, ocotillo, paloverde, mesquite, and other colorful desert vegetation characteristic of a dry, warm climate. This zone is subject to high-intensity thunder storms that can cause severe stream erosion and damaging floods.

The high mountain ranges of the National Forests produce over half of the usable annual water supply available to Arizona and New Mexico. However, much of the silt that clogs southwestern water courses today is the result of past abuse of desert lands. When the Coronado and Tonto National Forests were created, this situation was recognized and a large amount of desert land was included in these two Forests so as to assure adequate management along desert water courses within their borders.

The Desert Zone supports a wide variety of wildlife including coyote, rabbit, javelina, desert mule deer, quail, and dove. It is also valuable for grazing domestic livestock and informal outdoor recreation. Horseback riding, hiking, cookouts, rockhounding, and hunting, are popular during the winter, spring, and fall. The zone is attracting increasing numbers of recreationists from all over the country, particularly during the warm winter months.

In the Desert Zone, management emphasis is directed at maintaining the native desert flora and fauna for its recreation and esthetic values. Because of the delicate balance existing in this zone between soil and vegetative cover, a special effort is made to maintain a balance between wildlife and livestock numbers and available food supply.

Grassland Zone

This zone includes portions of the National Grasslands located in northeastern New Mexico, the Panhandle of Oklahoma and Texas, and western Oklahoma.

The Grasslands are the former "dust bowl" lands that were purchased by the Federal government in the 1930's, rehabilitated, and made productive once again. The zone ranges in elevation from 550 to nearly 6,000 feet and includes occasional areas of "rough breaks" and "badlands." In the western part of the zone several river and valley bottoms support small stands of oak, pecan, elm, and hickory trees. Lands in the zone provide food for cattle and a wide variety of wildlife including antelope, deer, turkey, and quail.

Hunting, hiking, and bird dog trails are important recreational uses in the zone. Stream fishing opportunities are relatively minor because of the scarcity of surface streams.

Due to climatic limitations and erosive soils, the Grassland Zone is suitable for forage production but not for cultivation. The Forest Service management objective is to promote and demonstrate good grassland agriculture on these lands and encourage adjacent private land owners to do the same. Management is also directed at maintaining the natural beauty of the zone and developing wildlife and fish habitat for recreational opportunities.

Chaparral Zone

The Chaparral Zone, ranging in elevation from 3,500 to 6,500 feet, includes extensive areas of brushy vegetation located in central Arizona. Also, southeastern Arizona and southwestern

New Mexico have scattered units of chaparral or brush.   Considerable use of this zone is made by livestock and wildlife.

Although the zone produces some grass, its vegetative cover consists principally of shrubs including manzanita, mountain mahogany, live oak, sumac, and hollyleaf buckthorn.   The plants in this zone generally grow close together and in many cases, form brush thickets so dense that travel through them is difficult or impossible.   In addition, the shrubs are highly inflammable and constitute the most dangerous wildfire hazard in the United States.

The Chaparral Zone receives from 16 to 25 inches of precipitation each year.   However, due to shrub density, runoff is strictly limited.   Research conducted by the Rocky Mountain Forest and Range Experiment Station has shown that by converting chaparral to grass, runoff can be substantially increased.   Such conversion also reduces the fire hazard and increases food for wildlife and livestock.

Management emphasis in the Chaparral Zone is directed at increasing water yield, reducing fire hazard, stabilizing soil, and improving forage for wildlife and livestock.

The Tonto National Forest has under way a program to increase water yield by converting selected areas of chaparral to grass through planned burning and reseeding.   After an area has been selected for treatment, a plan is carefully prepared which shows fire line location, time and technique of burn, and the procedure to be followed in establishing a forage cover of grasses and browse. The typical plan provides that patches of chaparral will be left untouched in the control area as escape cover for wildlife and for maintenance of the natural environment.   Studies show that costs of such treatment are a sound investment because water yield is increased, fire hazard is reduced, and habitat improved for game and livestock.

Woodland Zone

The Woodland Zone, which ranges in elevation from 2,500 to 7,000 feet, is the largest management zone in the Southwestern Region.   It includes 32 percent of the Region's total area.   The principal vegetation types are pinyon-juniper in Arizona and New Mexico and the live oak savannah on southern portions of the Coronado National Forest.   Annual precipitation varies from 7 to 20 inches, but water yield from this zone is very low.

The trees in the Woodland Zone, which are interspersed with shrubs and stands of grass, have little commercial value as sawtimber.   However, the zone is a source of fuelwood, Christmas trees, fence posts, and pinyon nuts, and it provides homes for many birds, small animals, and deer, and forage for livestock.   There is some mining activity in the zone.   It also offers opportunities for hiking, rockhounding, riding, and hunting.

Management emphasis in the Woodland Zone is directed toward forage production, game habitat, and improved watershed condition.   Because the balance between ground cover and bare soil in this zone is delicate, a management objective is to maintain and improve soil stability.

Pinyon and juniper control will be undertaken on selected areas where additional food for wildlife and livestock can be produced.   Control of pinyon and juniper where it has invaded natural grasslands is an approved management practice for providing and maintaining forage for livestock and big game.

Management also recognizes the need to further develop the zone's potential for Christmas trees, timber, fence posts, and fuelwood.

Intermediate Zone

The Intermediate Zone, ranging from 5,000 to 10,500 feet in elevation, includes areas favorable for the production of commercial sawtimber and forage.   It makes up about 30% of the Southwestern National Forests and is the so-called "backwoods."

The zone contains most of the commercial timber types including ponderosa pine, Douglas-fir, Engelmann spruce, limber pine, white fir, and aspen.   Grassy areas suitable for livestock and wildlife use are often interspersed with stands of timber.

The zone annually receives 15 to 35 inches of precipitation. Nearly 40 percent of the water produced by the Southwestern National Forests comes from this zone.

A wide variety of big and small game, upland game birds, waterfowl, and other small animals live in this zone.   Recreation opportunities of the back-country variety are plentiful, with big game hunting, stream fishing, hiking, and camping the major attractions.

The zone is attractive and frequently provides a backdrop of scenery which is visible from heavily-traveled roads and from lakes, rivers, and camp and picnic grounds.   The Intermediate Zone receives comparatively little public use.   Management emphasis is directed at producing sustained yields of timber, water, wildlife, and forage.

Travel Influence Zone

Travel in and through the National Forests is greatly increasing.   People are attracted to the National Forests by their scenic beauty, clean air, and opportunities for healthful outdoor recreation.

The Travel Influence Zone includes areas adjacent to roads, trails, railroads, tramways, ski lifts, and camp and picnic grounds. Obviously, this zone receives much public use.   The zone does not encompass work roads or trails which receive only occasional travel.

In this zone the objective is to maintain or enhance the natural beauty of the surroundings.   Camp and picnic grounds, winter sports areas, nature trails, vista points, and other recreation facilities will be developed to meet public needs.   The zone's timber and forage resources may be used, but in a way that will enhance the quality of the environment.

To illustrate, trees will be cut to improve the natural beauty of the Forest.   Overmature, dying, or dead trees, or those that create safety hazards will be removed.   Picturesque snags that add interest to the scene may be left.

Water Influence Zone

Water is undoubtedly the most important single product of the Southwestern National Forests, so Forest Service management of the Water Influence Zone is of vital importance to all citizens. This zone is made up of areas of varying sizes along streams, rivers, lakes, and reservoirs.   It is generally outstanding in scenic beauty. The zone provides a wide variety of opportunities for outdoor recreation, including fishing, boating, water skiing, swimming, hiking, camping, picnicking, and just plain sightseeing.   Waters which receive little or no public use are not included in this zone.

Water which supports fish life and provides recreation is also used for irrigation, industry, and human use.   Accordingly, management emphasis is placed on maintaining or enhancing water quality and the natural beauty of the zone.   Developed recreation sites and facilities will be made available in this zone.   Other resources in the zone will be managed to maintain scenic beauty and water quality.

Crest Zone

The Crest Zone, ranging in elevation from 10,500 feet to timberline and above, includes less than 10,000 acres of Southwestern National Forest land.   It is characterized by high peaks, rocky ridges, and limited stands of subalpine fir, dwarfed Engelmann spruce, and limber pine.   The San Francisco Peaks area of the Coconino National Forest is an example of the Crest Zone.

This zone experiences severe climatic conditions, has thin soils, and a short growing season.   It furnishes summer food for some wildlife and livestock.   Scenery is outstanding and attracts hikers and horseback riders.

The Crest Zone, with an average annual precipitation of above 30 inches, mostly in the form of snow, produces the greatest water yield per acre in the Southwest. Annual water yields vary from about one-half to two acre-feet of water per acre of surface.

Management emphasis in the Crest Zone is directed at protecting and improving water quality while safeguarding natural beauty and aesthetic values for back-country recreation. Proposed use of the Crest Zone for electronic sites or similar installations will be considered in terms of the effect of such developments on natural beauty and water yield.

Special Zone

Special Zones include areas which have been classified or formally designated by Congress, the Secretary of Agriculture, Chief of the Forest Service, or the Regional Forester. Those include wildernesses; primitive, scenic, and natural areas; experimental forests and ranges; and historical, geological, archeological, or botanical areas.

For example, in the Southwestern Region, the Gila, Pecos, Wheeler Peak, White Mountain, San Pedro Parks, Superstition, Mazatzal, Sierra Ancha, Chiricahua, and Galiuro Wildernesses are parts of the National Wilderness Preservation System. The Wilderness Act specifies how Congress wants these Wildernesses to be managed so as to preserve their pristine character. Primitive Areas, such as the Blue Range and Black Range, were established by the Secretary of Agriculture and are being studied for possible inclusion by Congress into the National Wilderness Preservation System. In the meantime, they are being managed under the regulations in effect when the Wilderness Act was passed.

The C. Hart Merriam Scenic Area located in the San Francisco Peaks of the Coconino National Forest has been designated by the Regional Forester under authority granted to him. As the name implies, this area has been given special recognition because of its outstanding scenic beauty.

The Monument Canyon Research Natural Area, Santa Fe National Forest; the Santa Catalina Research Natural Area; and Gooding Research Natural Area, Coronado National Forest, were established by the Chief of the Forest Service for scientific study and are to remain in an undisturbed or natural condition.

The Santa Rita Experimental Range, Coronado National Forest; Fort Valley Experimental Forest, Coconino National Forest; Sierra Ancha Experimental Forest, Tonto National Forest; and the Cloudcroft Experimental Forest, Lincoln National Forest were established by the Chief of the Forest Service. Research is being done on them in many phases of range and forest management.

In the Southwestern Region, historical, geological, and archeological areas have been inventoried but none have been formally classified.

In Special Zone areas, the documents, regulations, or laws establishing them tell how they are to be managed.

CHAPTER XXIII
Land Exchanges

Back in the 30's when land was still cheap in New Mexico, the Forest Service sought to obtain the 91,000 acres of the Rancho del Rio Grande Grant, in Taos County, then owned by a lumber company. This was part of a program authorized by Congress to consolidate National Forest lands. The Government appraiser set a value of $4.75 an acre on the land, and an exchange for timber and other lands of equal value was sought. The owners of the Rio Grande Grant were interested in disposing of the big block of acreage which was surrounded by National Forest, but decided to hold out for $5.00 an acre. The appraiser stuck with the $4.75 figure, and the deal fell through.

After World War II, the Forest Service again attempted an exchange. In the meantime, ownership of the grant had changed hands. Again the exchange fell through because of only pennies difference in the Government appraisal and the asked-for price.

Later the grant lands were sold to another timber operator, Rounds and Porter, a Kansas company. In 1960, the Forest Service decided to try again to bring about an exchange of timber and other lands elsewhere in the Region for the big block of forest lands within the boundaries of the Carson National Forest. Ralph Rounds, the head of the company, expressed an interest in the offer. But to put together a package of lands and timber which would interest the lumber company proved to be a problem. Then Ralph Rounds died, and negotiations had to be followed up with the Rounds estate.

The estate was interested in a cash sale, but not in a direct exchange. Under the law authorizing exchanges, the Forest Service could exchange lands and timber for other lands within the Forest, but could not make an outright purchase.

The only other method to bring about the exchange was to find a third person who would pay cash for the lands which were exchanged for the Rio Grande Grant. This turned out to be a very complicated procedure. No one purchaser could be located, and the third-person purchasers finally added up to 57.

The Rio Grande Grant was appraised now at approximately

$19.00 an acre for a total of $1,727,297.78.   This proved acceptable, and government-owned parcels of land on the fringes of the Forest elsewhere had to be put together in a package for exchange to the 57 willing purchasers.   These 57 were made up of people who had been applying for years to Rangers for an opportunity to obtain lands on which they were permittees or who wanted to develop summer home sites or obtain grazing lands adjoining patented lands, etc.   The Lands Division under the direction of the then-chief, Zane Smith, put together a total package of 52,870 acres in various parts of the State of New Mexico—Tijeras Canyon, Taos, Ruidoso, Cloudcroft, and grazing lands near Magdalena and Mountainair.   The next step was for the would-be purchasers to place their purchase price in escrow.

When all of the surveys had been made, the complexity of documents typed and checked, the Rio Grande Grant became government property, payments from 57 people went to Rounds and Porter, and the 57 in turn received deeds to the lands they had selected.

This complicated process took two years to complete, and in the final stages took intensive hours of work to meet final deadlines.

The completion of the Rio Grande Grant exchange brought a letter of commendation from Richard E. McArdle, Chief Forester, to then Regional Forester Fred Kennedy.

"When I discussed this case with you and Zane Smith a few years back, I frankly was quite doubtful that you could work it out," McArdle wrote.   "I am delighted that you have done so. I am impressed by your resourcefulness and ingenuity in working out the details of this exchange."   In a penned note at the bottom Chief McArdle wrote: "This is a real accomplishment.   I take my hat off to you folks."

The Regional Forester passed the letter along to Zane Smith, then Lands Chief, with a notation at the bottom of the letter, "I feel exceptionally proud of the folks in my outfit who did the work."

Alan Watkins, long-time career employee in the Forest Service, and one of those who had worked on the exchange, recalls that Zane Smith made copies of the Chief's letter for all who had worked on the exchange, and added a letter of his own.   They are cherished mementoes.

Smith in his letter to his staff said the exchange was "the most complicated case I have known" and that it was accomplished because of "fine work done by clerks, staff, stenographers, draftsmen, Rangers, Supervisors and the Regional Office."

Zane Smith noted that "the expression of appreciation is directed to the office workers as well as others. This was not accidental as everyone knows the exchange could not have been accomplished within the time limit without the extra effort and overtime by the girls."

This solving of a land problem is just one example of the activities dealing with the use, occupancy, and ownership of lands within the boundaries of the National Forests in Region 3. Such activities have been multitudinous and important almost since the establishment of the National Forests. Because of the relatively mild climate, people have been attracted to the Southwest ever since the first explorations by the Spanish *conquistadores.* Nearly every tract of land which was sufficiently level to be cultivated was occupied under the Homestead Laws during the years when homesteading was permissible. Any area with a showing of mineral was patented under the mining laws. Except for the Forest Homestead Act, the authorities for patenting both homestead and mining claims existed prior to the National Forest.

D. D. Cutler, of the Lands Division, reporting on land exchange problems, noted that in addition to such authorization to dispose of public land, an Act of 1866 for the Benefit of the Atlantic and Pacific Railroad authorized the company to select a right-of-way 100 feet in width along the entire length of its track and also the odd-numbered sections within a strip 40 miles wide on either side of the track to be used to offset costs of the construction of the railroad. This Act later was amended to extend the selection to the odd-numbered sections in an additional 10-mile strip on either side of the track if such was needed to offset the loss of land within the 40-mile strip where it crossed Indian and military reservations or had been otherwise patented. The railroad was completed from east to west across the entire region prior to the establishment of any National Forest.

The Act of 1897, which provided for administration of the National Forest Reserves, also authorized the railroad and others to reconvey their lands within the National Forest for unappropriated public domain anywhere in the United States. This was known as the lieu selection authority, and there was a very active program to consolidate the National Forest ownership with the Kaibab and Coconino National Forests until 1905 when this authority was repealed by Congress.

Water has been a most important asset in the use of land in the Southwest. By "hook or crook" each claimant for public domain attempted to include within his claim the available water. Thus, much of the water from springs and live streams was included within the homestead and mineral patents. Lands along stream bottoms controlled routes of easiest access to the remaining National Forest, and water controlled the use of adjacent land. As land management became more important and public pressures demanded better use of the land, impediments resulting from private ownership of water and access routes became more onerous. It soon was evident that many of these tracts should be returned to public ownership. The Act of March 20, 1922, for the purposes of consolidating National Forests, was Congress' recognition of the problem. Region 3 was quick to take advantage of this authority.

In addition to the above-mentioned problems, in New Mexico there were considerable areas of high-water yield, multiple-resource lands granted to private interests by the King of Spain or the Government of Mexico prior to the time Arizona and New Mexico were ceded to the United States. The abusive use of these lands by private owners resulted in considerable public criticism because of the great need for water coming from these watersheds. In 1925, special acts were passed by Congress which authorized the exchange for National Forest timber of two of these grants to the United States. In 1928, the 1922 Act was extended to authorize exchanges of any of the Spanish or Mexican Land Grants adjacent to the Carson, Santa Fe, and Manzano National Forests for National Forest land or timber. Upon consummation of the exchange, these lands automatically became part of the National Forests to which they were adjacent. Many land exchange cases have been processed through the years under this authority.

Also within New Mexico, the State acquired title to relatively large areas of public domain within the National Forest as a result of the Act of January 16, 1897. The State Land office was assigned the responsibilities for management of these tracts, but was never financed to carry out the responsibilities. As with the land grants, public opinion demanded something better. In 1926, the State Enabling Act of 1910 was amended to permit the State of New Mexico to enter into land-for-land exchanges with the United States in which it would offer its lands for either public domain or National Forest land or timber.

In the 1930's, cooperative agreements were signed by the State Land Commissioner and the Regional Forester under which the Forest Service would manage the timber resources. However, these agreements broke down for various reasons. In the late 1940's, as the result of discussions between the Forest Service and the State Land Commissioner, the Commissioner concluded that his office was not staffed to do the management job in the timber type, and for that reason he would proceed with a program to completely exchange out of the National Forests. This has resulted in a considerable load of lands work during the past 20 years. Only a few tracts of State land now remain within the Carson and Lincoln National Forests, and all of those within the Carson are in an active case.

In summary, 520 land exchange cases have been processed in the Region as of June 30, 1969, by which the United States has acquired 1,283,109 acres and granted in return 831,219 acres of land and 450,000,000 bd. ft. of timber. In addition, 25,265 acres have been purchased under Weeks Law and other authorities, and 275,390 acres have been given National Forest status through transfer from other Federal ownership.

Special land uses also have been a heavy lands workload throughout the history of the Forest Service. In all cases where parties other than the Forest Service wish to use parcels of the National Forest more or less exclusively, a special-use permit is issued. The Forest Service job consists of examining, issuing permits, and inspecting improvements for compliance with standards established to protect the National Forest land and resources against abuse. In the early history of the National Forests, many of these permits were for pastures to be used in connection with homesteads and ranch units, stockman cabins used in connection with grazing permits, irrigation ditches, reservoirs, telephone lines, powerlines, summer homes, and so forth. Because of the numerous homesteads and occupancies within the National Forests, these uses were numerous. More recently, the need for electronic sites has increased rapidly. Ordinarily, the highest elevations above sea level are the best suited. The National Forests occupying these high lands have experienced the greatest pressure for this special use. Each National Forest has specially designated and planned electronic sites. Many permits have been issued. Many of these sites are occupied by the military and other Federal agencies and universities with extremely expensive facilities costing hundreds of millions of dollars. Sac Peak for upper air research, near Cloudcroft on the Lincoln; Mount Hopkins and Mount Lemmon on the Coronado; portions of the Sandia Laboratory on the Cibola; and VELA Project on the Tonto are examples. Also, in recent years, there are powerlines transmitting tremendous voltages, high pressure gas lines, and a cross-country coal slurry line, all of which occupy considerable area. These require detailed engineering and considerable treatment to protect the National Forest resources. Many hours of work have been required to properly coordinate construction of these projects with the needs of the other National Forest resources and their uses.

Exploration for minerals in the Southwest has been and continues to be active. While the use of the surface of the mining claim for mining purposes is generally at the discretion of the claimant, the Forest Service is responsible for use of the adjoining National Forest for roads and other off-claim needs. Through close cooperation on the ground, it is often possible to direct the use of the surface on the claims in such a manner that the adjacent National Forest resources are not damaged. The Forest Service must also be assured that the claims are not being used for the non-mining purposes. Inasmuch as many of the National Forests were heavily involved with claims, estimated at one time to be several hundred thousand, the supervision of mining activities continues to be an important task. Also, the Forest Service was assigned the task of clearing the surface rights on all National Forest lands in accordance with the Multiple Use Mining Act of 1955. More recently, the exploration and development of oil and gas resources has increased tremendously. Few acres of National Forests in New Mexico and northern Arizona have not been under lease. The coordination of these activities with the use and protection of the other National Forest resources has required many hours of work.

With the tremendous increase in recreation time available to the ever-increasing population and the improvements in transportation, the pressures on the available land and resources will continue to increase accordingly. The importance of the lands activities will likely increase rather than diminish.

CHAPTER XXIV
Management

The National Forest System of the Southwest is big business. With more than five million acres of commercial forest and nearly 15 million acres of woodland (non-commercial forest) and grazing lands to administer, the Regional Office staff of 281 persons in Albuquerque supervises a tremendous amount of activity.

Revenues reached a record high figure in 1969. This was attributed to high lumber prices. Forest Service officials do not expect the high income to continue, since lumber prices may drop back more in line with the 1968 level.

Total revenues collected for the fiscal year ending June, 1969, were $7,910,624.34. These payments came from timber sales, grazing fees, land use, mineral leases and permits, recreation use, power line rights-of-way and non-locatable minerals. Of the amount collected, 25 percent is returned to the counties of the states in which the income originated. Arizona counties received a total of $1,269,799.80 and New Mexico counties, $676,679.07. In 1968, total revenues had for the first time in several years passed the $3,000,000 mark. The total was $3,274,395.71, of which nearly $800,000 was distributed to the forest counties in New Mexico and Arizona.

The Regional administration of Southwestern National Forests is the responsibility of Divisions in the Regional Office in Albuquerque. Recreation and Lands and Information and Education are discussed in separate chapters. The work of some of the other Divisions is reported on here.

Fiscal Control

The Division of Fiscal Control serves management of the Region by developing, coordinating and directing both the fiscal and law enforcement work of the Region. The organizational structure of the Division was sectionalized in 1964 to place specific duties under supervision of three branch chiefs: Accounting, Fiscal Management, and Review and Analysis. Another branch was added in 1967 when Law Enforcement was transferred from the Division of Fire Control.

There have been many significant changes in operational procedures throughout the years.   The year 1957 saw the conversion of the accounting system from a manual operation on National Cash Register accounting machines to automatic data processing.   This unit was established in the Division of Fiscal Control until August of 1966 when the operation was placed under the supervision of the Division of Operation.   In 1964 with the establishment of the Department of Agriculture automatic data processing payrolling unit in New Orleans, payrolls were no longer processed for payment in Fiscal Control but were mailed directly from field units to the centralized operation.

In 1965 permission was granted by the Chief's Office to establish a Coordinated Work Planning Budgetary, Accounting and Work Accomplishment reporting system in Region 3 on a pilot basis.   The system had been designed by Region and Washington Office Forest Service personnel to better fit the needs of the Forest Service.   The system with minor modifications is still in use.

The Law Enforcement Branch played a significant part in bringing to prosecution persons involved in violence and destruction of government property in northern New Mexico National Forests. These events are discussed in the final chapter.

Engineering

The engineering staff of the Southwestern Region is concerned with a variety of activities, everything from mapping and road building, to sewage disposal, construction of Visitor Information Centers, and landscaping.

Nearly half of the annual Forest Service budget goes into engineered construction on the National Forests, and the scope of activities requires in the Southwestern Region a staff of 57—the largest of all the divisions.

The engineers provide special skills that pay off in new and better ways to develop and utilize the wood, water, range forage, wildlife, and recreation resources of the Forests.   Environmental and esthetic considerations are being given more prominence than ever in engineered projects.

An important phase of the staff's activity is working with developers who establish facilities on National Forest lands.   These must meet Forest Service requirements.   An outstanding example of working with developers is the gondola lift on the Cibola National Forest, the Sandia Tramway, which is one of many installations by private industry for snow-related sports and recreation. Most of the major ski areas in the Southwest, as elsewhere, involve National Forest lands.

In general, the work of the engineers falls into three major categories: the work it handles itself; the work done in cooperation with other agencies; and the private developments authorized by permit or license and the public works by other government agencies.

Road building is the biggest activity. Cooperative programs include transmission lines, highways, power projects, conduits, dams, resorts, etc., and in all cases the engineers work with the designers and contractors to make sure that projects are safe, and located, designed and constructed to minimize impacts on Forest resources.

Range and Wildlife Management

Livestock production has been important in the Southwest since settlement by the Spanish more than 300 years ago. National Forest System lands provide approximately 13,000,000 acres of range extending from the lower desert, chaparral and plains to the subalpine vegetative types in the mountains. With its relatively favorable climate, the area is unique in that yearlong grazing is common for many permittees operating on these public lands.

Nearly 3000 permittees are authorized to graze more than two million animal unit months annually. Use by sheep has generally declined over the years and many permittees are gradually converting to cattle operations.

The Forest Service tries to develop the range resource to its potential consistent with other resource considerations and sustained yield principles. Encouraging sound range management practices and a stable livestock industry on public lands and nearby lands of other ownerships is an important part of this goal. Meeting these objectives involves administering the grazing permit system, constructing improvements, revegetating poor range, and related work in a multiple use land management program.

Wildlife management on the National Forest System lands is a highly cooperative program. The Forest Service is primarily responsible for management of habitat, and by cooperative agreement the U. S. Fish and Wildlife Service has primary responsibility for fundamental fish and wild animal research, propagation of fish in Federal hatcheries, and predator control projects. There are cooperative arrangements also with other Federal agencies and State Game and Fish Departments.

Watershed Management
and State and Private Forestry

The National Forests of Arizona and New Mexico produce

three-fourths of the available water of the two states, which offers an idea of the importance of watershed controls in the Southwest.

The Region's Multiple Use Management Guide notes that "water is a critical factor in the economy and future development of the Southwest.   The need for additional water is urgent.   Approximately 300,000 acres of potential agricultural land lies idle in Arizona for lack of water."

The Guide points out that underground reserves are being depleted, and as an example, "the annual pumping rate from this reserve in the Salt River Valley in Arizona is about three times the annual recharge.   Other water sources are being sought, including additional water from the watersheds within the state."

The annual water yield from the National Forest System lands in the Southwestern Region is estimated at three million acre feet.   Approximately half of this amount comes from summer storms, the balance from snow.

The guide notes that "there are opportunities to increase water quality and quantity. . . .   Research and new management techniques prove it possible to significantly modify water yields by delaying runoff, reducing sedimentation, and manipulating vegetative cover and snow pack.   Some water yield improvement activities may require a change in the land cover which could increase the opportunities for accelerated erosion."

As part of its plan for control of watersheds and to increase water quantity, the Forest Service has undertaken a number of research and pilot test development projects.

Watershed management is the direct responsibility of the District Ranger.   However, he is able to draw upon special scientific soil and water management skills as needed, and basic soil and hydrologic survey data is supplied for the Rangers to use in preparing watershed management plans and coordinating other resource programs with water resource.   Reconnaissance level hydrologic surveys have been made on approximately 18,000,000 acres.

Watershed restoration projects are carried out as funds are available.   During the past five years, 400 miles of gullies were stabilized, 75,000 acres of sheet erosion revegetated, and erosion on 1600 miles of abandoned roads controlled.   However, the Division's inventory shows this impressive backlog still to be done:

Gully stabilization	14,316 miles
Sheet erosion control	1,348,353 acres
Steambank stabilization	555 miles
Road stabilization	9,275 miles

As part of the Forest Service program of watershed protection, the Division's watershed scientists provide Rangers with analysis of water which flows from National Forest lands. Chemical, physical and biological analyses are made on samples collected at 172 operational stations on 12 National Forests, and more than 10,400 determinations are made annually and stored for automatic data processing. This sampling is an early warning system designed to prevent degradation of water quality from pollution. The program is coordinated with other state and federal agencies working on different facets of the Federal Water Pollution Control Program.

Soil survey and soil management, watershed protection, water yield improvement, resource development, river basin surveys and investigations are all part of the complex job of watershed management.

State and Private Forestry is a branch of the Division of Watershed Management. The objective of State and Private Forestry in the Southwestern Region is to further the protection, sound management, and wise use on non-federal forest and watershed lands. It is the general policy to work with and through state foresters in carrying out many of the State and Private Forestry programs. A major objective is to develop strong State forestry organizations which will conduct adequate forestry programs for all non-Federal forest and watershed lands in the State for harvesters, distributors and processors of forest products.

The Region uses the following cooperative programs to accomplish these objectives: Cooperative Fire Control, Cooperative Forest Management, Cooperative Tree Planting, Rural Areas Development, General Forestry Assistance, Four Corners Economic Development, Rural Environmental Assistance Program, Cooperative Forest Insect and Disease Control, Watershed Protection and Flood Prevention, Great Plains Conservation Program, Rural Fire Defense and the Resource Conservation and Development Program.

The New Mexico State Forestry Department was organized December 1, 1957. Arizona was the last state of the fifty to organize a forestry department, (July 1, 1966) which was placed under the Arizona Land Department. New Mexico has five district offices which cover the entire State and has responsibility for most aspects of forestry work on non-Federal lands. Arizona has no district offices but operates out of the State office in Phoenix, with a second office in Northern Arizona in Flagstaff. So far, Arizona is also involved in most of the cooperative programs and the management of State-owned commercial forest lands near Flagstaff.

At this time New Mexico State Forestry Department is protecting from fire all non-Federal lands in the State which amounts to approximately 40 million acres. The Arizona State Forestry Department has approximately 3,129,000 acres under fire protection at this time. They are managing the 35,000 acres of State timber lands for a sustained yield. Special emphasis is given to programs designed to improve rural conditions in poverty areas of the Region.

Timber Management

When the National Forests were established, one purpose was to furnish a continuing supply of timber for the use and needs of the people of the United States. Region 3, with more than 5,000,000 acres of commercial forest land under its management, helps to accomplish this objective without impairing the productivity of the land and at the same time considering other resource needs.

The timber management plan for each National Forest shows how much timber is available, how much can be cut, when and where it can be cut. Areas are divided into timber sale units, and before timber is offered for sale, the area is examined to determine what trees will be removed, the estimated volume that can be cut, the timber stand improvement needs, and what treatment may be desired to protect the area from fire, insects, disease, and erosion.

In making such determinations, the other specialists of the Forest Service are consulted—engineers, landscape architects, soil and water specialists, range conservationists. Oftentimes timber sales benefit other resources, by opening up timber stands and thereby permitting more plants to grow which provide forage for wildlife, and by increasing water yields, since snowpacks increase on cutover areas.

When timber is sold it is offered for bid by advertising for 30 days in local newspapers, and the minimum acceptable bid is the current fair market value.

The timber sale contract covers how timber will be cut, measured and paid for, what improvements will be constructed, how logging operations will be conducted, what fire precautions will be necessary, etc.

The management plan for the working circle outlines the silvicultural needs, that is, what is needed to place the forest and forest lands into its best growing condition. Existing stands are examined to determine what improvement work is desirable and what areas with scattered or no timber must be reforested.

The reforestation is accomplished both by natural regeneration from remaining trees that furnish seed, or by hand or machine seeding or planting.   Oftentime large area seeding is done by airplane.   Planting is done with seedlings from Forest Service nurseries.

Explaining the work of the Timber Management Division, F. LeRoy Bond reported that as an example, "Region 3 during the 1969 fiscal year planted 710 acres with ponderosa pine, Englemann spruce, white fir and Douglas-fir seedlings.   The total such acreage to date is 15,122 acres.

"Another 3,816 acres were sown with pine, spruce, and fir seeds.   The total acreage seeded to date is 24,858 acres.

"About 30,679 acres of young pine stands have been thinned. Thinning removes enough trees in dense young stands to give the optimum number of crop trees the needed growing space to put on the maximum growth the site can produce.

Division of Operation

The Division of Operation has the major responsibility of providing service to all other Regional Office divisions and to National Forests and Ranger Districts in the Southwestern Region. There are five broad program areas: Financial Management, Administrative Services, Administrative Management, Automatic Data Processing, and Manpower and Youth Conservation Programs.

The Financial Management unit is responsible for budget planning and execution of approved budgets, exercising management control over the obligation and expenditure of funds. Administrative Services is responsible for leadership, training, regional policy development and operational responsibility for contracting, procurement, real and personal property management, and records management for the Region.

Administrative Management is chiefly an analytical unit concerned with studies aimed at improving organization, workload measurement, performance, flow of work, inventories, etc.   Forest Service Manual directives by the various divisions are edited and published here.   This section also has overall responsibility for administration of the employee suggestion program.

The complexity of the Region's business operation brought about establishment of an automatic Data Processing Unit.   The Division uses a Univac business-type computer and has access through inter-agency agreements with larger computers for complex computations.   In December, 1969, the Region's Univac 1005 was connected via telephone line with the National Bureau of Standards Univac 1108 large-scale computer, thus greatly increasing the Regon's capability.

Manpower and Youth Conservation Programs is an important unit of the Division of Operation.   The Region is deeply involved in a number of manpower training programs as part of the overall effort to improve rural economy and train people to compete for jobs in the current labor market.   The programs include Operation Mainstream, Neighborhood Youth Program, Concentrated Employment Program, Willing to Work and Work Incentive—all of which have a common objective—to train people for better jobs and raise them above the poverty level.

From 1965 to 1969, a highly important major program was the Civilian Conservation Centers under the Job Corps Program, administered in Region 3 by the Division of Operation.   In 1971 and 1972 the Youth Conservation Corps provided practice and education in natural resource management to high school age youths.

Personnel Management

The Personnel Management program of Region 3 extends over 10 Divisions at the Regional Office level and 12 National Forests,—with total employment ranging from 1700 to 2800 at the peak.   This involves the 81 Ranger Districts, five Civilian Conservation Corps Centers (four now closed by Presidential order), and the Continental Divide Training Center.   The Division is staffed with 18 employees in the Regional Office and twelve at the Continental Divide Training Center.   Each National Forest is staffed with a personnel management specialist and one clerk to administer the personnel program.

The program as outlined by M. D. Ray, formerly Chief of the Division, has these objectives:

"To recruit and maintain a flexible, efficient, and productive force which will contribute directly and effectively to the accomplishment of the mission of the Forest Service.

"To motivate managers, supervisors and employees to render responsive service to the public.

"To improve our systems, practices and planning to obtain more effective and productive use of manpower.

"To provide a dynamic organization responsive to the accomplishment of work through people.

"To treat employees equitably and fairly and help them achieve personal satisfaction by enhancing their opportunities for career advancement through training and wise utilization of their abilities.

"To preserve the integrity and merit of the Federal Civil Service by carrying out public policy as expressed in laws, Executive Orders, and regulations."

As it has with other Divisions, increased interest and use of Forest resources has created tremendous management challenges. During the 1960's the employment level tripled to keep pace with expansion of programs and operating budget.

The Job Corps

The accomplishments of the Job Corps in New Mexico and Arizona were considerable, and brought high praise and recognition to Region 3. From their inception until four of the five Conservation Centers, as they were formally called, were terminated on June 30, 1969, they had produced better than $6,000,000 worth of improvements on public lands.

"But the real measure of accomplishment," according to Roy Gandy, who was the Job Corps administrator in Regional Headquarters, "was in what it did for the enrollees."

Since the Job Corps was essentially a training program, corpsmen were trained on actual, live, on-the-job situations in the National Forests as construction carpenters, bricklayer apprentices, cement masons, operating engineers, production line welders, cooks, auto mechanics and forestry aids.

"The average enrollee came to the Centers with a reading level below the fourth grade," Gandy noted. "Of those who stayed six months or more at any of the centers, we placed 70 percent of them in jobs in private employment."

Four training centers were established in 1965 at Grants and Mountainair, New Mexico and Alpine and Heber, Arizona. The fifth center was established at Camp Luna, Las Vegas, New Mexico in 1966. Alpine, which operated on the Apache Forest, had a capacity of 120 corpsmen. Heber, 125 miles northeast of Phoenix in the Sitgreaves Forest, has a capacity of 210. This camp is one of the group scattered throughout the United States which was selected to remain open after the main program terminated on July 30, 1969. The Grants Center, on the Cibola Forest had a capacity of 210 corpsmen, as did the Mountainair Center, also on the Cibola. The Luna Center, on the Santa Fe Forest, had a capacity of 224 corpsmen.

"The boys came from rural areas mostly." Gandy related. "The majority were Negro boys from the deep South of Louisiana, Arkansas and Texas. Most of them had never been outside their own neighborhoods before. They were willing to work. They just had not had the opportunity or know-how. The work program at the centers was a totally integrated vocational training program. Work habits, safety and work attitudes were high priority training items.

"The education program consisted primarily of basic remedial education and the 3 R's. Reading and math curriculums were especially designed for the populations that the Centers attempted to serve."

How well this was accomplished is indicated by the scores in the national achievement tests given at all centers. Mountainair and Grants stood among the top five in the nation.

The Job Corps administrators can point to some outstanding examples of construction achieved. They built roads, stock tanks, range fences, worked in timber stand improvement, juniper control, and building construction.

"The Corpsmen constructed the entire Ranger Station complexes at Mountainair and Tijeras on the Cibola National Forest, each of which would have cost more than a hundred thousand dollars if built on contract," Gandy said. "They built 10 miles of the Lobo Canyon road out of Grants and did such a good basic job that the Highway department followed up and paved the 10 miles then added another five. This is primarily a recreation road, but eventually this road will probably be completed by the Forest Service and provide a short cut route between Grants and Cuba."

The accomplishments of the Job Corps are all the more notable when it is pointed out that the trainees were enrolled under the following criteria: "16 to 21 years of age; school dropouts for three months or more; unable to find or hold adequate jobs; under-privileged from having grown up in impoverished surroundings; in need of change of environment to become useful productive citizens."

In addition to the accomplishment in improvements on public lands and the success of the training programs, the Centers had a substantial economic impact on the communities where they were located. The Centers had a total budget of approximately $5 million a year—a large percentage of which found its way into the communities.

When the Executive Order from the President brought about closure of four of the Centers, two of the New Mexico Centers were turned over to the State of New Mexico to operate a branch college at Grants, and a vocational training school at Luna (Las Vegas). The Alpine Center in Arizona was turned over to the State of Arizona for use of the State Department of Corrections. The Mountainair Center was used for several projects.

Job Corps Centers gave basic educational and vocational opportunities to thousands of young men and women.

Continental Divide Training Center, opened in 1962, provided facilities for intensive training of Forest Service employees in technical and administrative skills.

The Heber Center, which was selected to continue operations, undertook a program of operating under some rather unique concepts. The Center negotiated two contracts, one with the International Brotherhood of Carpenters and another with the Painters and Decorators Union, to do training in these two vocations.

Continental Divide Training Center

The Southwestern Region of the Forest Service operates its own training center at Continental Divide on the edge of the Gallup Ranger District of the Cibola National Forest.

Here in a new complex of classrooms, offices and dormitories, Forest Service employees have the opportunity to improve their skills and prepare for advancement in their chosen field. Classes are conducted throughout most of the year (except during the height of the fire season) and employees have a choice of more than 60 courses, everything from Beginning Spanish to Geodesy and Photogrammetry, and a variety of management courses.

Courses vary from four days to a month. Beginning Spanish, for example, is a four weeks course. Upon completion, the trainee will have a vocabulary of 2,000 Spanish words, be able to conjugate 100 common verbs, and have a basic idea of Spanish customs and culture. This course is designed particularly for employees in Northern New Mexico.

All new professional employees are required to take an indoctrination course, which lasts two weeks.

There is no tuition charge for Forest Service employees. Trainees other than Region 3 employees are charged $50 per course and $10 a day for room and board.

The Forest Service Museum is located at the Training Center.

Forest Service Museum

Undoubtedly one of the most unusual collections of historical materials in the Southwest has been brought together in the Forest Service Museum at the Continental Divide Training Center.

Here, the history of the Forest Service and its progress through 65 years of growth is told in the collection of photographs, tools, office equipment, correspondence, diaries, furniture, etc. Everything imaginable that was used by Forest Service employees is displayed, from a Washington wood-burning stove to a complete tack room. A 1910 Supervisor's office has been reproduced, complete with rolltop desk, a pioneer model Oliver typewriter, wooden files, and even a wire basket with an original letter from a

Supervisor. Old style grounded telephone and exchange, a tool room, and a collection of maps, photographs and old letters enhance the collection. One panel shows an exchange of correspondence between Supervisor Fred Winn and the western author, Zane Grey, relative to arrangements for a bear hunting trip with Ben Lily, the famous bear hunter and guide.

Just outside the door is a pair of giant logging wheels such as were used in the Forests in earlier years.

The historical collection has special interest for Forest Service personnel who visit the Continental Divide Training Center, but is also attracting tourists from Interstate Route 1-40. So much popular interest has been exhibited in the Museum that there is consideration for establishing it at a Visitors' Center, probably near Flagstaff.

Fire Control

In the Southwestern National Forests, 2,054 men (768 regular and 1,286 part-time) are trained and constantly ready to attack forest fires whenever and wherever they occur. In addition, other firefighters are employed as needed during the year to assist the regular firefighters. In the past year, this number totalled 8,000 who were employed for one day or more.

The fire control organization consists of the basic management unit, the Ranger District; the National Forest fire team, and the Regional fire team. Should it prove impossible for the Ranger District to suppress the fire, the National Forest fire team takes over the fire control task. Each of these fire control organizations is an expansion of another. As the organization expands, the more specifically trained men are placed in individual roles to insure an efficient team operation.

The basic fire tools that were used when the Forest Service was first organized are still efficiently used—shovels, axes, and fire rakes. In addition, the fire control organization has access to a variety of newly developed fire control equipment. Fire retardant chemicals are carried by air tankers, helicopters, trucks and water pumper units. Radio communication networks are available as well as other products of our modern technological society.

From its inception in 1905 until World War II, the primary mission of the Forest Service was to protect the National Forests from fire, disease, insects, theft and depredation. Land abuse and indiscriminate burning on public lands of the West had made protection necessary to stabilize exposed and eroding soils to maintain existing forests and ranges and permit re-establishment of desirable vegetation.

The Forest Service Museum displays tools, equipment and documents used by Forest Officers.

At the Museum's dedication Chief Forester Cliff and Regional Forester Fred Kennedy try out furniture used in Forest offices in the early 1900's.

The tremendous assets of the National Forests, which had hardly been tapped until they were needed by the requirements of war, went into a new phase of management use. By 1950, the management and use of National Forest resources was in full swing. The extensive harvesting of timber created additional fire hazard, requiring new methods of control.

The Forest Service in 1953 began to use fire as a tool in order to reduce the fuel volume existing in isolated areas where accumulations of dry, inflammable forests developed. Using prescribed fire, the fuel volume of these areas was reduced to the desired level. The first efforts were restrained and not always what were desired, but as attitudes about use of fire as a forest management tool changed, there was more extensive use of fire to reduce large areas of dead, dry vegetation.

This type of prescribed fire is now being used throughout the Southwest Region and has been steadily reducing some of the isolated areas of dead and highly explosive forest fuels.

Coupled with the prescribed burning program is the newly introduced fuel-break system. Together they form two parts of the three-part Conflagration Control System, which is designed to forestall escape of small forest fires or prevent their expanding into uncontrollable conflagrations.

The third part of the system is, of course, the employment of the skilled firefighters and their equipment.

No matter how modern or extensive the equipment, the real heroes of the Forest Service fire department are the Rangers, the firemen, the lookouts and equipment operators who respond to each fire emergency. Without them, forests and streams, mountains and vital soil would be lost forever, for forest and range management are impossible without fire protection.

Their dedication to their job, plus the effective use of all the resources of the Conflagration Control System, are helping to slowly overcome nature's awe-inspiring strength as witnessed in the hurricane force of large forest fires.

CHAPTER XXV
Public Relations

Public Relations was a rather neglected activity with the Service in its early years except as a byproduct of the Ranger's normal contacts with grazing associations and other organizations or individuals.

When Ward Shepard was in the Regional Office back around World War I days, he started a program of public relations. Then when Edward Ancona went to the Regional Office after World War I to become office manager, he handled what little public relations was accomplished. The first actual public relations division was set up in 1922 with Joseph C. Kircher, assistant district forester, in charge.

In 1924, John D. Jones was transferred from the Lands Division to the Public Relations Division. George H. Cook, who has been a Ranger at Tijeras from 1918 to 1920, before moving into the Regional Office, became Jones' assistant.

"He was my assistant for a long time," Jones recalled. "He was the one that originated the motion picture trips around the country. He was running that before I took over. He had a little generator and one projector.

"Our main job was to try to keep the public informed of what the Forest Service objective was, and why we were doing certain things. For instance, the stockmen were still undecided as to whether range management was of any value. They figured they'd been in the business all their lives and they knew more about it than we did. Our job was to convince them that we had made studies and knew how much of the grass could be harvested. I found that most of the old-timers had the idea that grass and water were indestructible, that the ground-water supply—you could pump it forever. It just replaced itself. And that the grass would replace itself, there'd never be any shortage. We finally convinced them through our studies that you could harvest bunchgrass about 40 percent of the volume and your range would stay in good shape forever, and you could harvest up to about 60 per cent of the grama grasses. It took a long time to convince those people of that."

The Public Relations Division had a traveling exhibit with motion picture projector which was called the Showboat.   George Russell, who had been a Ranger on the Datil and Lincoln Forests, had taken over the Showboat in the late 20's.

"There was an interesting incident that came up in connection with George Russell," Jones recalled.   "I had heard that he was a good shot.   We went over to Pinyon, and there was a group there that had been kind of troublesome.   They didn't like the Forest Service.   George said, 'If anything happens over here tonight while we're showing the picture, you turn out the lights and I'll do the rest.'

"I didn't know what he meant, but on the way home that night, up Weed Canyon on the way to the Ranger Station we were in this old Dodge truck rockin' along the road.   A little skunk dropped out in the road ahead of us.   George, hanging onto the wheel with one hand reached for his pistol with the other and killed that skunk—shooting him in the head.

"I didn't think too much of it, but we went a little further and a second skunk came out.   That time I held the wheel for him, and he did it again.   Then I knew what he meant when he had said, 'I'll take care of 'em if you'll turn the lights off.'

"George was a surprising character.   He was such a mild looking fellow, you'd have thought that he was a preacher or something.

"There was another interesting incident on George: We used to have a lot of trouble at the Ranger station at Monticello in the San Mateos.   There were a couple of Rangers driven out of there.   There were some people who were kind of troublesome down there in those days in that isolated village.   So they sent George down.   The first time he came into the village, as he rode in there were a bunch of boys—kids—playing out on the hill, just above town.   There was a can dump nearby, George turned to one of the bigger boys and said, 'You want to see some shootin'?   And the boys said, 'Oh, sure.'

"George told one of them to pick up a can and throw it in the air about 60 feet.   George put two bullets through it before it hit the ground!   He never had a bad word said to him all the time he was Ranger there.   He was extra good on propaganda. He knew just how to deal with people."

Jones said that one of the big problems of those days was erosion.

"I think I did the first original work on erosion in the Region," he recounted.   "I developed a lecture on that.   It dawned on me, the problem on erosion, when I was making a saddle-horse trip in California. I rode up a long valley east of Salinas, up to the San Bernito Forest, and I followed a little draw that had been a valley stream, and I noticed that it was cut out. I followed it for I guess 20 miles that day before I found any settlement. Then at the head of the valley there was a nice little farm, and there was no erosion beyond that. It stopped, and there was water. Well, I knew something was wrong. Then when I came down on the railroad from Portland I noticed when we came over the Stony Creek Wash that the railroad had been built up over a hump, and all that rock and gravel had come down from the Coast Range there. Well, those things began to percolate in my mind and I began thinking about it. When I came here from Montana where we had no erosion problems, my first trip was down on the Tonto and Coronado and, with the amount of grass they had there I couldn't see why a self-respecting cow would spend her time looking for it. I even suggested that they close the whole Tonto Basin to grazing, because its principal purpose then was irrigation, and the erosion was terriffic.

"So I developed my lecture on that. I gave it to some of the Indian pueblos. The Indian Service requested that I make a trip over to the Navajo Reservation, so J. S. Nave and I made that trip and I gave this talk. At Fort Defiance, old Chee Dodge was then chief, and he liked it so well that he had me give it three times and he interpreted it for me.

"Before that I used to attend the meetings at the State College when they'd have their meeting in the winter. I was put on the program by Dr. Kent down there one morning, and I decided to give my erosion talk. Well, Dr. Kent got off on something and he took up quite a bit of my time, so I had to crowd mine in. I didn't have time to show the pictures that I had. At noon he picked me up and took me to Kiwanis for dinner, and he said that was the best talk made at this convention. He said 'You folks have got a big problem.' I said, 'You've got a bigger problem.' He looked at me kind of surprised and said, 'What's that?' I said, 'The State of New Mexico owns 12 million acres, and your Land Office is nothing but an accounting office; they are doing nothing to protect the land. There's no limit on the number of stock that you can put on a unit, and I quoted a couple of instances that I knew about. He says, 'By golly, you're right. I'm going to do something about it.' So he called in his range men that he had there and they set out a little experiment station right there at the college farm. I told him that he could see ours on the Jornada right nearby, and get a lot of information from that.

"Later, when we started the program of the CCC's putting in these check-dams, I went down and looked over the one at Silver City and the work on that watershed there. Fortunately, the Forest Service had fenced that area two years before, and a year after they'd put in those little check-dams the old spring on the farm up there started running. It had been dry for several years. So that showed that the water had all been running down the wash through town.

"Fleming took over that work and he came in the office here one day and talked to me about it. I told him the only problem in solving erosion on the rangelands was a reduction in grazing, that all a check-dam did was stop the erosion until the dam filled up and then it ran over and it was worse than it was before, that unless you had enough grass by the time the dam filled up that you didn't need it, your work was all wasted. He still thought the check-dams were the stuff. He was flying to a range meeting up at Fort Collins cross-country. I told him, 'When you're going over, look at this Galisteo area there and you'll see those fingers just coming in all over, every one of them building an *arroyo,* and draining water out of the country that should be feeding the grass.'

"He looked at me kind of skeptical; I knew he didn't believe it. So when he came back he came up to the office and he looked pretty near all out of breath and he said, 'You're dead right! that's the problem.' So I worked on that. I think that was probably the most important thing I did in the public relations field at that time.

"In 1922 when I first started, Nels Field—he was from Magdalena—was with the State Land Commission. I went into his office and I said, 'Nels, you grew up, didn't you, down near Magdalena? Was the Rio Salado and the Rio Puerco a big wash then like they are now?" He said, "Well, no, there wasn't anything. As a boy I used to drive our sheep and follow the wagon up the Puerco. You could drive the full length of it. Now, by golly, it's 30 feet deep banks there." I said, "Well, there were little groves of trees, you remember. There at those groves, if you dug a little hole there'd be a little seep and you'd water your sheep?" He said "Yes." I said, "You'd take them out on the west side one day, bring them home at night. And the next day you'd take them out on the other side and you'd bring them home, and you'd stay there all summer. By the end of the summer there wasn't any grass there. And then the slope was like a tin roof and the water would all slide in and it'd start cutting."

"He said 'Heck, how did you know that?' I said, 'All you have to do is look at the country and you can see.' Then he said the floods would come down and gouge out holes, skip a ways and dig another hole and every year the holes would get bigger, and pretty soon the whole thing would sluff off. So I had that as evidence from an actual man. He didn't know what was happening, but he knew it had happened because he saw it.

"I sent a memo in to the investigator's committee; I imagine it's lost in the files, in which I made a statement that I had read all of the engineering publications in Arizona and New Mexico that I could get hold of on flooding and erosion and that I yet had never found a single person who had thought about what was causing it. All they were thinking about was putting some kind of structures in the way of dams to stop it. But the reason they were having these floods, never occurred to them; that the land had been overgrazed!

Discussing Forest Service operations, Paul Roberts, who spent 40 years in the Service, said he felt that "tremendous progress has been made, and is being made."

"I think one of the great things has been the public opinion concerning conservation," Roberts said. "I had always thought that the Forest Service was not a very good public relations organization. They never seemed to be able to put the story across too well, someway. But I think we must be doing that now. I think such things as 4H clubs and the other various agricultural activities among youths, so that a greater number of the younger generation who are going to college and studying husbandry and management—all this is contributing to what is almost a tremendous movement for the conservation of natural resources."

Gifford Pinchot, the "father" of the Forest Service, was a strong believer in aggressive public relations. For years after he left the Forest Service, he was a lecturer on forest policy at the Yale School of Forestry.

"Find out in advance what the public will stand for," Pinchot lectured students. "If it is right, and they won't stand for it, postpone action and educate them.

"Public support of acts affecting the public rights is absolutely required. Use the press first, last and all the time if you want to reach the public."

The Region 3 office in recent years has been a staunch advocate of taking the public into its confidence and has developed a highly effective public relations division. In 1937, it became the Information and Education Division, and the head of the division held status as Assistant Regional Forester.

Following John D. Jones' tenure the late Rex King became head of the Division in 1935 and remained in that position until 1950. King was a quiet, hard-working forester, who had been Supervisor of the Crook National Forest from 1923 to 1935, and a dedicated forester. After his retirement the I&E Division became part of Watershed Management and something of an orphan activity.

J. Morgan Smith was transferred from the Washington office to Region 3 in 1958 to assume charge of the I&E activities, and in 1961 a separate Division was created, with Smith in charge.

The importance of the I&E activities is stressed by Regional Forester William D. Hurst in his foreword to the current Multiple Use Management Guide:

"Forest Service program accomplishment and coordination hinges strongly upon an effective I&E program to gain the necessary public support and understanding of multiple use management. Full information relative to the needs and desires of local communities and Forest users groups must be understood and considered in the overall development of responsive coordination measures. Without full public cooperation, multiple use management cannot succeed."

Morgan Smith believes that the most important phase of his job is what he calls "preventive public relations." This is the development of I&E action plans in advance of undertaking projects or activities involving the public, rather than trying to explain them afterwards. Morgan Smith is a great believer in Gifford Pinchot's advice to educate the public by taking them into your confidence in advance rather than try to undo damage "after the fact."

The I&E Division is a many-faceted operation, and to carry out directions of the Multiple Use Management Guide the Division engages in a variety of activities running the gamut of public information activities such as booklets, maps, motion pictures, and talks to service clubs, conservation, farm and livestock organizations and other groups. An important phase of its work is relating public needs and desires to the activities of other divisions of the Forest Service, which may be of assistance in furthering policies of the Service. In a sense, every employee of the Forest Service is engaged in I&E work and the I&E Division of the Regional Office makes periodic inspections of the Forests within the Region to determine the effectiveness of the local public relations "climate."

In a recent inspection report, the I&E inspectors (the Chief of the I&E Division and his assistant) noted that they are "convinced that the Supervisor and his personnel are cognizant of the fact that there is an I&E aspect to practically everything we do. Several Multiple Use Impact surveys reviewed recommended that special I&E Plans of Action would have to be carried out before certain projects could be undertaken. This is solid 'PR.' "

In an inspection report, the I&E inspectors called attention to "broadcast burning of slash and debris" along a section of state highway, in which a considerable number of trees were scorched:

"This unsightly condition did not seem to bother local Forest officers, but to the inspectors, it looked extremely bad."

Reviewing the report, Regional Forester William D. Hurst noted that, "With all the emphasis the Forest Service is placing on natural beauty, we cannot live with a practice that leaves an unsightly condition in a Travel Influence Zone. We cannot tolerate a scorched appearance even for a year, if indeed the needles will fall off this season."

In another Forest, to preserve natural beauty a landscape architect prepared plans for a juniper eradication program so that all junipers were not merely eradicated, but rather done so in a pleasing appearance plan, which left some junipers for appearance sake and some as an "escape" route for wildlife which might graze in the open areas.

Such I&E activities are out of the ordinary but certainly effective public relations tools in the Forest Service's continuing campaign to keep the support of the public in its varied activities.

The I&E Division is diligent in "selling" its own Forest Service personnel on doing effective public relations work in the local communities.

A good example of its inspections to determine how well I&E policies are carried out is one last year on the Apache National Forest, the first on that Forest in several years. This was a seven-day inspection visit by the chief of the Division, J. Morgan Smith, and his assistant, George Worley. A full week was devoted to a variety of activities, which included visits to the Supervisor's headquarters and to Ranger Stations, a trip into the Blue Range Primitive Area, an inspection trip into the Mt. Baldy Primitive Area with the Regional Forester and Apache Forest personnel, interviews with prominent business men, state officials, permittees, conservation organization members, and attendance at a campground dedication.

From this inspection came a list of 21 recommendations, noting what is already being done from an I&E standpoint and and suggestions for further strengthening the public relations image of the Apache National Forest.

A few of the recommendations will indicate the extent of the I&E inspection activity:

"Overall, the 'public relations climate' of the Apache is favorable.

"The dedication of the Rolfe C. Hoyer Campground* and Memorial on June 22 provided the inspectors with an exceptionally good opportunity to talk with local people and a large number of state conservation organizations' representatives from the Phoenix area. The turnout of about 300 people for this event is testimony to the regard which most Arizonans have for Forest Service personnel and the Apache."

"The Forest's relationship with stockmen appears to be satisfactory. However (an attorney) was critical of the Forest Service because it had not done enough for the county in providing developed recreation facilities. . . .

"Outside of Greenlee County, there appears to be a general public support in the Springerville and Phoenix Area for reclassification of the Blue Range Primitive Area. Even in Greenlee County there are some supporters for reclassification. (Stockmen in the Clifton area and Greenlee County Supervisors were reported opposed to reclassification.)

"Some criticism was encountered about lack of adequate cleanup on a timber sale in the Bull Canyon area. There is a growing public insistence that there must be adequate cleanup after timber is harvested.

"Forest personnel's participation in community activities is outstanding and special mention should be made of the fact that two forest officers are president-elect respectively of the Rotary and Lions Clubs in Springerville."

There were numerous other comments and recommendations regarding the "public relations climate" of the Apache National Forest, but in general the inspection report was so favorable that Regional Forester Hurst wrote the Supervisor, H. L. Cox complimenting him on the "fine I&E work being accomplished under your leadership."

---

*The new campground was named for a former Ranger, Rolfe C. Hoyer, who had served on the Coconino, the Lincoln and on the Apache Forest, and who gave his life fighting the Slaughter fire on May 19, 1967. He was recreation and lands staff officer for the Apache National Forest at the time of his death. At the dedication Fred Greenwald of the Arizona Conservation Council gave a talk in which he related the debt he personally owed to Rolfe Hoyer. Greenwald had experienced a massive heart attack while in the Blue Range Primitive Area a few years ago and it took Hoyer three days to get him out.

CHAPTER XXVI
The Modern Ranger

C. A. (Heinie) Merker, who spent nearly 40 years in the Forest Service before his retirement a few years ago, once said he felt there were "actually only two jobs in the Forest Service that you might say are ideal. One of them is the Ranger, and the other is the Forest Supervisor."

His sentiments have been echoed by others. Over the years the Rangers have been considered kings of their Districts, the men who run the show. Men who have gone up through the ranks invariably have the most pleasant reminiscences of the days when they were Rangers.

Some of the old-timers preferred to remain Rangers rather than accept administrative positions, and oftentimes preferred to remain in one location when they could.

Today the modern Rangers are moved around fast in various assignments, to give them experience in various Districts and operations. Organizational directories are out-dated almost before they are off the press.

While the old-time Ranger might not have had more than an eighth grade education, today's is invariably a college graduate and usually from a university with a forestry school. The old-time Ranger started his job at anywhere from $75 a month to $1200 a year and had to provide his own horses and their feed. The Forest Service provided housing, such as it was—often merely shelter. Today, salaries are more in line with positions of like responsibility, and while all of the Ranger Station residences are not modern, the old ones are being replaced gradually, and new ones are being provided that are equal to homes in the better subdivisions of nearby cities.

While it used to be that the Forest Service would allot $500 to $600 to build a house—and often the Ranger had to help build it himself—today the maximum that can be spent to construct a residence is $22,000.

Henry Woodrow, long-time Ranger on the Gila wrote, in some reminiscences of his Forest Service years, that in 1912 he was allotted $75 to build a log cabin at the Ranger Station. With the $75 he hired a man to help him and they put up a cabin and covered it with shakes or boards split from a pine tree.

Edward Ancona remembers that when he first went to the Prescott National Forest in 1912 that he helped build the Willow Creek Station "with a limitation of $600 on the building construction." "I think we stayed within our $600 limit, if you can imagine building a house, a three- or four-room house for $600. It took some finagling."

The Ranger Station homes that were in existence even in the 30's and 40's were nothing to brag about. Dean Cutler, assistant chief of the Regional Recreation and Lands Division, recalls that when he first went to Reserve the house he was assigned was somewhat primitive. "We kept wondering why we'd find sawdust on the baby's blanket in the bedroom," he recalled. "We investigated and found that carpenter ants had eaten out practically the whole inside of a beam."

When Walter Graves, chief of the Regional Operation Division, was assigned to the Coyote District of the Carson National Forest in 1939—his first assignment as a full-fledged Ranger—he found that his home would be an *adobe* house without electricity and with mud-plastered interior walls.

Graves continued to have house problems and recalls that of five he occupied only one was in good condition. When he was moved to the Long Valley District on the Coconino in 1944, "One of my first jobs was to enclose the back porch and construct a new front porch and then put new oak floors in the living room and front bedroom," he related. "Incidentally, I understand that about three years after I had laid these floors the termites had eaten the floors to a point that when the Ranger's wife was vacuuming one day, the vacuum cleaner fell right through the floor. We found later, of course, that the entire house was just completely eaten up with termites."

Graves' experiences with poor housing had extended back to the time when he was given a temporary appointment as Assistant Ranger under J. W. Johnson, who had been Ranger on the Pecos District for many years.

"When we moved into the house we were to occupy," he related, "I found that it was about ready to fall down. As a matter of fact, the walls along the dining room on the south side of the house had fallen away from the ceiling so that there was a three-inch gap between the ceiling and the wall. Our first job was to correct this problem. We found the roof joints in the attic had not been tied to the walls and the weight of the roof was pushing the walls out. We went in with a jack from the basement and jacked the roof up, pulled the walls back in, and tied them together.

"The next problem was the well. There was an old windmill at the corner of the old office that supplied water to the Ranger station. We found that the water was so polluted with gasoline that my predecessor had been able to bail "water" out of the well and actually burn it in the trucks.

"I can remember that during that first winter we had a little tin stove in the office, and the way I started fires in the morning was to bail a bucket of water out of the well and throw it into the stove and toss a match in! And it burned real well.

"There was quite a lot of excitement around Pecos as a result of this. We had a number of geologists examining not only the well but the surrounding country, and the final decision was that there was a pocket of gas that had drained from some distant source into the area and that this was what we had tapped. This of course made the water completely unusable. On a hunch I sent a sample of the water to the University for analysis, and they found that there was not only gasoline in the water but there was also *Bacillus coli* in sufficient quantities to be very dangerous. When the Supervisor received the analysis on this, he was out at Pecos the next day locating a new well. A new well was drilled. We hit the same strata of gas about the same depth as in the old well, but this was cased off and the driller went on down several hundred feet farther and did bring in a very excellent well, which is still being used."

The well, with its stone pump house, is about the only thing at the Pecos Ranger Station that is left from early days. There is a completely new station, built in two sections in the past several years, a whole new complex of pre-fab warehouse buildings and several fairly new three and four-bedroom homes to house the professional staff members and their families. The attractive homes, well-built and well-insulated, had been moved in from the Continental Divide Training Center.

Because of his own experiences with housing conditions as a Ranger, Chief of Operations Graves is sympathetic to the needs of the Ranger staffs, but not optimistic about catching up.

"Unfortunately," he explained, "the funds that we receive for this work are very inadequate, and at the present time we are not able to do much more than meet our current needs. We are getting about enough money to construct one complete Ranger Station a year. This does not mean that we concentrate on constructing one station—office, a couple of houses, a warehouse, barn and other necessary facilities—but the equivalent of that."

The Pecos Ranger Station is one of the fortunate ones that has been rebuilt. It is also a good example of what has been happening all over the Forest Service in the Southwest in recent years. From the days when a Ranger and a couple assistants handled the work, today there is a permanent staff of 15, of whom seven are professionals—three of them, incidentally, graduates of the University of Missouri. During the summer the staff increases to as many as 60 people.

The professional foresters and the Ranger himself, Arthur Maynard, are young men—mostly in their thirties. They have 225,000 acres of forest and range to administer and protect from fires, something like 57,000 summer visitors to look after, and eight million board feet of logs to check out in timber sales.

In the old days, the Rangers covered this District on horseback. And it's still horseback country, for the Pecos Wilderness is part of it. Today, the District has a *remuda* of 27 horses, a fleet of trucks, a couple snowmobiles—and a heliport for helicopter landings. (The District has a cooperative agreement with the Air Force for search and rescue operations, using Air Force helicopters to bring ill or injured out of the Wilderness.)

But with all the different modes of transportation available, firefighters still find that there are a few places that they still can't reach by any means of travel except hiking in. A fire behind Penitente Peak last year took five and one-half hours to reach on foot.

The Ranger and his assistants may be better educated and better trained than the old-time Rangers, but they are still just as rugged. They are still men to match the mountains!

There are many modern Rangers who are "tall in the saddle"—of whom their old-time predecessors would be proud. There are some who have given their lives to their jobs . . . men like Rolfe Hoyer, of the Apache Forest, who was killed while fighting a forest fire, and Ken Sahlin, fire control officer on the Apache, who was killed in a plane crash. Sahlin had served earlier as a Ranger at Tres Piedras and on the Coronado.

Rolfe Hoyer lost his life fighting the Slaughter Fire in the Apache Forest on May 19, 1967. Born on a farm near Kalamazoo, Mich., he early developed an interest in the outdoors, and when he entered Michigan State University he studied forestry, and received his degree in that field. He joined the Forest Service in 1956 on the Coconino National Forest and later became an assistant District Ranger and then Ranger on the Mayhill District of the Lincoln National Forest in New Mexico. In 1962, Rolfe Hoyer was assigned to the Apache National Forest, where he served with distinction as recreation and lands staff officer until his untimely death.

Ken Sahlin was killed when he and Mayor Ernie Becker of Springerville, Arizona and their pilot were circling a small forest fire on June 25, 1962. The plane crashed and all three were killed.

An excerpt from a letter to the Forest Service staff from Mrs. Sahlin best described the kind of Ranger Sahlin was:

"Ken's life before we were married was crowded with worthwhile experiences . . . a good home, successful war record and college life. From the very first day of his Forest Service career, Ken loved to go to work—be it weekday, weekend, or three in the morning. Few men are so fortunate to find such a successful and personally satisfying way to raise and support their families. Because Ken was happy in his work, the Forest Service has my sincere gratitude. I would not have changed a minute of his life—except that last minute!"

After Sahlin's death, Mrs. Sahlin and their three children returned to Minnesota—his boyhood home—to live.

There are many other Rangers whose personal lives and work exemplify the best traditions of the Forest Service. It would be difficult to pick out the typical modern Ranger, for they come in all sizes and vary in age from the early thirties on up. Usually they have one very definite characteristic in common. They are dedicated men—with some men the Forest is almost a religion.

Mrs. Fred Swetnam, wife of the Ranger on the Jemez District of the Santa Fe Forest, has a little story that describes her husband's dedication to his job.

"We were at the El Rito Ranger District just before the birth of one of our boys," Mrs. Swetnam related. "It came time for Fred to rush me to the hospital at Espanola. On the way, he discovered some cows in trespass. There was nothing to do but stop and get the cows off the Forest and close a gate!"

"Oh, well," Fred put in, "it turned out to be a false alarm anyway."

Mrs. Swetnam is a typical Ranger's wife, or rather her experiences are typical—both of the old-time Ranger's wife and the modern Ranger's wife who usually plays a busy part in the life of a community.

They have lived under quite primitive conditions in times past, have spent 19 years of their lives on Ranger Districts, and have raised a happy family of three boys and a girl, all of them now teen-agers.

"Our place on the Lincoln National Forest at Mesa Ranger

Station was the bad one," Mrs. Swetnam remembered. "The plumbing wouldn't work, the place was cold, for the stove never worked properly, and I was almost afraid to step outside with baby because of the danger of rattlesnakes. For a city girl, I can tell you it was quite an adjustment."

Mesa was a one-man duty station, so Mrs. Swetnam had to become an auxiliary Ranger—taking telephone calls, relaying orders to fire guards, spotting fires, and a lot of other duties including cooking for emergency help and visitors.

Fred himself had to do everything that is done at a District from fire patrol, scaling logs, and handling permits to typing his own letters and reports.

Quite a difference today, when he has a work force of 23 men at peak periods and a professional staff of administrative assistants.

Fred Swetnam probably best exemplifies the transition period of the Forest Service—the changeover from the rough and ready ways of the early Forest Service to the highly complex multiple-use management operation of the present.

His work today is a far cry from his years on the El Rito and Ruidoso Districts when he personally fought fires, built fences, marked trees for cutting, and all the other variety of manual labor activities of a Forest district. Today, Fred Swetnam is an executive. Under the concept of today's operation he leaves much of the leg work and the routine to work crews and subordinates. His job is to manage the operation, to make decisions, to train and supervise, to become community involved.

He is probably as proud of this last category as any, for his service on the Technical Action Panel for Sandoval County brought a Distinguished Service Award from the Department of Agriculture. Only three of 3,000 counties won such recognition for their efforts to assist the economy of the community. As one of those Rangers who has what he calls "a limited knowledge" of Spanish, he has a rapport with the Spanish-speaking community and is *simpatico* to their problems and culture.

But Ranger Swetnam isn't the executive to the extent that he doesn't take a personal hand in the full operation of his District's activities. Having been exposed to all the problems, predicaments and emergencies that befall men in the woods, Swetnam is on constant alert and makes a daily practice of briefing his field crews and keeping in close touch with all that goes on in the 180,000 acres under his jurisdiction.

During the fire season he is especially close to his job, and every morning as his work crews and fire patrols prepare to depart, he gives his instructions over and over again, so that every detail is understood.

The Ranger not only has to worry about lightning strikes, but also careless people, for there is a tremendous influx of people into the Jemez country every weekend.

There are 15 campgrounds on the District, and just cleaning up after the weekend visitors is a big job.

To provide for the needs of maintenance and firefighting, there is a new warehouse full of equipment—everything from old-fashioned pack saddles and snowshoes to power saws and sleeping bags, and a variety of firefighting tools.

Swetnam is proud of the many Spanish New Mexicans who have worked with him over the years and their record with the Forest Service. He is particularly proud of the fact that his District has the distinction of having a third generation of one family on the payroll. He is Carlos J. Sandoval, fire dispatcher, who returned to the Jemez District office after service in Vietnam. Carlos' father, Simon Sandoval, retired after 31 years service, mostly as Cerro Pelado lookout. Simon Sandoval's father, Pete Sandoval, was employed on the District on trail and improvement maintenance and fire control work for 13 years prior to retirement in 1938.

The Ranger Station at Jemez Springs is a spanking new one—and perhaps that is one reason the Ranger would hate to leave this District. There are three new modern homes, too, but Swetnam and family decided they'd just as soon stay in the old house, which was built in 1928. "It's kind of like having a comfortable pair of old shoes," Swetnam explained. "You hate to give them up."

Like all modern Rangers, Swetnam is college trained. He was graduated from Colorado A & M in 1950 and took graduate work in range management in 1950-51. He went to work first at El Rito Ranger District, serving as assistant to a man he considers a great Ranger—Paul Martinez—then had three years as Ranger on the El Rito and Ruidoso Districts, and seven years at Penasco, headquarters of the southern district of the Carson National Forest, before being assigned to the Jemez District on the Santa Fe National Forest. On the Jemez he follows such outstanding Rangers as Leon Hill, Perl Charles and Len Lewis. Lewis, who had succeeded Charles in 1935, was killed November 1, 1938. Starting out at night with a truck and horse trailer for a camp where he would start a range and game survey next day, Lewis's truck and trailer slipped off a narrow curve and plunged down into Jemez Canyon. Both Lewis and his horse were killed. He was survived by his widow and nine children. They continued to make their home at Jemez Springs during the succeeding years.

A modern District Forest Ranger's Office, Springerville, Apache National Forest.

Modern buildings and equipment at the Jemez Ranger Station, Santa Fe National Forest

Talking about the difference between the old-time Ranger and the modern Ranger, Swetnam's superior, John M. Hall, Supervisor of the Santa Fe National Forest, thinks that the essential difference is that the old-time Ranger was strictly an outdoorsman. He carried on much of his job outdoors. Today the Ranger is a desk man by necessity. "I don't mean that he doesn't get out," Hall explained, "But the paper work and management problems tie him to his desk a great deal of the time. It's rare that I can't pick up the telephone and find one of my Rangers at his desk."

Supervisor Hall is something of a rarity since he skipped the Ranger phase of a career in the Forest Service. He had started as a timber scaler, then went into wildlife management and was for a number of years State Game Warden of Arizona before returning to the Forest Service in administrative work. But he is a strong booster for his Rangers and stresses the importance of the Ranger's job.

"It's the key to the success of the Forest Service," Hall said.

CHAPTER XXVII
Land Grant Country

It was a crisp October morning with a tang of autumn in the air. A bright sun kept breaking through the wispy clouds, giving promise of one of those beautiful fall days for which New Mexico is famous. All in all, it was an exciting kind of morning when you think it's a good day to be alive.

Before the morning was over, Ranger Walter Taylor had all the excitement he wanted for awhile. He knew that he was in deep trouble and that he might not even be alive to see the setting sun.

This was October 22, 1966, the day the Alianza Federal de Mercedes (an organization which included two or three hundred Spanish-speaking northern New Mexicans, including descendants of Spanish land grant heirs) had let it be known they planned a take-over of Carson National Forest lands—which they claimed were once part of a community land grant.

The organization led by Reies Tijerina, a militant ex-preacher, was seeking to stir up support for reopening land grant litigation, claiming community lands were taken over for public domain or obtained by fraud by private owners. The Alianza proposed to establish headquarters at Echo Amphitheater—a Forest Service picnic ground alongside U. S. 84, 65 miles north of Santa Fe.

This beautiful camp and picnic site, with its magnificent setting against the cream and pink colored cliffs where picnicking youngsters and their parents have for years been trying out their voices against the pulsating echoes, was to be their location of a new city-state, New Pueblo Republic of San Joaquin del Rio de Chama.

Since Echo Amphitheater is a public campground, the Forest Service had no intention of keeping anyone out, even people claiming title to the land. The visitors, however, were subject to the recreation-use fee.

The Forest Service assigned three Rangers to the campground: Walter Taylor, of Taos; Philip Smith, of Canjilon, and Chris Zamora from the Cibola National Forest. A few carloads of people arrived early, but when told they would have to pay the $1.00-a-day fee, they parked outside, along the highway.

State Police Officer Martin Vigil* was on duty outside the Forest boundary. He lectured the early visitors, announcing that he would not stand for any trouble. He told them the Forest Rangers were in charge inside the campground, and he was in charge outside. There was no trouble from this group.

Along about 10:30, a motorcade of cars approached Echo Amphitheater. Ranger Taylor was standing on one side of the cattle guard entrance to the grounds, Ranger Smith on the other. Turning into the campground, drivers sounded their horns, ignored the stop signs and the Rangers, then put on speed and headed through the gateway. The Rangers blocked the entrance, but had to jump out of the way or be knocked down. Probably 40 cars and trucks passed them as they stood helpless alongside the cattle guard. The cars pushed into parking areas, and a myriad of men, women and children erupted from the cars—laughing, talking, shouting.

Ranger Taylor remembered that he had left his pickup unlocked. He was afraid it might be looted if the crowd got out of hand. Among other things, a personal hand gun he usually carried in the car was lying on the seat under his jacket. He didn't want that to fall into someone's hands in this explosive situation, so he ran to the pickup. He had locked the door on the left side and was locking the door on the right side when Cristobal Tijerina, brother of the leader, came up to him and grabbed him by the necktie.

"Shut up," Cristobal Tijerina told the Ranger.

Ranger Taylor hadn't yet said a word.

"Don't talk to me like that," Taylor then told him.

"Shut up you son of a bitch," Tijerina said. "You're under arrest. "

If Cristobal was trying to provoke the Ranger, he had picked the right way to do it. Taylor clenched his fist and was just starting a swing when he was grabbed from behind. Hands clutched his arms, pulled at his shirt. There were shouts from men and women. . . . Get him. . . . kill him. . . ."

Taylor realized by now he had made a mistake in preparing to take a swing at Cristobal. Rifles and shotguns had made their appearance in the crowd. "I thought I was a dead man," Taylor related later. "I feel sure if I had hit him, someone would have shot me."

The men around him half dragged, half lifted him off his feet to take him toward a picnic table.

---

*Now Chief of State Police.

Ranger Smith, seeing the melee, rushed to help Taylor.   He was grabbed, too and up-ended and then practically carried along behind Taylor to the picnic table.   At the table was Jerry Noll, one of the Alianza leaders who had once proclaimed himself "King of the Indies."   He was hurriedly setting up court for the new city-state of San Joaquin.

Back in the crowd someone had grabbed Ranger Chris Zamora.   "Get your dirty hands off me," Zamora said in Spanish, pushing his "captor" away.

"Leave him alone," a voice said, "He's one of ours."   Being of Spanish extraction was the only "passport" needed to the Pueblo of San Joaquin on this day.

At the picnic table, "Judge" Jerry Noll was asking, "What are these men charged with?"

"Wilful trespassing."

"How about public nuisance?" the "judge" asked.

"Public nuisance, too."

About this time, Reies Tijerina, leader of the Alianza, got up on the picnic table bench to look over the crowd and the arrested men.

State Police Captain Martin Vigil came up to him, "Why are you holding these men?" Captain Vigil asked.

"Publicity," was the answer.

"If you're through with them, then let them go."

With Captain Vigil on hand to back them up, Rangers Taylor and Smith started to walk away.   "Judge" Noll was sentencing them, but the Rangers weren't paying any attention to him.

". . . . eleven months and 21 days—and $500 fine—all suspended on condition you leave the Pueblo and stay away."

Taylor and Smith got out their notebooks and started to write down the license numbers of cars parked in the area.

"If you do that we'll have to arrest you again," Tijerina told them.

All this time TV and news cameras had been grinding away, recording the scene of the take-over of the Forest.   People were milling around and setting up camp.

The Rangers, accompanied by Captain Vigil, Tijerina, and a group of Alianza "deputies" and followers, walked over to their pickups.   "You can't take them," Tijerina told them.   "They're impounded."

"Their personal things," Captain Vigil said.

Tijerina agreed they could take their personal belongings.

Taylor unlocked the door and reached in to get his coat and

gun from the seat.   He tried to keep the gun hidden under the coat and slide it out so he could shove it down inside his belt.

"As luck would have it," Taylor recounted later, "it slipped out of my hands and down to the ground.   A lot of people seemed to make a grab for it and got their hands on it, but I got my hand on the butt and hung on."

They were going to take the gun from Taylor, but Captain Vigil reminded Tijerina that the Rangers could have their personal articles.   The gun was a personal one.

By this time Taylor's anger was at the boiling point.   A soft voice said in a whisper from behind him, "Take it easy.   Take it easy."

It was Jim Evans, investigations officer of the Forest Service.

"He was wearing a black raincoat type of coat," Taylor explained, "and they must have taken him for a priest.   They never bothered him and he roamed all over the place, just as Chris Zamora did."

Some of the Alianza members even tried to talk Zamora into joining forces with them.

For the rest of the day, the Rangers remained outside the campground, observing from a distance what was happening inside.   During the afternoon, Tijerina stood on a picnic table and made a fiery speech in Spanish to his followers.

Taylor, who grew up in Western Colorado and speaks Spanish, heard him declaim that "Castro has what he has because he has guts.   Castro is getting every *gringo* out of Cuba, and we can do it here."

The blue flag of the Alianza, with its gold lettering proclaiming the Pueblo of San Joaquin was raised above the campground, and cardboard signs put over the Echo Amphitheater marker.

The Forest Service, fearing nightfall might bring violence, sent out a call for more Rangers, and they set up headquarters at Ghost Ranch Museum.   By 8 o'clock, the Pueblo of San Joaquin was as quiet as any other village in northern New Mexico, and the Rangers went home.

Forest Service officials swore out warrants for Reies Tijerina, Ezequiel Dominguez and Alfonso Chavez, charging them with assaulting the two Forest Rangers and conversion of government property.   They also applied to the Federal Court for an injunction restraining the Alianza membership from further occupation of the campground.   After a hearing the injunction was issued and the camp broke up.   The warrants against the five men were served and the men and their cause were headed for the courts.

Tijerina had claimed in press interviews that he was eager to get the land claims into the courts. "Our intention is to go to the Supreme Court."

The Forest Service issued a news release on October 29, 1966, stating that there was no Rio de Chama land grant. It was explained that the land of the original grant as confirmed by the courts is held under private ownership and is surrounded by National Forest.

The curtain came down—temporarily—on this first act in what has become a long drawn-out drama tinged with tragic overtones.

The basis for the plot of this modern drama goes back into history of the last couple of centuries. Millions of acres of New Mexico land had been granted by Spain and later by Mexico to individuals and to groups of colonists to establish settlements. One of these was the Cañon de Chama Grant, which had been given to 39 families who settled in the Chama Valley.

Confusion over the boundaries of this and other grants and also over the question of whether community lands as well as private lands were sold by heirs, and whether the United States government took over disputed lands for public domain, has kept the land grant issue alive for a hundred years.

After the American occupation of New Mexico when disputes began to arise over land grants, the Federal government undertook surveys of grants. In the 1870's, a surveyor general estimated the Cañon de Chama grant at 184,320 acres. Congress took no action on this, and it was re-surveyed in 1878. This survey estimated the grant at 472,000 acres. Again no action was taken by Congress to confirm the grant. In 1882, Congressman Hazelton introduced a resolution to confirm the grant, but the resolution was buried under hours of debate on technical questions in regard to grants, and again no confirming action was taken. In 1885, George W. Julian was appointed Surveyor General and sent to New Mexico to straighten out the land claims of various individuals and groups.

As an early history of New Mexico related, "The Territory was greatly wrought up in 1883, 1884, and 1885 over the extensive fraudulent operations in land in New Mexico. The matter was investigated under direction of Congress and the report of the special agents who performed the work showed that the registrar of the Land Office had entered into collusion with a ring of capitalists to get possession of vast areas of public land in the Territory by fraudulent means."

Surveyor-General Julian was aghast at the idea that the

Cañon de Chama Grant was surveyed to include 472,000 acres, contending that the lands involved were located only within the canyon as the name implied.

In the meantime, a British cattle syndicate had obtained possession. A newspaper account (Santa Fe New Mexican) in January 1887, said the English capitalists had paid $500,000 for 300,000 acres of land. When the U. S. Court of Land Claims was organized in 1891, the syndicate entered a claim for 472,000 acres. The Court confirmed only 1,422 acres and a patent was finally issued in 1905 in the name of the original grantees and the British syndicate, the Rio Arriba Land and Cattle Co. which passed into the possession of T. D. Burns of Tierra Amarilla, who had also purchased several thousand acres of the Manuel Martinez grant in Rio Arriba County.

When the Court of Private Land Claims finished its work after 13 years of hearings, it had confirmed only 2,051,526 acres of the 35,491,020 acres claimed in 301 cases. All lands not confirmed became public domain, and when the National Forests were established, they were created from public domain lands. The Carson National Forest, which encompasses lands that were claimed by the Cañon de Chama heirs, was established in 1908, taking in the Taos National Forest, established as Forest Reserve in 1906, and part of the Jemez National Forest, established as Forest Reserve in 1903.

The cattle firm which had bought Cañon de Chama appealed the Private Land Claims Court decision to the Supreme Court, contending the Claims Court allotment covered only the individual farming acreages and not the community lands. But the Supreme Court in one of its land claim decisions had ruled that common lands remained with the sovereign and could not be allocated to settlers.

In 1944, Congressman Antonio M. Fernandez introduced a bill in Congress to return to living heirs of the original grantees of the Cañon de Chama grant Federal lands within the boundaries of the grant as surveyed in 1878. The Department of Agriculture made a study of the grant legal history for the Committee of Public Lands of the House of Representatives.

In its report, the Department, over the signature of Charles F. Brannan, Assistant Secretary, stated that "while the Department believes that equity should be done in all cases, it is unable to find adequate equitable justification for the conveyance of even a limited interest in so large an acreage of publicly owned land, especially where such conveyance in all probability would quite adversely affect a considerable number of local and dependent people and a wide range of more remote state and national interests.   Accordingly, it recommends that the bill, H. R. 4797, be not enacted."

The report to the Committee summed up its findings as follows:

In essence the record may be summarized as follows: In 1806 Francisco Salazar on behalf of himself, his two brothers and 28 other persons, petitioned the Governor of the territory to grant them lands for purposes of residence.   On July 6, 1806 the Governor directed the proper Alcalde to make personal inspection of the land mentioned and make a report. On the 14th of the same month the Alcalde submitted his report in which he stated he had visited and personally examined a spot called the Chama River Canyon "over all of which I passed with the greatest care and observation."   He reported that the land was sufficient to care for the 31 families applying for it and land for the increase they may have in the way of children and sons-in-law.   Later, on March 1, 1809, the Alcalde reported that he had proceeded to the Chama River Canyon, accompanied by the 25 settlers, to which there were added 14 other citizens without land, and has assigned them certain lots or tracts.

The time expended by the Alcalde in making the necessary examinations, the small number of families involved, the restrictions which the Governor had placed upon the quantity of land to be allotted to each family, and the descriptions of the boundaries reported by the Alcalde, all showed the area covered by the Grant to have been of very limited extent.   At one point, the Surveyor General expressed the opinion that the area did not exceed four miles; the further opinion of the Surveyor General being that the Alcalde's report could not be construed to make the granted tract more than about three leagues square or the equivalent of about 40,000 acres in round numbers.

In 1878, a survey of the grant was made under direction issued in 1872 by Surveyor-General Proudfit.   The honesty, integrity, and validity of that survey later were challenged by a succeeding Surveyor-General, Julian, in 1886, in the strongest terms, as will be noted by reference to his report. As was too frequently the custom in that period the surveyor, instead of accepting the nearby landmarks described in the original grant, adopted more remote landmarks of similar name; the result being that the survey encompassed an area of 472,736,95 acres, or more than 10 times the maximum area that could be derived by the most liberal interpretation of the reports of the Alcalde upon which the grant originally was based. Apparently the protests of the Surveyor-General sufficed to prevent issuance of patent to the claimants based upon the survey made in May, 1878, by Stephen C. McElroy U. S. Deputy Surveyor and approved September 7, 1878 by Henry M. Atkinson, U. S. Surveyor-General.

Because of the number of cases of similar character then commanding attention, Congress by the Act of March 3, 1891 (26 stat. 854) established the Court of Private Land Claims. The specific function of that Court was to adjudicate claims to lands of the United States asserted or based upon prior grants by the governments of Spain or Mexico. By decree of September 29, 1894, in a case entitled "The Rio Arriba Land and Cattle Company (Limited) vs. the United States of America," the Court found for the petitioners "to the extent of the lands lying in the Canyon del Rio de Chama which were first apportioned among the settlers and no more"; the same thereby being confirmed to the heirs and legal representatives of the 39 persons specifically named in the decree. The names in the decree in large part correspond to those set forth in H. R. 4797, but that bill includes three parties not named in the decree and excludes three parties so named.

Upon entering of the above mentioned decree it became the function of the Surveyor-General to define the boundaries of the area which by the decree was confirmed to the petitioners. By letter of January 12, 1898 addressed to the Commissioner of the General Land office, the Surveyor-General protested that the decree was faulty in that the boundaries therein set forth were entirely insufficient and wholly indefinite. He accordingly recommended that the decree be returned to the Court for such corrections as would allow his office to execute a survey upon the ground with certainty.

In consequence, the Court of Private Land Claims later executed an amendatory or supplementary decree in which the lands confirmed to the petitioners were more specifically described. The understanding of this Department is that the area finally surveyed and patented as the Rio de Chama Grant, consisting of 1,422.62 acres, is the area precisely described by the Court of Private Land Claims in its supplementary or amendatory decrees.

By Section 9 of the Act of March 3, 1891, provision was made for the right of appeal to the Supreme Court of the United States, such appeal to be taken within six months from date of decision of the Court of Private Land Claims.   Accordingly, the Court of Private Land Claims, in its decree of September 29, 1894, specifically ordered that the petitioner be and thereby was allowed an appeal from the decision and decree of that Court to the Supreme Court of the United States. The Supreme Court on May 24, 1897 affirmed the decision of the Court of Private Land Claims. See Rio Arriba Land and Cattle Co. vs. United States (167 U. S. 298).

The Bill H. R. 4797 provides for the conveyance of title to the now living heirs of the grantees named in the bill. It should, however, be noted that the suit before the Court of Private Land Claims was in the name of Rio Arriba Land and Cattle Company, Limited, and the fact that the Court recognized that corporation as the legal plaintiff would indicate that the Corporation had succeeded to all rights in the property at some time prior to September 29, 1894. If the heirs of the original grantees had in fact disposed of all interests in the grant, an Act of Congress which would now vest such heirs with a right to the conveyance of title apparently would ignore the transfers of right or interest which apparently had occurred.

It seems evident the establishment of complete title to the lands to which H. R. 4797 would apply, hitherto could have been accomplished only under the provisions of the Act of March 3, 1891, (26 Stat. 854). The seventh provision of section 13 of the Act seems specifically to provide a maximum limitation of 11 square leagues for any claims under the Act. A Spanish league is 2 miles $48\frac{1}{2}$ chains; a square league thus containing approximately $7\frac{1}{2}$ square miles.   Eleven leagues, therefore, would amount to about 80 square miles or about 51,000 acres; consequently, the bill, if enacted, would apply to almost ten times the maximum area prescribed by Section 13 of the Act of March 13, 1891.

The big Manuel Martinez land grant in Rio Arriba county, which was sold and re-sold and its more than half million acres divided into many ranches, has triggered numerous court battles and violent acts in Rio Arriba County for the last 80 years.

Descendants of heirs of the Martinez family and other settlers had claimed community lands in the grant and were in and out of court over the years. Organized as the Corporation de Abiquiu in the 1940's, they sought to dispossess then-current owners and regain the lands but lost ot in Federal Court.   Then, in a hearing in state district court in October, 1964, Judge Paul Tackett stripped the Corporation of Abiquiu of all legality in connection with the Tierra Amarilla Grant.

So, the Alianza, which had been newly organized, began then to unite land grant claimants from the Abiquiu Corporation and from among the Cañon de Chama heirs, as well as any others who claimed any family connection with old Spanish or Mexican land grants.

The Alianza began to beat the propaganda drums to make its cause known.   Publicity campaigns were undertaken, using such phrases as "U.S.A. is Trespassing in New Mexico" and "Trespassers Must Get out of New Mexico."   Even a march to the capitol from Albuquerque was staged to present a petition to Governor Campbell demanding that he investigate their land claims.

The only gains made by Reies Tijerina and his Alianza in the next 18 months were publicity gains.   Tijerina and his Alianza were much in the news.   Then in October, 1966, the Alianza decided to take over the lands they could not get through legal channels.   The first confrontation was a quiet one.   On the weekend of October 15, about 300 or more members moved into the Echo Amphitheater to establish what they said was the ancient settlement of San Joaquin.   Don Seaman, Supervisor of the Carson National Forest, announced the Alianza camp was to be regarded merely as "visitors."   Next day the campers were gone.

But two days later the Alianza sent a delegation and a process server to the office of Regional Forester William D. Hurst with papers signed by Reies Tijerina proclaiming the establishing of the Pueblo San Joaquin del Rio Chama, and serving notice it was taking over the old grant lands.

The Regional Forester declined to accept the papers, and he told Tijerina and the others who had come to his office that the property they claimed belonged to the United States of America, and "I will not under any condition allow it to be claimed by an organization or group."

Tijerina and his delegation left the Forest Service office to plan their next step—and this was the confrontation at Echo Amphitheater on October 22 when Rangers Taylor and Smith were manhandled.

Trial for the five who were arrested was still to be a year off. In the meantime the Alianza leaders were having problems with State Police and District Attorney Alfonso Sanchez, of Santa Fe, who issued warrants for a number of the membership charging unlawful assembly growing out of a convention at Coyote, June 3. Then on June 5, 1967 when arraignments were to be held in Tierra Amarilla, an armed group of Alianza members raided the court house.   A state policeman was shot, the sheriff was disarmed, two of his deputies were wounded, a United Press International reporter and a deputy sheriff were kidnapped and held temporarily as hostages, and officials were rounded up and held prisoner in the county commission chamber. State Police cars were riddled with bullets; windows in the court house were broken. State Police got their second wind and began to make arrests as National Guardsmen were called in to keep order. It was weeks before all of the 14 charged had finally been arrested, including leader Reies Tijerina and his brother Cristobal.

The five who had been arrested at Echo Amphitheater went to trial in Federal court in Las Cruces in November, 1967. All five were found guilty on the charges of assaulting the Forest Rangers.

Reies Tijerina and Cristobal Tijerina were each sentenced to two years in prison. Jerry Noll, the "King of the Indies," who had presided over the "trial" of the Rangers at Echo Amphitheater, was sentenced to three years. "I am immune to prosecution in foreign courts," Noll announced. Esequiel Dominguez and Alfonso Chavez were sentenced to 60 days in jail.

The Alianza attorneys immediately announced appeals to the U. S. Circuit Court and the men were released on bond.

The next scene in this ill-omened drama shifted again to Tierra Amarilla where in early January, 1968, Deputy Sheriff Eulogio Salazar was murdered by being beaten over the head. His car was then run off the road into a 40-foot deep *arroyo*. Salazar was the deputy who had been shot in the cheek during the Tierra Amarilla raid. The mystery of Salazar's murder remains unsolved.

When he came to trial in district court on the State charges growing out of the raid, Tijerina claimed the raid was merely an attempt to make a citizen's arrest of District Attorney Alfonso Sanchez. He claimed to have taken no personal part in any of the shooting or violence. The jury believed him and brought in a verdict of not guilty.

Tijerina again made headlines when he went to Washington during the hearing on the appointment of Warren Burger as chief justice of the Supreme Court. Tijerina announced he would make a citizen's arrest of Burger. He did not get near Burger, but he did get the publicity which has seemed so important to the fiery Alianza leader in his effort to keep his cause alive. On Saturday, June 8, he also attempted to make a citizen's arrest of Governor David Cargo and of Norris Bradbury, director of the Los Alamos Scientific Laboratory, but was unable to locate either one. The next act took place next day in the Santa Fe National Forest, near the village of Coyote, a dozen miles from U. S. 84 which is a boundary for parts of the Carson and Santa Fe National Forests. In early June, 1969, members of Tijerina's Alianza had been encamped near Coyote for several days.

James H. Evans, investigations officer of the Forest Service Regional Office, was at the Coyote Ranger Station on June 8 and heard over the State Police radio that a Forest Service sign had been set on fire at Capulin, nine miles west of Coyote. Evans called U. S. Attorney Victor Ortega to ask his advice on how to proceed. The U. S. Attorney advised him not to make any arrests at that time but to try to identify the sign burners. Later, Evans was informed that a crowd was gathering around a Forest Service sign on the highway, a couple hundred yards below the Coyote Ranger Station and preparing to burn the sign.

This time Evans went down with the intention of making arrests. State Police Officer Robert Gonzales later testified that he saw a woman dressed in yellow slacks and flowered blouse put brush and twigs around the Forest Service sign. (She was later identified as Mrs. Tijerina.)

The sign erupted in flames and Evans, a carbine in his right hand, walked over to Tijerina. He was backed up by two State Police investigators, Robert Gilliland and Jack Johnson.

"I'm Jim Evans," he told the Alianza leader. "I'm a Federal officer. You're under arrest for destruction of government property."

"You," Tijerina replied, "are under arrest for conspiracy against the poor."

The crowd moved in between the two men, and Tijerina walked hurriedly to his car and pulled out a carbine. The crowd scattered, and Evans stepped behind an automobile. Evans saw Tijerina put the rifle to his shoulder and aim it directly at him.

"Drop it or I'll kill you," he shouted to Tijerina. When Tijerina hesitated, Evans called out, again, "Drop it or you're a dead man!"

Tijerina rested his carbine against his car and the State Police officers then moved in and took him into custody.

Meanwhile, State Police had arrested Mrs. Tijerina.

The Associated Press the next day quoted Tijerina in the Santa Fe New Mexican as saying Jim Evans "has 24 hours to get out of the state." The AP reported that Tijerina and his Alianza are "going ahead with plans to make a citizen's arrest" and "this time we are not going unarmed." That night four members of Tijerina's group sought to make a citizen's arrest of Evans at his home, but he was not present when they arrived.

As a result of the sign burning incident, and the alleged threats against Evans, Federal Judge Howard Bratton was requested to revoke the bond under which Tijerina was free while awaiting action on the appeal of his conviction in the Echo Amphitheater case.   Judge Bratton ordered Tijerina held without bond, and he was taken to the Federal Penitentiary at La Tuna, Texas to await court action.

In late September, 1969, Tijerina went to trial in Albuquerque in connection with the sign burning.   After nearly a week of testimony, he was found guilty of aiding and abetting destruction of government property and assaulting a Forest Service officer.   He was sentenced by Judge Bratton to three years in prison.   His lawyers immediately announced an appeal.

The previous appeal from the Echo Amphitheater conviction had been decided against Tijerina in U. S. Circuit Court of Appeals and was then carried to the U. S. Supreme Court.   In early October, 1969, the Supreme Court refused to hear the appeal.   A rehearing was next requested.

Tijerina's court trials were not over.   He was still scheduled to go on trial in connection with additional charges growing out of the Tierra Amarilla court house raid.   Since his bond was still revoked, he was being held in jail in Albuquerque but allowed to go to the Federal building under guard each day to use an office for interviewing witnesses to prepare his defense in the raid case.

Just before the trial opened the Alianza met in Albuquerque in annual convention and elected Ramon Tijerina, brother of the jailed leader, as president.   It also issued a map of southwestern states showing land grant areas, which it announced it would petition President Nixon and Congress to separate from the United States for a separate nation.

The jailed leader disagreed with the latest switch in policy and announced to the press his resignation from the organization.

Before the District Court trial got well under way, a mistrial was declared by District Judge Garnett Burks because of what he termed "impermissible separation of jurors" disqualifying two or more from hearing the evidence.   The trial was reset for the November, 1969 term of court.

On November 26, Tijerina was convicted on two counts of false imprisonment of a deputy and assault with intent to kill or maim the jailer Eulogio Salazar.   Tijerina was acquitted on other charges growing out of the Tierra Amarilla raid.   His attorney filed notice of appeal.

It is ironic that the Santa Fe and Carson National Forests have been the scene of violent demonstrations in recent years, since the rapport between the Forest Service and ranchers and residents of northern New Mexico had been generally good over the years.

While there were misunderstandings and oftentimes some resistance to Forest rules and regulations, in general there had been good cooperation. Forest Service officials learned early in its existence that it made good sense to assign people to northern New Mexico who could speak Spanish. Some Rangers and deputy Rangers, aides, fire guards and work crews have been of Spanish extraction. Most of the Anglo Rangers were men who spoke Spanish—men like Elliott Barker, Tom Stewart, and Dick Wetherill (who spoke Spanish and Navajo as well as English.) One of the Santa Fe's outstanding Rangers was the late Joe Rodriguez, who knew his Coyote District like his own backyard and knew every man, woman and child in the District. The adjoining Carson National Forest had such Rangers as Paul Martinez, L. P. Martinez, Chris Zamora, and Steve Romero.

Because the Carson National Forest has so many small ranches bordering the Forest, and because it has been used by northern New Mexico residents for two centuries, the Carson has the largest number of permittees of any Forest in the Southwestern Region.

As Elliott Barker once related, "four-fifths of our dealings were with Spanish-speaking people. They would listen to a person who could talk their language and explain things to them, whereas if it had to be done in English or through an interpreter, you could never put it over at all."

The appearance on the scene of a Spanish-speaking, fire-eating orator who aroused the people in what most legal minds regard as a hopeless cause brought about an era of bitterness, discontent, and violence.

It is all the more ironic since only two or three hundred people are involved as so-called land grant claimants, but the organized group keeps up a constant barrage of publicity and agitation.

As the administrator of lands that were once claimed as grants, the Forest Service has sought to administer them for the greatest good for the greatest number. The small ranchers in the neighborhood of the Forests have been given permits to graze, work crews have been hired from the village, projects have been sought to upgrade the economy of the area.

Years ago the Forest Service began the organization of livestock associations made up of permittees on the Forests in order to deal with representatives of the Forest users rather than a large

290 Men Who Matched the Mountains

number of individuals singly.   The associations were designed to
help the permittees and to improve relations.

Chief of Operation Walt Graves has explained how they
operated:

"On the Coyote District (where he had once served as Ranger)
the livestock associations were limited usually to one grazing allotment and were made up of permittees on that particular allotment.
In a few instances, the association covered two allotments, primarily because we had permittees who grazed on one of them in the
summer and another in the winter, and we combined the two into
one associaton.   They were strictly local associations.   They
elected their own officers.   I, as Ranger, had to act as secretary
and keep the thing going, but they conducted their own meetings
which I always attended.   To the extent that we could, we accepted
their recommendations for range management practices and that
sort of thing on the allotment.   We could not always accept their
recommendations because they were continually requesting increases in numbers, and this, of course, we could not accept."

The livestock associations are still operating, and on the Coyote
District, for example, there are three associations.   Many of the
permittees are small farmers, with two or three or a half dozen
cows grazing on the Forest.   But having that forest permit is very
important to them, and it has been said that most of them would
sell anything else they owned before they would part with their
Forest permit.   It is something of a status symbol to be one of the
permittees.   Presently the grazing fee on the District is 43 cents per
cow per month, although a sliding scale of increases will take it
above a dollar in the 1970's.

Eddie Rael, range conservationist on several Districts in
recent years, and currently Ranger on the Coyote District, thinks
the cooperation between permittees and the Forest Service today
is better than it has been in many years, in spite of the Alianza
activities, or maybe because of it.

There has been a backlash among Spanish New Mexicans in
the area because of the Echo Amphitheater incident, the Tierra
Amarilla raid and the sign burning.

"Our people here at Coyote saw what an ugly thing it was,"
Rael related, "and many of them have turned their backs on the
Alianza.   In fact, before the recent convention of the organization
when a meeting was called here, only a very few people showed up."

Even on the day of the sign burning, the people of Coyote
were onlookers rather than participants, according to Rael.
"Manuel Martinez, the State Police officer who covers this district, was here that day," Rael said.   "He told me that he looked

the crowd over and the Coyote people were just spectators scattered around in the background looking on.

"Many people are actually embarrassed that they ever had anything to do with the Alianza. They say that when they go to Santa Fe to shop, they even hesitate to say they are from Coyote. And they have always been so proud of their village."

Rael also credits improved relations between the Forest Service and residents of the area to more cooperative efforts by the present professional staff of the Ranger District, who have been assigned there in the past two years.

Rael explains it this way:

"Years ago, the old-time Rangers were close to the people. Probably in more recent years when new Rangers were assigned to the Districts they seemed less approachable to the villagers who looked upon them as very important people, and they hesitated to take their little problems to the Ranger or his staff—or to ask for a free-wood permit or make some complaint. So perhaps they got caught in some violation of regulations and were pretty unhappy about it. Then along came Tijerina and capitalized on their discontent."

Because he is a native New Mexican—born and brought up in Santa Fe and one of the native Spanish American professionals in the Forest Service—Rael understands the problems on both sides. As a result, much of his work the past two years has been visiting and listening to people of the District, explaining the Forest Service operations and trying to iron out minor differences.

"You know, it's a funny thing," he said, "but I think I do more business just before and after church on Sunday than anytime during the week."

As a devout Catholic, Rael attends church every Sunday. He recalled that one very elderly lady came up to him one Sunday morning to congratulate him. When he asked what she was congratulating him for, she replied in Spanish: "For working for the Forest Service. I didn't know that they employed Catholics."

In his present assignment, Rael could probably have moved back to Santa Fe to work out of the Forest Supervisor's office, but he asked to remain in Coyote.

One of the reasons is that he wants his children to learn and speak Spanish fluently. "I don't have the time or the patience to teach them, and my wife is from Wisconsin, so she can't help them. But they are certainly picking it up at school." The Raels have six children, and three of them are now in school.

Spanish is the language of rural northern New Mexico, although most of the people except the elderly are bilingual. Since the beginning years of the Forest Service, Rangers have been encouraged to learn Spanish if they did not know the language before taking assignment in various parts of New Mexico and Arizona.

When Bill Edwards, formerly Ranger at Coyote, was moved to the District from Ruidoso, he took a cram course in Spanish. At Coyote, he told Eddie Rael he wanted to continue to use his Spanish so he could become more fluent and not let it lapse. Rael then suggested that they conduct their conversations in Spanish and that he give his instructions and orders to work crews in Spanish.

Rael helped it along by telling permittees to "talk to the Ranger in Spanish when you see him."

"Word got around that the *guardia,* as they call the Ranger, could talk their language," Rael explained. "It made all the difference in the world in the relations with people generally."

Rael's current assignment as this was written is another activity that is improving the Forest Service's image among the people of the District. He is researching land titles to attempt to clear up titles on a large number of small plots of land—about 600 acres in all—that were included in the general survey of the Polvadera Grant when it was purchased by the Government in 1937 as part of the Land Utilization Projects. Tracing ownership and occupation of the lots by families over the past 150 years has been a time-consuming task since it means tracing and examining legal documents, parish and family records and personal interviews with old time residents. But the Forest Service is trying hard to assist the people in securing clear title to their land.

In the fall of 1969, the Forest Service purchased ranch lands on the Chama River which will provide tremendous recreation facilities in the Coyote District since the 3,000-acre ranch has seven miles of river frontage. The ranch was purchased from the Guy C. Scull estate and comprised lands that had once been part of the T. D. Burns Ranch.

The Forest Service still has land problems to be solved. One involves the 1,750,000 acres of non-Federal lands intermingled and within the boundaries of the National Forests and Grasslands of Region 3. In addition there are nearly 2,000,000 acres of Spanish Land Grant lands adjacent and surrounded by Forest lands.

Congress has authorized land purchases, and as parcels within National Forests become available efforts are made to acquire them. Lands within Wildernesses have first priority in this regard. The Forest Service is also seeking to acquire by exchange, lands within old Spanish land grants, since they are valuable watershed and have substantial recreation development potential.

It has been noted in the Service's Management Guide that "the Spanish land grants have been largely stripped of timber under past ownerships and management. Fifty to 100 years of restoration and protection are needed for them to again contribute fully to the Nation's economy and to the welfare of locally dependent people."

Fortunately for generations yet to come, the Forest Service takes the long view in the conservation, protection and rehabilitation of our land resources.

END

www.ingramcontent.com/pod-product-compliance
Lightning Source LLC
Chambersburg PA
CBHW031501270326
41930CB00006B/187